Federal Antitrust Policy During the Kennedy-Johnson Years

Federal Antitrust Policy During the Kennedy-Johnson Years

James R. Williamson

Contributions in American History, Number 162
Jon L. Wakelyn, Series Editor

GREENWOOD PRESS
Westport, Connecticut • London

Library of Congress Cataloging-in-Publication Data

Williamson, James R.
    Federal antitrust policy during the Kennedy-Johnson years / James
R. Williamson.
        p.   cm. — (Contributions in American history, ISSN 0084–9219
; no. 162)
    Includes bibliographical references and index.
    ISBN 0-313-29641-3
    1. Trusts, Industrial—Government policy—United States—History.
2. Antitrust law—Economic aspects—United States—History.
3. Public interest—United States—History.   4. Monopolies—United
States—History.   I. Title.   II. Series.
    HD2795.W68   1995
    338.8'0973'09046—dc20   95–7908

British Library Cataloguing in Publication Data is available.

Library of Congress Catalog Card Number: 95–7908
ISBN: 0–313–29641–3
ISSN: 0084–9219

First published in 1995

Greenwood Press, 88 Post Road West, Westport, CT 06881
An imprint of Greenwood Publishing Group, Inc.

Printed in the United States of America

The paper used in this book complies with the
Permanent Paper Standard issued by the National
Information Standards Organization (Z39.48–1984).

10 9 8 7 6 5 4 3 2 1

TO JIM

—for all he was;
—for all he might have been.

Contents

Tables and Figures

Preface

The Kennedy-Johnson years witnessed the third and greatest merger movement to that time in the history of the United States, when over 9,400 formerly independent firms were absorbed into other corporations. An overwhelming number of these mergers were of the conglomerate variety, bringing together companies from differing rather than similar industries. By 1968, 200 corporations held over 60 percent of the nation's manufacturing assets and total annual profits. The diminution of competition and corresponding increase in economic concentration that accompanied this great merger wave were contrary to America's historical commitment to competition and aversion to monopoly power.

Presidents Kennedy and Johnson knew they could expect little public support for a crusade against the increasing concentration of economic power. World War II production, and America's industrial leadership since that time, had made big business acceptable to the American public. Moreover, the success of the New Frontier and Great Society programs, and America's involvement in Vietnam, were dependent upon a strong and growing economy, which in turn was dependent upon business optimism and support. This realpolitik view of government-business relations had its effect on the antitrust activities of the Justice Department and the Federal Trade Commission. Faced with a shortage of resources and the lack of a White House commitment to antitrust, only 170 of the thousands of mergers during these years were challenged by the two agencies.

Congress was generally indifferent to antitrust during this period. Despite the efforts of a few Senators and Representatives, and years of hearings into the effects of economic concentration, no significant antimerger legislation was enacted.

Only the Supreme Court was consistently procompetition and anticoncentration during these years. In the 16 merger cases that came before it, the Court interpreted the antitrust laws so as to strike down every actual or potential threat to competition and to prevent further concentration.

Thus, during the Kennedy-Johnson years, both the Executive and the Congress, reflecting the apathy of the electorate, generally ignored the historical commitment to the preservation of competition.

This study is not intended to be a business history of the Kennedy-Johnson Administrations, or a history of antitrust during that period. Nor is it an analysis of Supreme Court decisions in selected cases. It will not include financial institutions, nor antitrust activity in the individual states or in the international arena. Anti-price-fixing activity will not be included. It is a study of the federal government's response, during the Kennedy-Johnson years, to the Third Great Merger Movement.

A considerable part of the narrative is based on information contained in the John Fitzgerald Kennedy and Lyndon Baines Johnson Presidential Libraries. Each institution awarded me a small grant for travel expenses while using their resources. I am grateful for the financial support and for the prompt and courteous assistance provided by the staff of both libraries. My deepest thanks are extended to Professor William H. Becker, of The George Washington University, who directed this project from its beginning, and whose guidance and recommendations, along with those of Professors Edward D. Berkowitz and Leo P. Ribuffo, also of George Washington, were of significant value in the completion of this study. I also wish to thank Harold E. Cox, Professor and Chair, History Department, Wilkes University, for his advice and assistance; the administration of Gwynedd-Mercy College for time to pursue this project; and Josephine Glass, Secretary of Gwynedd-Mercy's Business Division, who typed the initial draft. Special recognition is hereby given to Linda Fossler, who typed and proofread the final manuscript, and without whose priceless assistance this work might not yet have been completed.

This book is dedicated to my son, who died in an automobile accident at age 23, while serving on active duty as an attorney in the United States Army. To him, to my wife and other children, and to those friends who have shown interest and encouragement, I extend sincere thanks.

Clarks Green, Pennsylvania   James R. Williamson
December 1994

Federal Antitrust Policy During the Kennedy-Johnson Years

1

Introduction: A Brief History of Antitrust Policy to 1950

THE AGE OF LAISSEZ-FAIRE CAPITALISM

During the last third of the nineteenth century, the rapid expansion of the railroad and telegraph transformed local markets into regional and national ones, and provided ready access to them. In addition, the development of capital intensive, mass production manufacturing techniques increased production costs, especially fixed costs, and compelled manufacturers to seek economies of scale in order to reduce fixed costs per unit of output. It was also a period of fierce competition, when violence and cutthroat pricing policies were regularly employed to destroy economic rivals. Gradually, in order to overcome this disruptive competition, to stabilize output and prices, and to gain increased profits, corporations began to combine, first into "loose" arrangements such as pools, then into "tight" agreements such as trusts, and eventually into holding companies. Finally, toward the end of the century, they resorted to mergers as the most effective method to gain control over production costs and market prices. These combinations, coupled with the collapse of thousands of small firms during the recessions of the 1870s and 1880s, began to concentrate market power in certain industries in the hands of large producers. Liberal state incorporation laws in New Jersey and Delaware also contributed to the growth of large-scale enterprises.

This great growth of economic concentration and corresponding monopoly power took place within an environment of laissez-faire and Social Darwinism. The monopolies that had been so abhorrent to the nineteenth-century consumer and small businessman were those that were granted by state decree. Those monopolies had their origins in the patents given by the British sovereigns. This new power, however, seemed to be the inevitable outcome of a natural business evolution whose inequities eventually would be solved by society. Besides, not big business, but the tariff and the silver question, veterans' pensions, and civil service reform were the major political-economic issues of the day.

To the farmer and the small businessman, however, the major issues were artificial prices—low when selling and high when buying. To the factory worker and craftsman, the primary concerns were long hours and low wages, and possibly replacement by machine. As consumers, the people faced arbitrarily high prices, or went without. Theoretically, the common law would protect them from artificial prices. As a practical matter, however, the courts acted only in response to suits brought before them. Legislation appeared to the aggrieved as the only way to deal with the problem of corporate power.[1]

The farmers, dependent upon the railroads for movement of their crops, yet subject to various types of rate discrimination, began to pressure their state legislatures for laws to regulate shipping rates. Their efforts resulted in the Grange Movement and the Granger Laws, a series of regulations pertaining to rail and warehouse rates passed by Illinois, Iowa, and other states in the 1870s. The farmers, joined by factory workers and small businessmen, then began to press for federal regulation of the railroads. After the U.S. Supreme Court, in its famous *Wabash* case of 1886,[2] declared that the individual states had no authority to regulate interstate commerce, the U.S. Congress enacted the Interstate Commerce Act of 1887 to prohibit rebates and unfair price discrimination in interstate commerce. The act also established the Interstate Commerce Commission, the first federal regulatory agency.

In addition to the railroads, other huge combinations in the petroleum, sugar, lead, and whiskey industries had aroused the historical antimonopoly feelings of the general public to such an extent that the trusts were denounced in the platforms of both major political parties in the presidential election campaign of 1888.[3]

Although the tariff issue remained the primary political concern when the new Congress took office in 1889, both parties were committed to antitrust. The Democrats, seeking lower tariffs, claimed that high tariffs aided monopoly. Therefore, antitrust legislation would support their antimonopoly position. The Republicans, seeking high tariffs to protect American industry from external competition, sought antitrust legislation to promote domestic competition. Thus, a series of bills proposing a wide range of antitrust prohibitions were put forth, among which was one sponsored by Senator John Sherman of Ohio. Although considerably rewritten during committee discussion, the Sherman Act, signed by President Benjamin Harrison on July 2, 1890, became the first antitrust law of the United States. Its two main provisions follow:

Section 1. Every contract, combination in the form of a trust or otherwise, or conspiracy, in restraint of trade or commerce among the several states, or with foreign nations, is hereby declared to be illegal. Every person who shall make any such contract or engage in any such combination or conspiracy shall be deemed guilty of a misdemeanor . . .

Section 2. Every person who shall monopolize, or attempt to monopolize, or combine or conspire with any other person or persons, to monopolize any part of the trade or commerce among the several states, or with foreign nations, shall be deemed guilty of a misdemeanor.[4]

THE TURN OF THE CENTURY MERGER WAVE: 1895-1904

Ironically, the passage of the Sherman Act, far from halting the increasing concentration of industry, was followed by the first of the great merger movements in U.S. history.[5]

In 1889 New Jersey amended its general incorporation law to become the first state to permit manufacturing companies to purchase and hold stock in other enterprises, that is, to become holding companies. This change allowed corporations chartered in New Jersey to own stock in other companies, whether chartered in New Jersey or elsewhere, and to pay for property purchased with stock issued for that purpose. Following the advice of their attorneys, the "trusts" (i.e., large corporations) began to incorporate themselves as holding companies, and to await the courts' interpretation of the Sherman Act. Despite widespread use of the word *trust*, the actual number of trusts was small. Chandler has identified only eight that operated nationally, although others may have existed in regional markets. Nevertheless, the words *trust* and *antitrust* have remained in the vocabulary of business and government.[6]

In the first case prosecuted under the Sherman Act, the *Jellico Mountain Coal* case, the federal government filed suit against a combination of coal miners and coal dealers in Tennessee and Kentucky known as the Nashville Coal Exchange. The combination had been formed to regulate the production, pricing, and distribution of coal. On June 4, 1891, the District Court declared the combination illegal under the Sherman Act. In the following year, however, the government failed in three cases—one against a lumber combination, and the other two against the Distilling and Cattle Feeding Company, commonly referred to as the *Whiskey Trust*. In all three cases, the court was not persuaded that interstate commerce had been restrained.[7]

Meanwhile, continued prosperity plus the new holding company device contributed toward a mini-merger wave in the early 1890s. It appeared that American business was on the threshold of an even greater concentration, as 57 holding companies were formed between 1890 and 1893. In 1893, however, prosperity abruptly gave way to depression. The failure of the Philadelphia and Reading Railroad in March began a run of panic proportions on bank reserves. Domestic and European banking houses began to call in their loans, reducing the availability of credit. In May the stock market collapsed. Before the year was out, over 500 banks and 16,000 businesses had failed, and hundreds of railroads had gone into receivership. Unemployment reached 18 percent. Excessive speculation, overbuilding, and depressed agricultural prices were among the causes contributing to the Panic of 1893, up to then the worst depression in U.S. history. During the next four years, only 27 new holding companies were formed.[8]

Also during the depression, the first Sherman Act case, the *E. C. Knight* case, reached the Supreme Court. The American Sugar Refining Company of New Jersey, the *Sugar Trust*, which had been producing approximately 65 percent of all sugar refined in the United States, had purchased the E. C. Knight Company and three other Pennsylvania corporations, which accounted for an additional 33 percent. The federal government filed suit to force the divestiture of the four Pennsylvania companies. Both the District Court and the Circuit Court of Appeals acknowledged the existence of a monopoly, but did not see it as a restriction on interstate commerce. When appealed to the Supreme Court, Chief Justice Fuller, delivering the opinion of the Court on January 21, 1895, declared that manufacturing was not commerce and therefore the acquisitions did not violate the Sherman Act.[9]

Improved economic conditions, following soon after the *E. C. Knight* case, ushered in the great turn-of-the-century merger movement. During the peak years of 1898 to 1902, over 2,600 firms disappeared (Table 1.1). Of those disappearing, 75 percent were absorbed into consolidations made up of five or more previously independent firms. The horizontal merger was the dominant form of this movement, although the vertical merger also played a significant role.[10] Some of these organizations, such as U. S. Steel (now USX), International Harvester (now Navistar), U. S. Rubber (now Uniroyal), and American Can (now Primerica), still rank among the leading American manufacturers.

Meanwhile, additional Sherman Act cases made their way to the Supreme Court, the first of which was the *Trans-Missouri Freight Association* case, decided in 1897. This association was formed in 1889 by 18 railroads to fix prices and regulate their operations. Challenged by the federal government as a combination in restraint of trade, the trial court upheld the association's claim that since it was subject to the Interstate Commerce Act, it was beyond the scope of the Sherman Act. On appeal, the Circuit Court, finding it unnecessary to determine whether transportation was subject to the Sherman Act, stated that contracts made for a lawful purpose that were not unreasonably injurious to the public welfare were not illegal. The case was appealed to the Supreme Court. Justice Peckham, delivering the opinion of the Court, emphasized that *every* contract in restraint of interstate and foreign commerce is subject to the act. Further, there is no inconsistency between the Interstate Commerce Act and the Sherman Act; both are applicable to railroads. In addition, referring again to the Sherman Act, Peckham stated that its language is plain enough to include *all* contracts, not just those that result in an unreasonable restraint of trade. The Trans-Missouri Freight Association was found in violation of the Sherman Act.[11]

Justice White opposed this broad interpretation. In his dissent, distinguishing between reasonable and unreasonable restraints of trade, he pointed out that every contract must restrain trade to some degree, and that only unlawful restraints would be in violation of the act. White was to maintain this opinion until, fourteen years later, it became accepted doctrine.[12]

In the following year, the Supreme Court ruled on the constitutionality of the Sherman Act. Attorneys for the Joint Traffic Association, a combination of over 30 eastern railroads formed to fix prices and proportion freight traffic, argued that if the *Trans-Missouri* decision was allowed to stand, the Sherman Act would prohibit ordinary contracts, deprive the defendants of their liberty and property without due process, and also deprive them of equal protection of the law. Justice Peckham, again delivering the opinion of the Court, declared the constitutionality of the Sherman Act and the power of the Congress to legislate for interstate commerce. The Joint Traffic Association was found to be in violation of the act.[13]

Six manufacturers of cast-iron pipe had entered into an agreement to fix prices and divide sales territory in over 30 southern and western states. The federal government filed suit charging a conspiracy to enhance prices and eliminate competition. On February 8, 1898, Appellate Judge William Howard Taft, in *United States v. Addyston Pipe and Steel Co.*, delivered one of the landmark opinions in American antitrust history. Clearly challenging the *Whiskey* and *Sugar Trust* opinions, Taft declared that the making of sales which necessarily involve delivery of merchandise across state lines is interstate commerce, and so within the regulatory power of Congress even before the transit of the goods has begun. He further stated, in reference to the agreement to fix prices and divide sales territory, that no matter what defense might be given for the agreement, the illegality of the means makes it a conspiracy and so brings it within the terms of the federal statute.[14] On appeal, the Supreme Court in 1899 upheld Taft's opinion in its first unanimous decision in an antitrust case.[15]

Thus, by 1899 the Supreme Court had invigorated the Sherman Act and established a firm basis for antitrust policy. Moreover, the American public continued to express concern over the increasing concentration of business. From September 13 to 16 of that year, more than 700 people, including Governors, business and labor representatives, journalists, and university economists, attended a conference called by the Civic Federation of Chicago to discuss the "trust" problem. Over 90 individuals addressed the conference, covering a variety of economic and political attitudes, ranging from laissez-faire to strict antitrust enforcement. The general outcome was that the advantages of large-scale enterprise should be retained, but potential abuses prohibited. Ideas exchanged at this conference would eventually bear fruit in the Clayton and Federal Trade Acts of 1914.[16]

In 1901 the Hill-Morgan-Harriman interests formed the Northern Securities Company, a holding company, to control the Great Northern and Northern Pacific Railroads (the major routes in the northwestern United States) and their important feeder route, the Chicago, Burlington, and Quincy Railroad. Farmers, shippers, and smaller railroad operators were fearful of the potentially disastrous power of this new giant. So too was Theodore Roosevelt, the new President of the United States, who had frequently voiced his concern about the trusts, and who directed his Attorney General to bring suit to dissolve the holding company. This case drew the attention of the American people as no other antitrust case to that time. The fact that the President was willing to oppose the financially powerful Hill-Morgan-Harriman interests indicated that no person or group, no matter how powerful or manipulative, was above the law. On April 9, 1903, the Circuit Court found the

Northern Securities Company to be in violation of the Sherman Act.[17]

The year 1903 marked the institutionalization of antitrust. Not only had the President triumphed over an important "trust," but Congress, for the first time, appropriated funds especially for antitrust enforcement, and the Antitrust Division was established within the Department of Justice. In addition, Congress passed the Expediting Act to enable the immediate appeal of antitrust cases directly from the District Courts to the Supreme Court. And finally, also in 1903, the Bureau of Corporations was established within the Department of Commerce and Labor to conduct investigations and compile data concerning corporations and economic concentration that might assist the President to make recommendations to the Congress concerning antitrust legislation. Underlying this activity was the hope that the light of publicity would prevent the abuse of concentrated economic power and vitalize the forces of potential competition. The final act in this series of events was provided by the Supreme Court when, on March 14, 1904, it upheld the lower court's finding in the *Northern Securities* case.[18]

After 1899, the peak of the first great merger wave, merger activity began to decline as Supreme Court decisions and public concern, plus a high incidence of failure among many of the recent mergers, took their toll. Bankers, industrialists, and the stock-buying public turned away. By the end of October 1903, the market value of 100 leading industrial stocks had shrunk by 43 percent. The Panic of 1903 marked the end of the first merger movement.[19]

THE PERIOD BETWEEN: 1905-1918

Roosevelt, leaders of the major political parties, and some members of the public continued to be concerned about business concentration.[20] For many, including Roosevelt, Standard Oil was the prime example of the potential evils of business concentration. More than 30 corporations had been combined to form the Standard Oil Company, which by 1899 refined 90 percent of the oil produced in the United States. Although producing only about one-tenth of the national output, it controlled the industry through its refining and ruthless marketing techniques, including rebates and ruinous price competition. It had become the nation's most detested industrial combination. Not surprisingly, in 1906, the Justice Department filed suit against The Standard Oil Company.

On November 20, 1909, the Circuit Court convicted Standard Oil of being a combination in restraint of commerce by preventing competition among its various subsidiaries, and ordered it dissolved into its component parts. On May 15, 1911, that decision was upheld by the Supreme Court. Justice Edward White, who had distinguished between reasonable and unreasonable restraints of trade in his dissent in the *Trans-Missouri Freight Association* case, was now Chief Justice. Delivering the majority opinion, he stated that not *every* contract or combination should be considered illegal per se under the Sherman Act, but only those in which the *intent* was to restrain trade. Large size and concurrent market power gained through efficiency and normal internal growth would not be considered illegal, but that gained through "predatory" practices and "unreasonable" methods would be. Thus was enunciated what has come to be known as the "rule of reason." The Chief Justice, applying the rule of reason, found the Standard Oil Company to be in violation of the Sherman Act because its size and monopoly power were not the result of operational efficiency, but of illegal methods.[21]

In 1907, the Justice Department filed suit against the American Tobacco Company. Despite the continued existence of thousands of small tobacco producers, American had absorbed 250 firms and dominated the U.S. tobacco industry. In the following year, Judge Lacombe, delivering the opinion of the Circuit Court, stated that "every aggregation of individuals or corporations, formerly independent, *immediately upon its formation terminated an existing competition*, whether or not some other competition may subsequently arise." The company was found in violation of the Sherman Act and ordered dissolved.[22]

Upon appeal to the Supreme Court, Chief Justice White, immediately following the *Standard Oil* case, delivered the majority opinion. Again applying the rule of reason, White upheld the Circuit Court opinion and found the tobacco company guilty of predatory pricing, erecting barriers to entry, and other abuses. Thus, the strict interpretation of the Sherman Act, as delivered in the *Trans-Missouri* case, had been replaced by the rule of reason. Henceforth, the courts would judge the reasonableness of a merger and the intent of its participants.[23]

In July 1911, Senator Francis G. Newlands introduced a bill to create an Interstate Trade Commission, replacing the Bureau of Corporations, and requiring all interstate corporations with receipts in excess of $5 million to furnish organizational and financial data to it. Although the bill did not gain serious political attention, it did maintain the oft-discussed idea of a federal commission to oversee business in interstate commerce. In November, a National Civic Federation questionnaire, sent to 30,000 businessmen, indicated that those responding favored a federal incorporation law by four to one, some type of federal licensing by two to one, and a commission by three to one. In December, in his annual message to Congress, Taft called for a federal interstate commission and clarification of the Sherman Act.[24]

Antitrust was a major issue in the 1912 election. Big business sought either legislation, federal incorporation, a commission, or all three to eliminate the vagueness of the rule of reason, to protect themselves from a hostile public, to escape state regulation, and to stabilize conditions within their own industries. Small businessmen sought protection from what they saw as predatory pricing, and the right to establish their own price and output agreements without fear of antitrust prosecution. Labor unions and farm organizations sought exemption from the Sherman Act.

Shortly after the Wilson Administration took office, the revelation of attempts by Morgan, Rockefeller, and others to monopolize New England transportation through control of railroads, trolley lines, and coastal water transportation companies startled the nation and brought renewed cries for federal legislation to prevent such concentration of economic power. Both the Secretary of Commerce and the Commissioner of Corporations called for legislation prohibiting corporations from owning stock in competing corporations and prohibiting interlocking directorates, and for the establishment of a federal commission to which corporations would have to report the names of their directors and officers, stockholdings in other corporations, and various financial data. Although much of Wilson's attention in 1913 was directed toward passage of the Federal Reserve Act, in his December State of the Union message and in a speech to both Houses of Congress in January, 1914, he called for more explicit antitrust legislation, prohibition of interlocking directorates, and a commission with broad powers to investigate trade practices and prohibit those that tended to promote monopoly.[25]

Hearings on the issue of antitrust legislation were held by both the Senate and House during the first half of 1914. In March, legislation proposing a commission was separated from that proposing antitrust clarification; in April, Representative Henry D. Clayton combined his previous antitrust bills into one. Finally approved by both Houses, Wilson signed the Federal Trade Commission Act on September 26 and the Clayton Act on October 16.[26]

Following are portions of the Clayton Act specifically important for this study:

Section 2. The act forbade any person to discriminate in price, either directly or indirectly, between purchasers of commodities whenever such discrimination would lessen competition or tend to create a monopoly.

Section 7. Corporations were forbidden to acquire stock in another corporation where the effect was to substantially lessen competition.

Section 8. Interlocking directorates were forbidden among firms in interstate commerce whose capital, surplus, and undistributed profits aggregated more than $1 million, if such firms were competitors. In addition, directors, officers, or employees of a bank or savings institution were forbidden to serve as such in a similar institution.

In addition, Section 6 specified that labor unions and farmers' organizations would not be considered illegal combinations or conspiracies in restraint of trade under the antitrust laws.[27]

The key section of the Federal Trade Commission Act states that "unfair methods of competition in commerce" are hereby declared unlawful (Section 5).[28]

Although the background of these acts indicates an intent to clarify federal antitrust law, especially after the introduction of the rule of reason, and to prevent illegal actions before they take place, Bork and others have pointed out that phrases such as "substantially lessen competition" or "tend to create a monopoly" again left the courts to decide the reasonableness of the actions and the intent of those who take them.[29]

Perhaps the most obvious defect of the Clayton Act was the confinement of Section 7 to stock acquisitions. Merger-minded businessmen avoided that prohibition by buying the assets of the company they wished to acquire. The "assets loophole" was not remedied until the Celler-Kefauver Act of 1950.

Wilson, trying to minimize the effects of a brief depression in late 1913 and 1914, and to ease the tension that had existed between business and his administration, began to seek the counsel of businessmen and bankers, to invite them to the White House, and to express his confidence in them. In addition, World War I had begun in Europe, and the President knew that the United States, as a leading economic power, would play a crucial role in the outcome. Now was a time for close relations between business and government. Moreover, Wilson had envisioned the Federal Trade Commission (FTC) as an aid to business. He therefore appointed businessmen as the first commissioners, and a period of mutual cooperation to settle disputes and promote business efficiency began.[30]

THE SECOND GREAT MERGER MOVEMENT: 1919-1930

Encouraged by its victories in the *Standard Oil* and *American Tobacco* cases, the Justice Department filed suit against the United States Steel Corporation on October 26, 1911. The government claimed that between 1901 and 1911 the corporation repeatedly violated the Sherman Act through restraint of trade, including price fixing and attempts to monopolize the market in steel products. The government asked for dissolution.

The United States Steel Corporation had been formed in 1901, as a holding company, to bring together ten large producers that had previously merged over 150 formerly independent companies with 300 plants. Although competition remained, the new corporation, vertically and horizontally integrated, controlled approximately 50 percent of the nation's annual steel output (with up to 75 percent in some products) and 80 percent of the ore reserves of the Mesabi Range.

On June 3, 1915, the U.S. District Court of New Jersey found the corporation not guilty. Judge Buffington, speaking for the Court, explained that U.S. Steel's position in the market in almost every category of finished products had actually declined from 1901 to 1911, and that at least 80 firms competed domestically, producing 60 percent of the national output. He also noted that the corporation did not have an ore monopoly, since large domestic and foreign deposits were available. In addition, Buffington noted that U.S. Steel's prices on all products decreased during the period and that no competitor had charged the corporation with price discrimination. Finally, the District Court noted that the famous "Gary Dinners," where prices supposedly were discussed, had been abandoned before the initiation of the case.[31]

Upon appeal to the Supreme Court, Justice McKenna, writing for the majority, ruled against the government. Although he found U.S. Steel to be "of impressive size," he stated "we must adhere to the law, and the law does not make mere size an offense or the existence of unexerted power an offense. It, we repeat, requires overt acts," and he found no such acts.[32]

The reasoning of the Court in the *U. S. Steel* case was sufficiently consistent with its findings in the *Standard Oil* and *American Tobacco* cases to reaffirm the rule of reason and distinguish between "good" and "bad" trusts. In all three cases the Court looked for a dominant market position achieved by abusive practices. In the two earlier cases the government was able to demonstrate both dominance and abuse; in the *U. S. Steel* case it was not. Following this decision, the government withdrew its appeals in several pending cases.[33] The acquittal of U.S. Steel and the Court's distinction between "good" and "bad" trusts eased the way for the coming of the Second Great Merger Movement.

A postwar business boom, though somewhat subdued by the recession of 1921–1922, ushered in a new wave of merger activity that was to reach an extent during the late 1920s that exceeded the great turn of the century wave. From 1919 to 1930, over 8,000 formerly independent manufacturing and mining firms disappeared through mergers, with over 2,300 disappearing in the peak years of 1928 and 1929 (Table 1.1). Although steel and machinery manufacturers accounted for about one-fifth of the total, the chemical, oil, food, textile, and automobile industries were actively merging during this period.[34]

Among the reasons for this great merger movement was the widespread industrial prosperity of the period, especially from 1923 to 1929. Increasing profits stimulated business expansion, prosperity eased the sale of new securities, and, as during the turn of the century movement, investment bankers promoted mergers. Unused plant capacity, resulting from the wartime expansion, stimulated mergers for economies of production. In addition, vertical integration through merger grew in importance as firms sought increased technical proficiency, freedom from dependence on others for raw materials, and consolidation of sales and distributing organizations. This latter purpose was especially significant in the growing awareness of marketing, as the home radio audience in the country increased from 75,000 to 40 million during this period and automobile and truck registrations exceeded 30 million by 1930, expanding the sales area beyond the small local market and making consumers more mobile. Moreover, the distrust of business concentration that had been widespread at the beginning of the century had decreased by the third decade as business-government cooperation during the war, a generally rising standard of living, and an increasing variety of consumer goods made the population more tolerant.

This Second Great Merger Movement, like the first, was largely horizontal, with strong elements of vertical integration and diversified combination also present. Unlike the earlier movement, the new goal was explicitly oligopoly. Although dominant firms such as U. S. Steel may have made small acquisitions, they did not attempt to increase their share of the market. Instead, mergers by second-level firms, large but not dominant such as Bethlehem Steel, created larger corporations

Table 1.1
Disappearance by Merger, Manufacturing and Mining, 1895–1968

Nelson, 1895–1920		Thorp, 1919–39		FTC, 1940-68	
Year	Number	Year	Number	Year	Number
1895	43	1919	438	1940	140
1896	26	1920	760	1941	111
1897	69	1921	487	1942	118
1898	303	1922	309	1943	213
1899	1208	1923	311	1944	324
1900	340	1924	368	1945	333
1901	423	1925	554	1946	419
1902	379	1926	856	1947	404
1903	142	1927	870	1948	223
1904	79	1928	1058	1949	126
1905	226	1929	1245	1950	219
1906	128	1930	799	1951	235
1907	87	1931	464	1952	288
1908	50	1932	203	1953	295
1909	49	1933	120	1954	387
1910	142	1934	101	1955	683
1911	103	1935	130	1956	673
1912	82	1936	126	1957	585
1913	85	1937	124	1958	589
1914	39	1938	110	1959	835
1915	71	1939	87	1960	844
1916	117			1961	954
1917	195			1962	853
1918	71			1963	861
1919	171			1964	854
1920	206			1965	1008
				1966	995
				1967	1496
				1968	2442

Sources: Federal Trade Commission, Staff Report, *Economic Report on Corporate Mergers* (Washington: U. S. Government Printing Office, 1969), 665. Figures for 1895–1920 are from Ralph R. Nelson, *Merger Movements in American Industry, 1895–1956* (Princeton, N. J.: Princeton University Press, 1959), 37; those for 1919–1939 are from Temporary Economic Committee, *Monograph No. 27: The Structure of American Industry* (Washington: U. S. Government Printing Office, 1941), 233; those for 1940–1968 are from the Federal Trade Commission.

that could compete more effectively with the leaders, changing the structure of the industry from near-monopoly to oligopoly. The motive for merger—market power —remained, but the antitrust laws and fear of court-ordered dissolution caused these firms to halt their merger activity after gaining control over a smaller share of the market than they might otherwise have sought.[35]

The first three Clayton Act Section 7 cases to reach the Supreme Court—*Western Meat, Thatcher Manufacturing*, and *Swift*—were decided together in 1926.[36] These cases originated in 1922 and 1923, when the FTC ordered the divestiture of assets acquired by the companies. In each case, the companies had first purchased the stock of a competitor and then, through the voting rights obtained, had approved the sale to themselves of the former competitor's assets.

Justice McReynolds, delivering the opinion of the Court, focused on the timing of the FTC's order. In the *Western* case, the Court upheld the FTC, because the latter had ordered the divestiture when the respondent actually owned the stock in violation of the law, that is, before the assets had been transferred to the acquiring firm (Western). In the other two cases, the Court denied the FTC's appeal, since the assets had been transferred prior to the issuance of its divestiture order and the former competitors were already united. "The [Clayton] Act has no application to ownership of a competitor's property and business obtained prior to any action by the Commission, *even though this was brought about through stock unlawfully held*."[37] Thus, the Clayton Act was seriously injured, and with it the antitrust activity of the FTC. By the end of the decade, the prevention of false and misleading advertising had become the primary function of the commission.[38]

Meanwhile, the Harding-Coolidge-Hoover Administrations had fostered a "New Era" of government-business cooperation. This cooperation took two forms: administration encouragement and assistance to the trade association movement, and the appointment of probusiness individuals to the antitrust agencies.

The various mobilization agencies established by the federal government during World War I, and business-government cooperation to facilitate the war effort, convinced business leaders that industrial coordination could achieve production efficiencies, and that government could be an ally rather than an antagonist. As a result, prominent businessmen, economists, and politicians began to speak of voluntary business cooperation and industrial self-government in the form of trade associations, which would rationalize the economy without government direction or monopolistic concentration.

The best-known spokesman for the associationists was Secretary of Commerce Herbert Hoover. He accepted the antitrust framework within which business was to operate, and agreed that such activities as price fixing and output restrictions were illegal. But Hoover believed that it was the proper function of trade associations to rationalize their industries, and that it was entirely legitimate for government to investigate economic problems, to gather and distribute economic information, and to encourage and assist businesses in cooperative activities. Through the resources of the Commerce Department, he was able to achieve considerable success in the collection and dissemination of statistical information regarding prices, costs, and volume of production, the establishment of standards for the simplification of sizes and designs, and the development of efforts to eliminate waste. Eric Goldman has noted that in 1920 there were only a dozen trade associations; when Hoover left the White House there were over 2,000. And Thomas McCraw has pointed out that the lenient attitude of members of the Antitrust Division encouraged associational activities.

Hoover was also instrumental in the appointments, in 1925, of William E. Humphrey as Chairman of the Federal Trade Commission and of William Donovan as Assistant Attorney General for Antitrust. Under the admittedly probusiness Humphrey, a former Congressman and lumber lobbyist, the FTC actively fostered industrial self-regulation. Through a series of trade practice conferences, the commission assisted industry associations in developing their own codes of fair and unfair trade practices, which would be supported by the FTC. The ideas of industry self-regulation and codes of conduct would be carried into the National Industrial Recovery Act and Franklin D. Roosevelt's National Recovery Administration.[39]

Meanwhile, influenced by probusiness Republican sentiment and the unpredictability of Supreme Court rulings, the Department of Justice shifted its energies from prosecution of violations to prevention of them. In a speech on October 28, 1927, William J. Donovan, the Assistant Attorney General in charge of the Antitrust Division, noted that while some mergers may seek to eliminate competition or affect prices, others may correct the evils of "destructive" competition and better adjust to the needs of the economy. Thus, the Antitrust Division would investigate mergers when they were proposed, before a violation had been committed. "This method is at once fair to the businessmen who wish to avoid conflict with the law. . . . It is effective also in serving the public interest by ascertaining the facts and assuring that illegal combinations shall be dealt with at once."[40]

The success of this new approach was indicated by a marked increase in the number of consent decrees obtained by the government during the next few years. Moreover, the number of mergers that had been under discussion and subsequently abandoned, or modified to satisfy the Antitrust Division's objections, cannot be known. However, as Thorp observed, "This new policy, by removing a large element of uncertainty concerning the attitude of the government from the field of the promotion of mergers, has undoubtedly done more to encourage rather than to discourage the movement."[41] The increasing strength of the movement in 1928 and 1929 and its continuance into 1930 confirmed Thorp's analysis. It remained for the Great Depression to end the Second Great Merger Wave.

DEPRESSION DECADE

Following the stock market crash of 1929, a decline in mergers accompanied the decline in stock prices and general business confidence. From a peak of 1,245 during 1929, the number of firms disappearing through merger decreased from 799 to 203 during the next three years. The number dropped below 200 in 1933 and remained around 100 through 1942 (Table 1.1).[42] Nevertheless, significant antitrust activity took place during the depression decade.

In 1930, in *International Shoe Company v. Federal Trade Commission*, the Supreme Court addressed, for the first time, the concept of *substantial* competition. In 1923, the FTC ordered the International Shoe Company to divest itself of the recently acquired stock and assets of the W. H. McElwain Shoe Company. Even though the International Shoe Company maintained that McElwain was insolvent at the time, the Appeals Court considered possible alternatives to merger and upheld the FTC.[43]

The Supreme Court, however, found that there had not been substantial competition between the two companies prior to the acquisition and thus no substantial lessening of competition after the merger. The Court indicated that 95 percent of McElwain's sales were in towns having a population of 10,000 or more, while 95 percent of International's sales were in towns having a population of 6,000 or less. Moreover, their products did not compete geographically in many states. "Mere acquisition by one corporation of the stock of a competitor, even though it results in some lessening of competition, is not forbidden; the act deals only with such acquisitions as probably will result in lessening competition to a substantial degree . . . that is to say, to such a degree as will injuriously affect the public." Addressing the concept of potential competition, the Court also found that the precarious financial position of McElwain made remote the probability of future substantial competition.[44] Thus, the highest court interpreted the concepts of market share and potential competition, which were to be of considerable importance in later cases.

The next significant case in the evolution of antitrust enforcement was *Arrow-Hart and Hegeman Electric Company v. Federal Trade Commission*, delivered by the Supreme Court in 1934. In 1927, the Arrow-Hart and Hegeman Company was organized as a holding company for acquiring the stock of the two electric companies bearing those names. Because the new company was now the largest producer of electrical wiring devices in the United States, and all competition between the two previous companies had been eliminated, the FTC filed a complaint. Before the commission could pursue its investigation, two new holding companies were established to hold the stock of the two previously independent companies and the original holding company dissolved. Then the two holding companies were merged into one new company, the Arrow-Hart and Hegeman Electric Company, Inc. The FTC found the company to be in violation of Section 7 of the Clayton Act and ordered it to divest itself of the stock and assets of one of the two formerly independent companies. The Circuit Court upheld the FTC.

Upon appeal to the Supreme Court, however, Justice Roberts, speaking for the majority in a 5-4 decision, although acknowledging that the stock had been acquired contrary to the Clayton Act, reversed the lower court and found for the company. In a minority opinion, the four dissenting justices noted that "however gross the violation of the Clayton Act, the celerity of the offender, in ridding itself of the stock before the Commission could complete its hearings and make an order restoring the independence of the competitors, leaves the Commission powerless to act against the merged corporation." The minority also noted that the offender can evade the statute "by taking refuge behind a cleverly erected screen of corporate dummies."[45]

Following these decisions, the FTC reduced its inquiries into the legality of corporate mergers, but continued its efforts to have the Clayton Act amended. The commission issued only eleven complaints and no divestiture orders from 1935 through 1950, the year of the Celler-Kefauver Amendment.[46]

The Great Depression brought a new awareness of the monopoly problem, and a growing belief that the misuse of business power was responsible for the economic breakdown and the persistence of depressed conditions. President Roosevelt's advisors were divided on the subject of remedial action; some recommended rigorous antitrust prosecution, while others, believing that antitrust was obsolete, recommended national economic planning and control. These latter, however, were divided as to who should do the planning and the degree and type of control that would be necessary. On the other hand, both groups recognized the need for maintaining democratic values, private initiative, and business confidence. The solution, attempted through the enactment of the National Industrial Recovery Act (NIRA), in June 1933, was to seek the cooperation of business, both large and small, labor, and the federal government in establishing "codes of fair competition" to revitalize the economy. In return for this mutual cooperation, the antitrust laws would not be invoked, except for the most flagrant abuses. The provisions of the NIRA would be carried out by the National Recovery Administration.[47]

By the time the Supreme Court declared the NIRA unconstitutional in May, 1935, almost all groups had found the experiment to have been a disillusioning and frustrating experience. Consumers, small businessmen, labor, and antitrust advocates had come to believe that the codes, instead of preserving competition, had curtailed free markets, solidified prices, hurt the small producer, ignored labor, and further entrenched the power of big business. The national government had become a partner to monopoly.

These beliefs were reinforced by the findings of the National Recovery Review Board, chaired by Clarence Darrow, which was established by FDR in March 1934 to study monopolistic tendencies in the codes. Its report, issued two months later, though hasty and superficial, found a general trend toward monopoly and oppression of small business. In the meantime, reports from various sources between 1933 and 1937, such as Gardiner Means' study, *Industrial Prices and Their Relative*

Inflexibility (1934), the Brookings Institution's four volume inquiry into the economy (1934–1935), and the writings of prominent economists, linked the depression to oligopolistic concentration and administered prices.[48] In response, as early as 1935, several of FDR's advisors began calling for an investigation into economic concentration, Congressmen were talking of establishing an investigating committee, consumer interests were calling for an inquiry, and in 1937 the Attorney General recommended a broad study of the antitrust laws.

By the beginning of that year, however, the economy seemed well on the way to recovery, with some areas reaching or exceeding 1929 levels. Nevertheless, by late summer a recession had begun, which was followed during the next few months by one of the most rapid and severe declines in the history of U.S. business activity. This "Roosevelt Recession," as it was sometimes called, again brought to the fore the dilemma over concentration and antitrust that had preceded the NIRA. Unable to get the President to take some action on the worsening situation, Robert H. Jackson, the Assistant Attorney General for Antitrust, supported by Harold Ickes and other Administration officials, decided to act. Beginning in December, Jackson and Ickes spoke out against the concentration of monopoly power and blamed the "plutocrats" for the recession. Members of Congress, consumers, business leaders, and the media all had their own, frequently conflicting, recommendations. It soon became evident that a congressional investigation should be undertaken. When 16 leading businessmen indicated their willingness to cooperate, the President agreed.[49]

On April 29, 1938, Roosevelt sent a message to Congress asking it to vote funds for an investigation into the concentration of economic power. The country, he said, was threatened by "a concentration of private power without equal in history" that "is seriously impairing the economic effectiveness of private enterprise." Although the President declared that "The power of a few to manage the economic life of the Nation must be diffused among the many or be transferred to the public and its democratically responsible government," he stated that he did not propose to abandon the traditional antitrust approach, but indicated that the antitrust laws were inadequate to solve the problem. He proposed a thorough study of the concentration of economic power in American industry, including mergers and interlocking relationships, financial controls, pricing policies, and the improvement of antitrust procedures. On June 16, the Temporary National Economic Committee (TNEC) was officially established.[50]

The investigation continued for almost three years, including 18 months of public hearings, and resulted in over 30 volumes of testimony, studies, and recommendations. The committee concluded that "monopoly has greatly increased in American industry during the last fifty years," and denounced administered prices and other forms of market control. Recommendations pertinent to this study included:

- Amendment of Section 7 of the Clayton Act to prohibit the acquisition of the assets of competitors
- Legislation to prohibit mergers above a certain size, to be determined by

Congress, unless beneficial to the economy (This recommendation included six suggested guidelines)

- Legislation that would eliminate the holding company as a device to combine competitors, without disturbing it as a device for control between parent company and subsidiary
- Federal charters for national corporations
- Congressional action to strengthen the authority of the antitrust agencies and increased funding to enable them to perform their mission[51]

During the latter months of the TNEC investigation, the economy had been revitalized by the industrial response to the increasing prospect of war in Europe. The problems of concentration and antitrust, which had given birth to the TNEC, were overlooked as the national government exacerbated the problems of industrial and geographic concentration by its contract awards largely to the giants of industry as the United States began to improve its defense posture. The value of the TNEC's findings and recommendations were to be in the information they would provide for future studies and inquiries into economic concentration.

Meanwhile, in March 1938, following the appointment of Robert Jackson as Solicitor General, Thurman Arnold, a Yale law professor, became the Assistant Attorney General for Antitrust. Although Arnold had previously written about the ineffectiveness of antitrust, he believed that its inadequacy was due, at least in part, to the lack of personnel and adequate funding which he promptly set out to correct. Following the recession of 1937 and the establishment of the TNEC, he believed the nation was sufficiently aroused to support a vigorous antitrust campaign. Beginning in May, the Antitrust Division began to issue public statements, explaining conditions that would be investigated and the results expected. Arnold believed that such investigations would develop a body of procedures and precedents to aid in the formation of a consistent antitrust policy, which would also assist businessmen and the general public. Arnold also wanted prospective cases compared and evaluated so that those having the greatest public interest and consumer benefit would be selected for prosecution. In addition, he wished to make more use of consent decrees. By the end of the year, Arnold had received an increase in appropriations and personnel, and morale was high in his division.[52]

In the next four and a half years, the division filed approximately 200 cases, as Arnold attacked monopolistic practices in the chemical, oil, food, drug, insurance, and other industries. Most of these cases were concerned with price fixing; only four mergers were challenged. He also instituted investigations into patent abuses, monopolistic practices by both business and unions in housing construction, and rate fixing in the transportation industry. As America's involvement in World War II increased, Arnold kept insisting that antitrust enforcement could be used to prevent abuses of wartime controls, restrictive agreements, and excessive profits, and to protect small businesses. However, the War Production Board had been granted power to exempt war production activities from the antitrust laws, and the government had to turn to the giant corporations to fulfill its military needs. By January 1943, antitrust had become a casualty of the war, and Arnold left the Justice Department to accept an appointment as a Circuit Court Judge.[53]

Although World War II ended Arnold's antitrust campaign, his tenure as Assistant Attorney General marked a transition in antitrust enforcement. Arnold was concerned with using the American tradition of free enterprise, the "folklore" of capitalism as he called it, to further the production and distribution of goods and services. He was concerned with protecting the consumer from high prices, and with protecting the worker, the farmer, and the small businessman from the power of the large corporations. His approach, however, was not to attack big business, or mass production, or efficient marketing. Rather, he sought to prevent businesses from keeping new products and processes off the market, to prevent businesses from setting unnecessarily high prices, and to demonstrate the vitality and usefulness of the antitrust laws. Richard Hofstadter stated that even though World War II intervened, Arnold's efforts were successful in three ways. He showed that strong antitrust enforcement could affect the conduct of business within the existing framework of the American economy; that it could win from Congress increased financial support; and that it could provide a firm foundation for future antitrust operations under both Democratic and Republican administrations. And Corwin Edwards noted that when Arnold took office it was common to encounter the view that the antitrust laws were obsolete; when he left office public interest in antitrust had been reawakened and public support for competition reaffirmed.[54] This renewed public interest in competition and antitrust enforcement would contribute to the passage of the Celler-Kefauver Act in 1950.

TOWARD THE CELLER-KEFAUVER ACT

A relatively modest merger movement took place from 1943 through 1947, when 1,693 formerly independent companies disappeared (Table 1.1). Fifty-seven percent of the mergers took place in the machinery, transportation equipment, petroleum, chemical and drug, food and beverage, and textile industries. Although the 200 largest corporations accounted for 27 percent of the acquisitions, this merger activity did not significantly alter the concentration of U.S. industry. Unlike the earlier great merger movements, in which some very large corporations merged with each other, the vast majority of all firms acquired during this period were relatively small, over 94 percent being under $5 million in assets and 73 percent under $1 million. The number of small companies losing their independence simply reflected the preponderance of small firms in the economy.[55]

The Smaller War Plants Corporation (SWPC) Report, March 5, 1946, noted that many of the mergers were of the conglomerate type, in which large companies, with established names and distributive organizations, acquired smaller firms engaged in auxiliary or unrelated products. The FTC, indicating that approximately

21 percent were of this type, warned "there are few greater dangers to small business than the continued growth of the conglomerate corporation."[56]

Merger activity subsided with the recession of 1948 and reached a postwar low in 1949, when 126 firms lost their identity through merger. The immediate postwar years, however, witnessed two landmark antitrust cases—*ALCOA* in 1945, and the *Columbia Steel* case in 1948. In April 1937, the government brought suit in District Court against the Aluminum Company of America (ALCOA), seeking dissolution of the company. ALCOA was founded in 1888 and the aluminum production process was patented in the following year. By various manipulations and control of raw materials, the company was able to preserve itself as the sole domestic producer of virgin aluminum. The government presented 140 charges stemming primarily from ALCOA's monopolization of virgin aluminum ingot production and certain aluminum products. In 1941, District Judge Francis G. Caffey found for the company, stating that ALCOA had not illegally excluded others from production, charged extortionate prices, or made exorbitant profits, and that the government had not proved its charges.

The Supreme Court was unable to hear the government's appeal, because it could not provide a quorum of six justices, four having been involved previously in ALCOA cases. Therefore Congress, in June 1944, passed a special act allowing the U. S. Court of Appeals for the Second Circuit to hear the case as a court of last resort. Judge Learned Hand, delivering the decision, noted that ALCOA controlled about 90 percent of the virgin or primary aluminum production, and about 64 percent of the combined virgin and secondary, or scrap, production. He further noted that since ALCOA's control over the primary market necessarily gave it substantial influence over the secondary market, the relevant market under consideration in the case was the primary one. The company, he observed, controlled 90 percent, which constituted a monopoly. He also noted that the Sherman Act condemned monopolizing, regardless of whether one or more companies share market control, and regardless of whether or not the power is used to oppress consumers or exclude potential competitors. Judge Hand declared that Congress "did not condone 'good trusts' and condemn 'bad' ones, it forbade all."[57] Thus, the rule of reason was overthrown.

Nevertheless, those who believed the Courts were now determined to prevent the concentration of economic power received a surprise in *United States v. Columbia Steel*, decided in 1948. In this case, the federal government had sought under the antitrust laws to enjoin the United States Steel Corporation from purchasing, through its Utah subsidiary, Columbia Steel, the assets of the Consolidated Steel Corporation, the largest steel fabricator on the West Coast. Although U. S. Steel had steel finishing facilities in California, and 51 percent of the total Pacific States capacity, it had no plants in that area for fabricating heavy structural steel, and its eastern locations were at a freight-rate disadvantage vis-à-vis western producers. Before buying Consolidated, it had planned to build structural steel plants in California.

Following the District Court's denial of the injunction, the government appealed to the Supreme Court, where, in a 5–4 decision, the lower court was upheld. In reasoning similar to the *International Shoe* decision, the Supreme Court found that prior competition between Consolidated and U. S. Steel was not "substantial." In addition, by considering the acquisition and westward movement of U. S. Steel to be only an appropriate business expansion, the Court failed to address the preservation of, and potential increase in, competition between the two companies if U. S. Steel had built plants instead of purchasing Consolidated.[58]

The steady increase in economic concentration, the unpredictable interpretations of the antitrust laws by the Supreme Court, and the apparent threat to competition and to small business led to periodic calls for legislation to restrict merger activity and to correct the "assets loophole" in Section 7 of the Clayton Act. Twenty-one bills to amend the act were introduced in Congress between 1921 and 1950, the main effort coming after the Final Report of the TNEC, with 16 bills between 1943 and 1949. However, three events—the 1943–1947 mini-merger wave, the FTC's 1948 Summary Report on the merger movement, and the Supreme Court's decision in the *Columbia Steel* case—provided the impetus for the amendment to the Clayton Act, the Celler-Kefauver Act, signed by President Truman on December 29, 1950.[59] The most important changes were the rewording of Section 7:

—That no corporation engaged in commerce shall acquire, directly or indirectly, the whole or any part of the stock or other share capital and no corporation subject to the jurisdiction of the Federal Trade Commission shall acquire the whole or any part of the assets of another corporation engaged also in commerce, where in any line of commerce in any section of the country, the effect of such acquisition may be substantially to lessen competition, or to tend to create a monopoly.

—No corporation shall acquire, directly or indirectly, the whole or any part of the stock or other share capital and no corporation subject to the jurisdiction of the Federal Trade Commission shall acquire the whole or any part of the assets of one or more corporations engaged in commerce, where in any line of commerce in any section of the country, the effect of such acquisition, of such stocks or assets, or of the use of such stock by the voting or granting of proxies or otherwise, may be substantially to lessen competition or to tend to create a monopoly.[60]

Thus, 36 years after passage of the Clayton Act and nine years after the final report of the Temporary National Economic Committee, Congress assumed that in the Celler-Kefauver Amendment they had enacted legislation to halt the steady increase in economic concentration and preserve competition in the American economy. The following decades would test this assumption.

2

The Issue: Business Concentration in the 1950s and 1960s

THE THIRD GREAT MERGER MOVEMENT: 1951-1968

Ironically, a vast merger movement followed the enactment of the Celler-Kefauver Act in 1950. This Third Great Merger Movement, exceeding the previous two, began with a disappearance of 235 formerly independent firms in 1951, and steadily increased until 1968, when a staggering total of 2,442 corporations disappeared into mergers during that year alone (Table 1.1). Another indication of the enormity of this merger wave was the disappearance of 1,261 large firms, defined as those with assets of $10 million or more.[1] The number of large firms acquired grew from nine in 1951 to 99 in 1966, then jumped dramatically to 167 in 1967 and to 201 in 1968. The transfer of assets accompanying these acquisitions averaged well over $1 billion through 1960, averaged $3 billion from 1961 through 1966, and reached almost $13 billion in 1968 (Table 2.1). Especially significant is that 46 percent of these large firms, representing 64 percent of their total assets, were acquired by the 200 largest industrial corporations, thus increasing the degree of concentration in the American economy. Indeed, by the end of 1968, the 200 largest industrial corporations controlled over 60 percent of the total assets held by all manufacturing companies in the United States, an amount equal to that held by the 1,000 largest in 1941 when the TNEC warned of the growing concentration of economic power (Table 2.2).[2] It is not surprising that academicians, small businessmen, members of Congress, and the antitrust agencies viewed with alarm this accelerating concentration of economic power.

This great merger wave took place during a period of prosperity marked by a rapidly expanding economy, easy money, and a buoyant stock market. As in the mini-wave of the 1940s, over half of the mergers took place in the machinery, chemical, food, transportation equipment, and textile industries. Once again, investment bankers and financial consultants were active, but to a greater extent than in previous movements, corporate management initiated merger activity, and

Table 2.1
Disappearance by Merger of Large Manufacturing and Mining Firms,
1951–1968

Year	Number	Assets ($millions)
1951	9	201
1952	14	338
1953	23	679
1954	35	1426
1955	67	2117
1956	55	1991
1957	51	1442
1958	37	1077
1959	64	1959
1960	62	1708
1961	55	2056
1962	72	2174
1963	71	2956
1964	89	2707
1965	90	3827
1966	99	4167
1967	167	9062
1968	201	12800
Total	1261	52684*

* Detail does not add to total due to rounding.
Note: Large acquired companies are those that had $10 million in total assets at the time they were acquired.
Source: Adapted from Federal Trade Commission, Staff Report, *Economic Report on Corporate Mergers* (Washington: U. S. Government Printing Office, 1969), 185.

Table 2.2
Percent of Manufacturing Assets Held by the 200 Largest Corporations, 1951–1968

Year	Percent
1951	47.7
1952	49.2
1953	50.3
1954	52.1
1955	53.1
1956	54.1
1957	55.6
1958	56.6
1959	56.0
1960	56.3
1961	56.3
1962	56.0
1963	56.3
1964	56.6
1965	56.7
1966	56.7
1967	59.3
1968	60.9

Source: Adapted from Federal Trade Commission, Staff Report, *Economic Report on Corporate Mergers* (Washington: U. S. Government Printing Office, 1969), 173.

established offices for "Corporate Development" or "Acquisitions." Firms with solid, though not spectacular, earnings records, frequently with the book value of their assets far below their liquid market value, became the prey of a new breed of corporate executives—financiers, not industrialists—who sought rapid profit enhancement through acquisitions rather than the slower route of internal growth.[3] In 1951, acquisitions by large firms represented less than 3 percent of the investment in new capital, and remained around 20 percent from 1959 through 1966. In 1967 and 1968, however, acquisitions rose to 39 and 55 percent of new capital investment. It appeared that growth by merger, rather than by investment in new plant and equipment, increasingly occupied the attention of management. This situation was characteristic of the most prominent feature of the Third Great Merger Movement, the conglomerate firm.[4]

CONCENTRATION

Aggregate Concentration

By the end of 1968, the 200 largest industrial corporations controlled over 60 percent of the total assets held by all manufacturing companies in the United States, an amount equal to the 1,000 largest in 1941. In fact, by the end of 1968, just 87 corporations, each with assets in excess of $1 billion, held 46 percent of all manufacturing assets and received 50 percent of the net profits earned by all manufacturing corporations in the United States. In addition, these 87 represented an increase, in only ten years, in the number of billion-dollar firms (assets) from 24, with 26 percent of the assets and 36 percent of the net profits (Figure 2.1). Moreover, by 1968, 384 of the 1,000 largest corporations in 1941, including 37 of the 200 largest in that year, had disappeared by merger. These figures substantiate the increase in aggregate concentration—the centralization of economic power, usually in the 200 largest manufacturing firms—in American business during the Third Great Merger Movement.[5]

Of the 14,877 firms disappearing by merger from 1951 to 1968, 1,261 were large firms. A further examination of the importance of mergers in this period of increasing concentration indicates that of the 1,261 companies, 101 had assets in excess of $100 million. Included in these were 24 very large firms—those with $250 million or more in assets—six of which were acquired in 1967 and 12 in 1968 alone.[6]

During this period, mergers accounted for approximately 75 percent of the increase in assets of the 200 largest manufacturing corporations, with about 25 percent attributable to industrial growth. And within the 200, the 70 most merger-active companies represented about two-thirds of the increase. Moreover, this increasing concentration in assets took place while over 50,000 new manufacturing companies, and entire new industries, were added to the industrial population. In

Figure 2.1
Distribution of Assets and Profits by Size of Company, First Quarter of 1959 and 1969

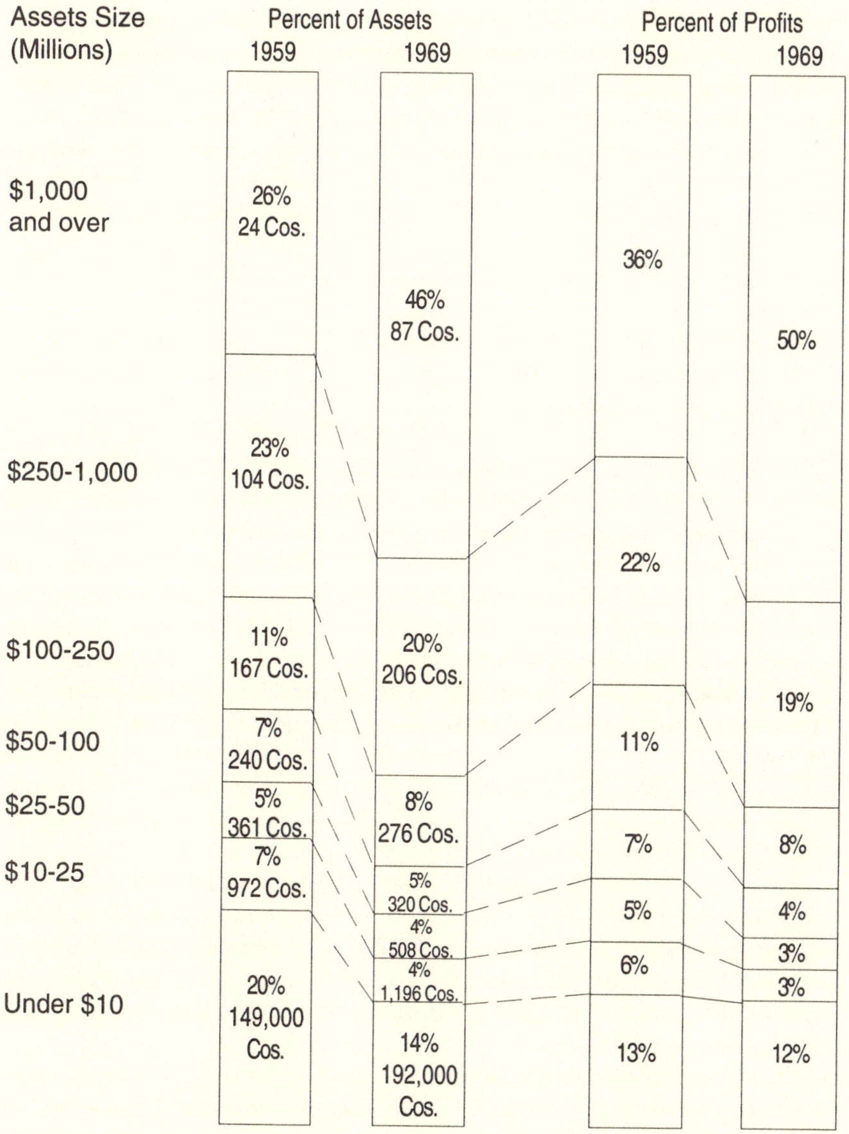

Assets Size (Millions)	Percent of Assets 1959	Percent of Assets 1969	Percent of Profits 1959	Percent of Profits 1969
$1,000 and over	26% 24 Cos.	46% 87 Cos.	36%	50%
$250-1,000	23% 104 Cos.		22%	
$100-250	11% 167 Cos.	20% 206 Cos.		19%
$50-100	7% 240 Cos.		11%	
$25-50	5% 361 Cos.	8% 276 Cos.	7%	8%
$10-25	7% 972 Cos.	5% 320 Cos.	5%	4%
		4% 508 Cos.	6%	3%
Under $10	20% 149,000 Cos.	4% 1,196 Cos.		3%
		14% 192,000 Cos.	13%	12%

Source: Adapted from Federal Trade Commission, Staff Report, *Economic Report on Corporate Mergers* (Washington: U. S. Government Printing Office, 1969), 163.

other words, a statistical universe of 200 corporations was significantly expanding its share of an immensely larger universe, which was itself expanding at this time. Between 1951 and 1968, the largest 0.1 percent of all American manufacturing corporations had increased their share of total manufacturing assets from 41 to over 60 percent.[7]

It is important to note that acquisitions by the largest corporations have generally been of profitable companies. A study of 234 of the large manufacturing and mining firms acquired between 1961 and 1968 indicates that 111 had profits greater than their industry average, and 17 were twice as profitable as their industry average. Only eight, less than 4 percent, were not profitable at the time they were acquired. Moreover, these companies often held leading positions in their industries. Smaller corporations usually acquired the less profitable firms.[8] Thus, most acquisitions by large corporations did not involve the purchase of failing companies, nor did they represent "toehold acquisitions" of smaller firms that might have been expanded to challenge the market position of the dominant companies. Instead, they added to the already considerable market power of the large acquiring firms and to the aggregate concentration in the economy.

In addition, corporations became increasingly entwined through jointly owned operations, known as joint ventures. From 1960 to 1968, the 200 largest manufacturing companies formed at least 705 joint ventures, which involved 1,153 intercorporate ties, approximately 20 percent with each other. The 50 largest companies participated in 608 of these joint ventures, 178 with companies among the largest 200. Such activity further intensified the degree of aggregate concentration in the economy.[9] By strengthening already existing relations or establishing new ones, joint ventures contained the potential for reducing both actual and potential competition, especially among those large companies that were the leading firms in their industries. Business partners in one market may be less inclined to compete aggressively when they meet as rivals in other markets.

The actual degree of aggregate concentration, or centralization of corporate decision making, is even greater than that indicated by asset control. Many of the largest corporations, including the largest 200, are related to each other and to other corporations, both manufacturing and nonmanufacturing, and to legal and financial institutions, in ways that may infringe upon totally independent decision making. Probably the most frequent and widespread example of this relation is that referred to as interlocking directorates or interlocking managements, achieved through common board members or corporate officers. Although Section 8 of the Clayton Act prohibits direct interlocks—those among competing firms— corporations establish many indirect interlocks with suppliers, customers, potential competitors, and with each other through these indirect links.

A 1962 study prepared for the House Antitrust Subcommittee showed that 29 of the largest corporations had interlocking arrangements with 745 industrial corporations, 330 banks, and 51 other corporations. General Motors, for example, was interlocked with 63 companies with assets exceeding $65 billion; U. S. Steel with 89 companies with assets exceeding $100 billion. An FTC study in 1965 revealed that the top 200 industrial corporations had 476 interlocks among themselves, and 974 with the next 800 largest.[10]

Corporate interlocks are especially significant for aggregate concentration, not only because of their impact on independent management decision making, but also because of their frequency among the largest corporations. These large corporations are leading firms in their own industries and could be potential entrants, that is, competitors, in many of the industries of the corporations with which they are interlocked.

Market Concentration

Whereas aggregate concentration deals with the control of assets and centralized decision making, market concentration refers to the share of total industry output, sometimes called "value of shipments," produced by the four leading firms within an industry. This four-firm share is often called the "concentration ratio."

Census Bureau figures indicated that by 1966, 33 percent of all U.S. manufacturing took place in industries in which four companies accounted for 50 percent of output. The Census Bureau's survey covered 382 of the 417 manufacturing industries. Of the industries surveyed, 14 percent of production ($66 billion) took place in industries in which the top four firms accounted for 75 percent or more of output; 19 percent ($89 billion) took place in industries in which the top four produced between 50 and 74 percent of total output. The survey further revealed that 40 percent of manufacturing was in industries in which the four leading firms produced 25 to 49 percent of total shipments, and that only 27 percent took place in industries with a four-firm concentration ratio under 25 percent.[11] Fifty percent and above is considered to be highly concentrated, 25 to 49 percent to be moderately or intermediately concentrated, and below 25 percent to be low or unconcentrated (Figure 2.2).

Comparison with previous years is difficult because total and average figures do not indicate changes among specific industries, producers, or products over time, nor the presence of new industries that came into being. Moreover, in periods of increasing demand and general economic growth, it is easier for new competitors to enter an industry, and for fringe firms to expand at the expense of industry leaders. The years of the Third Great Merger Movement, and especially the 1960s, were marked by general prosperity and economic growth. In addition, the Census Bureau did some redefining of industries and products for the introduction, in 1963, of its new Standard Industrial Classification (SIC) System. Also, as will be discussed later, the passage of the Celler-Kefauver Act, resulting in a decline in horizontal and vertical mergers, apparently gave impetus to the conglomerate variety, which would affect aggregate and market concentration. Further, concentration is understated in industries in which firms specialize in specific

Figure 2.2
Distribution of Manufacturing Industries by Four-Firm Concentration Ratio, 1966

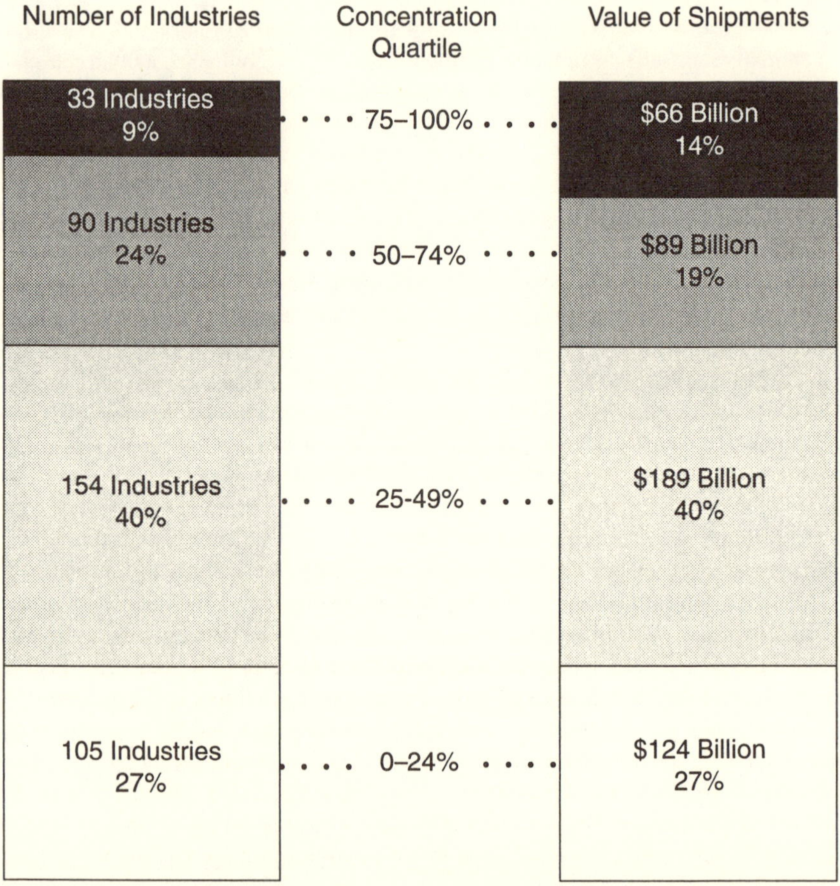

Number of Industries	Concentration Quartile	Value of Shipments
33 Industries 9%	· · · 75–100% · · · ·	$66 Billion 14%
90 Industries 24%	· · · 50–74% · · · ·	$89 Billion 19%
154 Industries 40%	· · · 25-49% · · · ·	$189 Billion 40%
105 Industries 27%	· · · 0–24% · · · ·	$124 Billion 27%

Source: U. S. Cabinet Committee on Price Stability, *Study Paper Number 2: Industrial Structure and Competition Policy* (Washington: U. S. Government Printing Office, 1969), 57.

Note: The manufacturing sector is composed of 417 industry categories. Excluded from the above tabulation are: 15 industry categories composed of products "not elsewhere classified" within major industry groups, 18 local and small regional market industries, and the newspaper and periodical industries. The Census did not publish 1966 concentration ratios for 29 industries. For these 29 industries, 1963 concentration ratios were used.

products rather than produce an entire line. In such cases, the degree of concentration would be higher for the individual products than for the industry as a whole. Finally, national concentration figures, in a nation as geographically large as the United States, may understate concentration in particular regional markets and may distort the market impact of a firm or product in that area.

Nevertheless, the Census Bureau was able to report on 213 industries that remained essentially comparable during the period 1947 to 1966. This comparison indicates that from 1954 to 1966, those industries in which a four firm concentration accounted for 50 percent or more of all shipments increased from 71 to 73, those with a four-firm output of 25 to 49 percent increased from 73 to 80, and those below 25 percent concentration declined from 69 to 60 percent.[12] Thus, there was an overall increase in high and moderately concentrated industries, accompanied by a decline in the low or nonconcentrated ones, indicating a general increase in market concentration. This would be consistent with the increase in aggregate concentration and the growth in the number of large and very large manufacturers in the economy.

These 213 industries were divided into 132 producer goods industries and 81 consumer goods industries. From 1954 to 1966, the high and low concentrated producer goods industries declined by three and two respectively, while the moderately concentrated rose by five. During this same period, the high and moderately concentrated consumer goods industries increased by five and two respectively, while the low decreased by seven. These figures, considering the uncertainties mentioned above, reflect the beginning of a decline in heavy industry and the increasing demand for consumer goods, indicative of prosperity and a growing economy. During these years, average four-firm concentration, or market concentration, in 213 industries increased from 40.6 to 41.9 percent, a further indication of the growth of large and very large manufacturers in the economy.[13]

Consumer goods industries are further divided into undifferentiated (e.g., government-graded fresh meat) and differentiated (e.g., breakfast cereals). Usually the degree of product differentiation is positively associated with the amount of advertising expended. Industry increases and decreases are based on a minimum change of three percentage points in four-firm concentration. Between 1947 and 1966, concentration increased in 14 of 17 highly differentiated industries (82 percent), in 21 of 36 moderately differentiated ones (58 percent), and in 12 of 28 undifferentiated ones (43 percent). These figures coincide with an overall increase in average four-firm concentration from 35.4 in 1954 to 39.6 in 1966.[14] Economic analysis of this increased concentration in consumer goods industries indicates that even when such factors as economies of scale and industry growth rates were considered, the most significant factor was television advertising. (There was little or no relation between concentration and other forms of advertising.) This finding reflects not only the growing importance of television advertising in the 1950s and 1960s, but also the enormous promotional resources, both human and financial, that the large and very large manufacturers were able to bring to the market.[15]

Table 2.3
Concentration Ratios for Representative Industries, 1972

Industry	4-Firm Ratio (%)	Number of Firms
Motor vehicles and car bodies	93	165
Electric lamps	90	103
Chewing gum	87	15
Cigarettes	84	13
Household laundry equipment	83	20
Primary aluminum	79	12
Aircraft engines and engine parts	77	189
Photographic equipment and supplies	74	555
Tires and inner tubes	73	136
Calculating and accounting machines	73	74
Primary copper	72	11
Aircraft	66	141
Metal cans	66	134
Motorcycles, bicycles, and parts	65	219
Soaps and other detergents	62	577
Environmental controls	57	117
Railroad equipment and locomotives	56	128
Watches and clocks	55	183
Radio and TV receiving sets	49	343
Farm machinery and equipment	47	1465
Motors and generators	47	325
Blast furnaces and steel mills	45	241
Toilet preparations	38	593
Flour and other grain mill products	33	340
Petroleum refining	31	152
Footwear, except rubber	30	153
Bread, cake, and related products	29	2800
Pharmaceutical preparations	26	680
Cement	26	75

Source: Adapted from "Concentration Ratios in Manufacturing," Bureau of the Census MC72 (SR) -2, issued October 1975, Table 5 items.

As would be expected, the largest corporations held prominent positions in the most concentrated industries. By 1963, companies among the 200 largest produced 73 percent of total shipments in the highly differentiated consumer products market, and were responsible for 87 percent of output in all highly concentrated industries where the four leading firms accounted for 75 percent or more of total shipments. Each of the 100 largest manufacturers held at least one of the leading positions in one five-digit product class, and on the average, each occupied over ten leading positions. In total, the 100 largest held 1,052 leading positions in individual product markets.[16]

By 1968, the 200 largest manufacturers had greatly increased their presence in all production categories, from the five-digit product class through the two-digit major industry group. One hundred twelve of the 200 participated in five or more of the major industry groups, with 32 participating in over ten. One hundred ninety seven participated in over five product classes, 181 in over ten, and 32 in over 50 product classes.[17] This increased participation also increased the number of contact points at which the largest manufacturers would meet each other, thereby affecting independent decision making and competitive behavior. Thus, during this period, the largest 200 had a profound impact on market concentration. They not only accounted for an increasing share of total shipments, but they greatly diversified, spreading their power and resources into many areas of the economy.

Mergers played an important role in the increase in market concentration. Between 1950 and 1968, 327 of the 1,000 largest manufacturers disappeared by merger, 190 of which were acquired by the 200 largest. Of these 190, 22 had been among the largest 200, and 42 had ranked among the 201st to 400th largest. Further, these 190 companies had operated in 1,404 product classes and held leading positions in 374. (They held fifth to eighth positions in 315.)[18] Therefore, the largest manufacturers substantially increased their leading positions. Moreover, mergers eliminated actual or potential competition between the merging parties. In addition, the acquired firms may have been potential competitors in other product classes or even other industries. Thus, mergers impacted directly upon market concentration, the number of leading positions held by the 200 largest manufacturers, and the amount of competition in the economy (Table 2.3).

Concentration of Corporate Headquarters

In addition to aggregate and market concentration already discussed, the 200 largest U.S. manufacturing corporations were responsible for a headquarters concentration, with socioeconomic and political ramifications little investigated by 1968. By that year, the headquarters of 82 of the 200 were located in New York State. Only four states had more than ten: California, Ohio, Illinois, and Pennsylvania, with 19, 19, 17, and 12 respectively. Michigan followed with eight. Thus, 157 (78.5 percent) of the 200 largest corporations had their headquarters in

Table 2.4
Acquisitions by Location of Corporate Headquarters, State of Acquired and
Acquiring Companies, Net Gain or Loss of 80 Firms, 1955–1968

State	Firms headquartered in State that were acquired		Acquisitions made by firms headquartered in State		Net gain or loss
	By firms outside State	By firms inside State	Of firms outside State	Of firms inside State	
CA	1541	1052	1030	1052	-511
CO	187	14	55	14	-132
CT	392	72	310	72	-82
FL	367	110	191	110	-176
GA	240	44	136	44	-104
IL	910	435	1394	435	484
IN	296	43	214	43	-82
KS	121	6	32	6	-89
MA	578	179	494	179	-84
MI	567	188	456	188	-111
MN	190	59	280	59	90
NJ	727	136	627	136	-100
NY	1346	1386	3078	1386	1732
NC	198	41	76	41	-122
OH	788	317	908	317	120
PA	842	261	929	261	87
VA	191	17	107	17	-84
Total	12798	5096	12798	5096	0

Source: Adapted from Federal Trade Commission, Staff Report, *Economic Report on Corporate Mergers* (Washington: U. S. Government Printing Office, 1969), 697–698.

Note: Columns do not add to total due to omission of states.

just six states, with the remaining 43 spread over 44 states.[19]

An FTC study investigating 17,894 manufacturing and mining mergers between 1955 and 1968 revealed that 12,798 (71.5 percent) of these involved acquisitions by companies whose headquarters were outside of the state of the acquired company. The remainder were acquired by firms within the same state (Table 2.4). The survey further indicated that in every state except New York, more firms were acquired by out-of-state companies than by those within the home state, and that 40 of the 50 states showed a net loss of corporations. Only New York, with 1,732, Illinois, 484, and Ohio, 120, had a net gain exceeding 100. California, Florida, and Colorado had net losses of 511, 176, and 132, respectively.[20]

During this Third Great Merger Movement, apparently little research had been available concerning the impact of mergers on local communities when the acquiring firm is located out-of-state, or located at a significant distance in the same state. Community populations, number and kinds of industries in the area, and number of workers in the acquired firms, are but a few of the many and varied factors that must be considered. The FTC Staff Report briefly discussed a 1969 report prepared for the Governor of Wisconsin which indicated that out-of-state companies acquiring Wisconsin firms tended to use the financial, legal, and accounting services of the parent firm rather than local professional services. The report also found that companies acquired by in-state firms grew less rapidly after the merger than before, despite a general growth within the state, and that companies acquired by out-of-state firms showed generally negative growth. Nevertheless, opinion surveys taken in conjunction with the study indicated that a majority of the general public, including newspaper editors, were unaware of any adverse impact on these communities.[21]

In a book published in 1965, Senator Estes Kefauver stated that "the area of social effects of monopoly and high industrial concentration upon community life is particularly barren of study and analysis." He then discussed a 1959 Rochester, New York, study entitled *Out-of-Town Acquisitions of Rochester Companies*. The study reported that the outside owners were not sensitive to community needs nor imbued with the same sense of loyalty and responsibility as local owners had been. The newly installed local management had little feeling of community identity. Local banks, lawyers, and insurance companies reported that the major portion of the merged firms' business now went to the institutions and agencies of the parent company. Thus, local banks received fewer deposits and had fewer funds to loan to local businesses and homeowners. Further, because the large parent companies engaged in various types of reciprocity regarding parts, supplies, and raw materials, sometimes involving many types of products and industries, the local Rochester suppliers received less business from their previous customers, no longer locally owned.[22]

Senator Kefauver also discussed an earlier study prepared by the Smaller War Plants Corporation. Although published in 1946, the study was concerned with economic concentration and the effect it would have on the general welfare of cities and their inhabitants. The report spoke of the local businessman as a civic leader concerned with community health, better schools, streets, parks, and playgrounds, concerns that are sometimes absent for officials of absentee-owned corporations. If the latter are ambitious and successful, their stay in the local area is short as they move up the corporate ladder. Professional interests and family ties may be elsewhere. Further, the out-of-town corporation can usually get its own way regarding civic projects or various concessions simply by the exercise of its power, such as threatening to close the local factory, or by maneuvering the election of local officials favorable to itself.[23]

In 1947, during congressional hearings on the Celler-Kefauver Act, Senator Kefauver stated, "The control of American business is steadily being transferred from local communities to a few large cities in which central managers decide the policies and fate of the far-flung enterprises they control. . . . Through monopolistic merger the people are losing the power to direct their own economic welfare."[24] Begun only a few years after that statement, the Third Great Merger Movement, snowballing to its great peak in 1968, brought about a degree of economic concentration, including that of major corporate headquarters, undreamed of by Senator Kefauver.

THE CONGLOMERATE MOVEMENT

Background

The most prominent feature of the Third Great Merger Movement was the explosive growth of the conglomerate form of merger, a form which, in its purest sense, united producers of totally unrelated products. The term *conglomerate* seems to have first appeared in a TNEC monograph discussing central control over "establishments having no apparent relationship" to one another. The FTC identified three types of conglomerate mergers. The first is the geographic *market extension* type, in which the acquired and acquiring companies manufacture the same products but in different geographic markets, such as Florida and California. The FTC admits that these resemble horizontal mergers. Second is the *product extension* type, in which the acquired and acquiring companies are similar in production and/or distribution, but the products are not the same nor in competition with each other, such as personal soaps and household cleaners. The third type is the *other* or *pure* conglomerate, which involves the merger of companies having "neither a buyer-seller relationship nor a functional relationship in manufacturing or distribution, such as a ship builder and an ice cream manufacturer." There may be some elements of all three types, or of horizontal and vertical, depending on the size and diversity of the acquired and acquiring firms.[25]

Conglomerates of the product and market extension types were recognized to have existed as early as the Second Great Merger Movement, representing about 27 percent of larger mergers during the years 1926 to 1930, and certainly existed

Figure 2.3
Distribution of Total Acquired Assets in Large* Mergers, by Type, 1948–1968

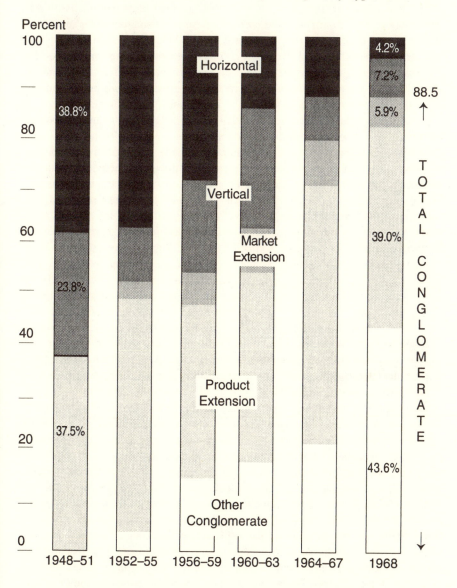

Source: Federal Trade Commission, Staff Report, *Economic Report on Corporate Mergers* (Washington: U. S. Government Printing Office, 1969), 61.

* Firms with assets of $10 million or more.

much earlier. They began to receive specific attention following World War II and in discussions leading to the Celler-Kefauver Act. By the end of 1968, however, conglomerate mergers represented 88.5 percent of all large mergers, with 43.6 percent being the other or pure type.[26] This "explosion" of conglomerates contributed to the alarm generated by the Third Great Merger Movement (Figure 2.3).

Many large and established companies in the automobile, steel, dairy, electrical, chemical, and other industries had been conglomerates, some for decades.[27] Nevertheless, the major part of their operations were usually within one industry and they were identified with that industry. The "new" conglomerates, however, not only disregarded industry boundaries, but extended their activities into a variety of financial and personal services. Some had been large and long established in specific industries; others were not even among the largest 500 ten years earlier.

Ironically, the Celler-Kefauver Act encouraged the growth of the conglomerate type of merger. The act, which gave the antitrust agencies a firm legal basis for opposing horizontal and vertical mergers, was less clear regarding the anticompetitiveness of the conglomerate, which operated in many markets rather than in the same or related ones.[28] Indeed, Donald Turner, who served as Assistant Attorney General for Antitrust from 1965 to 1968, did not believe that the Celler-Kefauver Act extended to conglomerate mergers, nor did Alfonso Everett MacIntyre, a Federal Trade Commissioner during the Kennedy-Johnson years.[29] Thus, the antitrust agencies did not seriously oppose the conglomerate movement during those years. In 1969, Representative Celler noted that "the success of the Celler-Kefauver Act, which prevented horizontal and vertical mergers . . . has probably encouraged conglomerates." And in that same year, Richard McLaren, Assistant Attorney General for Antitrust during the early years of the Nixon Administration, stated that the Celler-Kefauver Act did not reduce merger activity but redirected it into the conglomerate form.[30]

Whereas traditional market power was, and is, derived from the characteristics of a particular market—the number of sellers and each seller's position in the market, product differentiation, and so forth—the power of the conglomerate is internally generated, a combination of its diverse units and their products and services. The multimarket nature of a conglomerate gives it the potential to engage in practices not generally available to the single-market operator, especially the smaller businessman. Although the acquisition by a conglomerate may not immediately affect the concentration in the market of the acquired company, nor its customers, the merger may ultimately impact upon that market and its customers, and even the entire economy. In markets where the conglomerate lacks traditional power, it may temporarily exercise its overall power to weaken or repress rivals, or force them to take expensive defensive action, and to discourage entry of potential competitors into the market. Specifically, the conglomerate has a greater potential for reciprocity and cross-subsidization than its nonconglomerate rivals, and to act interdependently with those large corporations with which it meets at many contact points across many markets.[31]

Potential Impact on Competition

Reciprocity

Reciprocity, a common business practice dating to the days of barter, occurs when a firm purchases goods or services from companies that are actual or potential customers for its products. In concentrated markets, however, where producers acknowledge interdependence and engage in nonprice competition, a small producer, or single-line producer, would have relatively few opportunities for reciprocity, whereas a multiindustry conglomerate would have the potential to use reciprocity to expand its sales, entrench its own position, and injure its smaller competitors.

The conglomerate may, but does not necessarily have to, hold a large market share in a particular industry or product, nor does it have to have a direct buyer-seller relation for each of its products. For example, firm A in industry X has many suppliers who seek firm A's purchases and over whom A therefore has some oligopsonistic power. Firm A owns or acquires firm B in industry Y, which produces a product that firm A's present or potential suppliers use and must purchase from someone. A lets it be known that the best way to sell supplies to it is to purchase from B. Thus, reciprocity, buying from firm B, is a condition for selling to A. As a result, B's sales increase to the detriment of its rivals, and A's suppliers become more dependent upon both B and A. This example may be repeated many times as firms buy and sell various amounts to the subsidiaries and joint ventures of the multiindustry conglomerate. Interlocking directorates may be established to further solidify the reciprocal relation. Thus, it is the conglomerate's total sales and purchases, over a variety of industries and products, that gives it the potential impact on competition.

Reciprocity does not increase production, but rechannels it in favor of those firms able to exert sufficient market power to demand and receive reciprocal favors. It thereby reduces competition based on price, quality, and service, and further rigidifies the administered prices of oligopolistic markets. This in turn can structure or restructure markets by increasing concentration and raising barriers to entry. Firms without substantial market power would have opportunities for entry, or expansion, foreclosed to them. Although this can be especially serious for small firms, even billion-dollar corporations can be denied entry when their larger rivals have foreclosed a dominant share of the market through reciprocity and other arrangements. For instance, in 1962, Cities Service Corporation found its entry into the rubber-oil market blocked because the major tire companies had developed reciprocity arrangements with other large petroleum companies.[32] Companies finding themselves increasingly squeezed out of a market, or denied entry, may seek a merger with a more powerful firm, possibly a conglomerate, in order to be able to compete. Such a merger would, to some degree, further increase concentration and impact on competition.

By the mid-1960s, reciprocity had become sufficiently important that many large corporations had established "Trade Relations" departments and a Trade Relations Association had been formed. A reciprocity official of General Dynamics explained that prospective reciprocity partners were usually willing to enter such arrangements for mutual advantage and without coercion. And a representative of ALCOA's reciprocity program testified that ALCOA carefully reviewed its acquisitions to find opportunities for reciprocity among the previously independent companies' buyers and sellers. In an article published in 1965, Donald F. Turner, soon to be appointed Assistant Attorney General for Antitrust, stated that "even in the absence of formal or informal pressure . . . some producers . . . will voluntarily favor the conglomerate firm with their purchases in the hope of substantially increasing their own sales."[33]

By this time, however, the courts had begun to oppose reciprocal trading agreements. Then, in 1965, in the *Consolidated Foods* case, the Supreme Court struck down Consolidated's acquisition of Gentry, a manufacturer of dehydrated onion and garlic, on the theory that Consolidated, a large food processor and distributor, might base its purchases from food suppliers on their purchases from Gentry. The Court upheld the FTC's finding that the acquisition violated Section 7 of the Clayton Act because it gave Consolidated the "threat and lure of reciprocal buying in its competition for business and the power to foreclose competition from a substantial share of the market."[34]

Cross-Subsidization

Cross-subsidization is the use of profits obtained in one product, industry, or geographic location to offset losses incurred in another, and is but one type of price discrimination or predatory pricing. The deliberate use of cross-subsidization to injure or destroy competitors was one of the reasons for the enactment of the Interstate Commerce Act in 1887, which sought to prevent discriminatory freight rates imposed by powerful railroads. Although large size alone may give a firm such power, the conglomerate, selling in many markets, with products and profit centers relatively insulated from each other, would have more opportunities to engage in cross-subsidization, especially when it holds leading positions in highly concentrated industries. Thus, by using profits in area A to subsidize operations in area B, a firm may force its competitors in area B to choose between bankruptcy or merger, either of which would increase both concentration and barriers to potential entry in area B. Moreover, the mere presence of a powerful conglomerate in specific markets may intimidate potential entrants and thereby stifle competition and rigidify prices.[35]

Beginning in the 1950s, coinciding with the Third Great Merger Movement, television advertising soon became the most powerful weapon for domination, cross-subsidization, and intimidation in consumer goods markets. Unlike newspaper or magazine advertising, the supply of television time, especially major network prime time, is severely limited; it cannot be varied with demand. Consequently, with few exceptions, prime-time national advertising is dominated by a small number of very large corporations, with the smaller firms unable to compete or limited to a few less-desirable spots. Moreover, the multiproduct conglomerate can contract for large blocks of time and offer a variety of goods, changing with the weather, shopping seasons, or prearranged schedules, an option not available to the small or limited-line producer. In addition, the multiproduct conglomerate can use profits from its more successful items to subsidize increased advertising for new or slower-selling products.

Advertising is directly related to another limited commodity—display space in the retail outlet. Since sales for many consumer products, and perhaps their survival, depend on their visibility and ready availability in the market, rivalry for display space—shelf, floor, and checkout area—is keen. And since retailers depend for their continued existence on sales, products that are low-volume sellers are removed from display, while high-volume sellers may be given more space, and especially more prominent space. Thus, intensive advertising may not only increase consumer demand, but may also induce retailers to give additional space to the particular product. In addition, leading manufacturers may produce and actively promote different brands of the same product, in order to further squeeze their small competitors. A conglomerate, able to shift its advertising emphasis and resources to concentrate, for a limited time, on one or a few products, can preempt a major portion of limited display space, seriously harm its smaller competitors, and erect formidable barriers to entry.

Advertising and cross-subsidization may also be used by conglomerates to enhance the market position of recent acquisitions. The Supreme Court struck down the acquisition of Clorox by Proctor and Gamble because of the latter's ability to cross-subsidize, through extensive advertising, and thereby injure actual and bar potential competitors to Clorox.[36] Thus, the conglomerate corporation, through cross-subsidization, may have a potentially injurious impact on competition, injuring smaller businesses, barring entry to potential competitors, and increasing market concentration.

Interdependence, Forbearance, and Potential Competition

In a market of a few large sellers, firms tend to behave interdependently, that is, to take into consideration the consequences of their market decisions. The individual seller realizes that an independent market decision, for example, a decision to reduce prices, invites retaliation from its competitors, which could be to match the reduced prices, or to engage in a concerted action to drastically lower prices so as to injure their rival. Thus, in concentrated markets, firms rapidly develop a mutual awareness of common interests and operate like cooperating monopolists rather than individual competitors. Moreover, mergers increase the number of contact points at which competitors, suppliers, and customers meet, thereby increasing the mutual awareness or community of interest between them. Interlocking directorates and joint ventures further increase these contact points and further centralize corporate decision making. Finally, the increasing conglomeration that accompanied the Third Great Merger Movement greatly broadened the number of contact points and the opportunities for concerted action.

In addition, firms that meet in many markets are likely to treat each other with great deference, resulting in a condition of mutual forbearance. In other words, a conglomerate that is a dominant firm in a geographic market or a particular product may decide not to adopt a new market strategy—pricing, advertising, or whatever— for fear of retaliation in other markets where it does not hold a leading position. The same pertains to conglomerates that are both customers and suppliers of each other, since a price or production change by company A in one product or area may severely affect sales to it of raw materials by company B or purchases from it by company C in another product or area.[37]

When a few corporations dominate a market, they tend to refrain from vigorous price competition. Any increase in competition, therefore, must come from a firm not in that market. However, even if a potential entrant does not enter, its presence could affect the competitive behavior of firms in the market, especially if it is a large manufacturer or conglomerate. Thus, merger with or acquisition of the potential entrant would eliminate the threat to the status quo and maintain the price and concentration level in that particular market. In 1964, the Supreme Court acknowledged the importance of potential competition in ruling against the acquisition of Pacific Northwest Pipeline Corporation by the El Paso Natural Gas Company. El Paso, the only out-of-state producer to supply natural gas to California, acquired Northwest, which had once tried to enter the California market and remained a potential entrant. The Court, however, stated that Northwest "had a powerful influence on El Paso's business attitudes" and that its potential competition should be preserved.[38] And in 1967, potential competition was one of the issues in the Supreme Court's directed dissolution of the Proctor and Gamble-Clorox merger. In that case, the Court noted that since liquid bleach was a natural area of diversification or product extension for Proctor and Gamble, Proctor and Gamble was a potential competitor of Clorox. Their merger, if allowed to stand, would reduce the potential competition in the liquid bleach market as well as increase the barriers to entry by smaller, less powerful potential entrants.[39]

Thus, by 1967, as the Third Great Merger Movement, and the conglomerate movement within it, rushed to its peak, the Supreme Court had given warning that it would closely scrutinize potential competition, reciprocity, cross-subsidization, and the conglomerate threat to competition in the American economy.

Table 2.5

Assets Acquired by the 25 Most Active Acquiring Companies Among the 200 Largest Manufacturing Corporations, 1961–1968

Company	Number of firms acquired	Assets of acquired companies (millions)	Rank among largest companies according to assets 1960	1968
Gulf & Western	67	$2882	-	34
Ling-Temco-Vought	23	1901	335	22
IT&T	47	1487	35	15
Tenneco	31	1196	-	16
Teledyne	125	1026	-	136
McDonnell Douglas	8	864	242	62
Union Oil	11	825	56	30
Sun Oil	3	808	54	28
Signal Companies	10	770	126	66
Occidental Petroleum	15	767	-	41
Continental Oil	19	686	45	24
General Telephone	40	679	13	9
U. S. Plywood-Champion Papers	27	649	176	74
Litton Industries	79	609	275	67
Atlantic Richfield	9	543	46	25
North American Rockwell	6	534	103	58
FMC	13	497	121	89
Studebaker-Worthington	13	480	222	138
General American Transportation	4	453	94	123
Textron	50	454	132	98
White Consolidated Industries	28	443	-	133
Phillips Petroleum	11	440	17	20
Colt Industries	9	437	238	140
RCA	2	402	47	27
Georgia-Pacific	45	396	128	64
Total 25	695	$20227		

Source: Adapted from Federal Trade Commission, Staff Report, *Economic Report on Corporate Mergers* (Washington: U. S. Government Printing Office, 1969), 260–261.

MOST ACTIVE ACQUIRING FIRMS: 1961-1968

Three Conglomerates Reviewed

The Third Great Merger Movement brought a marked increase in aggregate concentration, especially that represented by the 200 largest industrial corporations. From 1961 to 1968, $40 billion in assets were acquired, with over $34 billion acquired by the 200 largest. Of this group, the 25 most active acquiring firms made 695 mergers, totaling over $20 billion or 59 percent of all assets acquired by the 200 largest. Table 2.5 lists these 25 by asset acquisition, indicates their rank among the largest manufacturing corporations, and shows the importance of mergers as a source of asset growth. In 1961, only 15 of the 25 were among the 200 largest, and only nine were among the 100 largest. By 1968, all 25 were among the top 200 and 20 were included in the top 100. Of the 25, eleven, including the three most active, were conglomerates. A brief review of these three follows.[40]

Gulf & Western (now Paramount Communications, Inc.) was the most active during this period, acquiring at least 67 companies with assets exceeding $2.8 billion. Energized in 1957 by new management under Charles Bluhdorn, Gulf & Western (G&W) rapidly expanded its original business, automobile and truck parts, becoming by 1968 one of the country's largest manufacturer and wholesaler of automotive parts. Until 1965, however, its expansion was largely automobile related. In that year, G&W made its first major conglomerate acquisition, New Jersey Zinc Company, one of the leading firms in domestic zinc production and a substantial manufacturer of chemical and fertilizer products. Among G&W's significant acquisitions in the next three years were Paramount Pictures in 1966, and Desilu Productions in 1967. Other acquisitions in the entertainment field included phonograph records, visual displays, and music publishing. In 1968, G&W acquired the Brown Company, a manufacturer of paper and wood products, and owner of extensive timber areas in upper New England and Canada. Also in 1968, G&W acquired two large financial institutions, Associates Investment and Providence Washington Insurance Company, which provided a variety of financial and insurance services throughout the United States. In addition to its consummated mergers, G&W gained considerable attention over acquisitions it was unable to complete— Armour, Allis-Chalmers, Pan American World Airways, Sinclair Oil Company, and others—some of which ran afoul of the FTC or Justice Department. Nevertheless, G&W made a considerable short-term profit between the purchase and sale of shares of these organizations.[41] Thus, by 1968, G&W had diversified far beyond the automotive parts market into entertainment, publishing, chemicals, wire and cable, real estate, paper products, and financial services. It had become a major player in the conglomerate movement.

Ling-Temco-Vought (LTV), the second most active acquiring firm during this period, rose from 335th to 22nd place among the largest industrial corporations in the United States. Having established his own electrical contracting business in

1946, James Ling acquired several electronics companies during the following years, and by 1959 was a prominent producer of radio transmitters, loudspeakers, and other sound equipment. In that year he purchased Temco Aircraft Corporation, a leading manufacturer of military reconnaissance equipment. In 1961, Ling acquired Chance Vought, an aircraft and missile producer. His renamed Ling-Temco-Vought Corporation now controlled a complete aerospace and electronics complex capable of competing in many areas, especially in defense contracts. LTV's products were used in air defense, the Polaris missile, and lunar exploration systems, and its space flight simulators were used to train astronauts. The 1965 acquisition of the Okonite Company, a producer of high quality copper wire and cable, followed by three additional electronic equipment manufacturers, completed LTV's rapid expansion in the broad electronics industry. Ling now rushed headlong into diversifying conglomeration. The first step was the takeover of Wilson & Company, a leading meat packer, which was also the country's largest sporting goods manufacturer as well as a producer of animal-derived chemicals, pharmaceuticals, and soaps. Next was the purchase of Greatamerica Corporation, itself a conglomerate, whose major holding was Braniff Airways, a domestic and Latin American carrier. The biggest plum, however, was the 1968 acquisition of the billion-dollar Jones and Laughlin, the fourth largest steel corporation in the United States. By the end of that year, LTV had become one of the most spectacular conglomerates, and James Ling a Wall Street hero. LTV, like the Third Great Merger Movement of which it was a part, peaked in 1968.

The third most active acquiring firm during this period was the International Telephone and Telegraph Company (ITT). Unlike G&W and LTV, ITT was already a huge organization in 1961, a worldwide communications-electronics company employing almost 300,000 people, which ranked 35th among U.S. manufacturing corporations. Nevertheless, under the leadership of Harold Geneen, ITT was committed to diversification. In the early 1960s, however, ITT's acquisitions were concentrated on communications-electronics firms, or technologically related companies, some of which were leading producers in specific product markets. Its first major diversifying acquisition was the purchase of Aetna Finance Company in 1964, which brought ITT into consumer loans, mutual funds, and insurance. Another consumer finance company was absorbed in 1968. In 1965 ITT acquired Avis, the world's second-largest car rental system, and in the next year obtained Airport Parking Company, one of the nation's largest parking companies, which also operated airport limousines and airport motels.

The merger mania that peaked in 1968 saw ITT acquire, in that year, 20 domestic corporations with combined assets approximating $1 billion. Most significant were the Continental Baking Company, the nation's largest bread and cake baking company; Levitt & Sons, Inc., a leader in home construction and planned communities; Pennsylvania Glass Sand Corporation, a leading producer of silica, electrical porcelain, high-voltage insulators, and products used in the chemical industry; and the Sheraton Corporation of America, operator of hotels and motor inns throughout the country. The largest of Geneen's 1968 acquisitions was Rayonier, with almost $300 million in assets, a major producer of wood pulps used in such products as rayon, acetate, cellophane, and plastics. A merger not consummated, however, with the American Broadcasting Company, received the most publicity. This acquisition would have made ITT a leader in radio and television broadcasting, phonograph records, and publishing. Under continuous pressure from the Justice Department, the merger attempt was abandoned. Nevertheless, by the end of 1968, ITT had further entrenched itself as a leader in the communications-electronics industry and had diversified into a variety of nonrelated businesses, usually by the purchase of leading firms in their markets. It had become the 15th-largest industrial corporation in the country.

Eight other conglomerates were among the most active acquiring firms. At the beginning of the Third Great Merger Movement, some were not even in existence, only slightly known, or single-line producers. By 1968, the conglomerates had electrified the financial community, frightened small businessmen, and challenged the antitrust agencies. They were the most prominent feature of the Movement.

TOWARD THE KENNEDY-JOHNSON YEARS

Following the passage of the Celler-Kefauver Act in 1950, there appeared a number of articles in the *American Bar Association Journal, Journal of Public Law, Fortune*, and other publications calling for a review and revision of the federal antitrust laws. Prominent among these was an article by S. Chesterfield Oppenheim, Professor of Law at the University of Michigan Law School, in which he noted that no attempt had been made to provide a comprehensive review of the various antitrust laws, their relevancy to current business conditions, and national enforcement policy.[42]

Undoubtedly influenced by this concern, Attorney General Herbert Brownell, in a speech on June 26, 1953, affirmed the Eisenhower Administration's commitment to antitrust enforcement and proposed the establishment of the Attorney General's National Committee to Study the Antitrust Laws. Stanley Barnes, the Assistant Attorney General for Antitrust, and Professor Oppenheim were selected as Co-Chairmen, aided by 61 attorneys, economists, and representatives from government agencies. Their report was submitted to the Attorney General on March 31, 1955.

Although the report strongly endorsed strict enforcement of the antitrust laws, it was neither a blueprint for broad legislation nor a call for changes in enforcement policy. The committee, however, indicated that court interpretations had frustrated the congressional purpose of the Clayton Act, which was to stop in its incipiency undue concentration of economic power. It therefore reaffirmed that Section 7 does not require findings of *actual* anticompetitive effects, but merely a *reasonable probability* of a lessening of competition, and that mergers must be studied in regard to their impact on the relevant markets and the foreclosure of competition. The report also recognized that Section 7 applies to all types of mergers and acquisitions, vertical and conglomerate, as well as horizontal. Addressing the courts as well as the antitrust agencies, the committee recommended four areas to consider in determining the competitive consequences of a particular acquisition: the character of the acquiring and acquired companies; the characteristics of the markets affected; the immediate change in the size and competitive range of the acquiring company and the adjustments required of its competition; and the probable long-range impact on companies actually or potentially operating in these markets.[43] Acknowledging that the Justice Department was handicapped in a civil investigation because it could not compel the submission of evidence, the committee recommended that the Attorney General be empowered to issue a Civil Investigative Demand, which would require the corporation or party under investigation to submit pertinent documents to it. Immediately espoused by the Eisenhower Administration, this recommendation became law during the Kennedy years. Finally, some committee members felt that "we need a law requiring advance approval of mergers when carried out by industry leaders, and placing upon the proponent the burden of proof that the transaction has technological justification and serves the public interest. This was proposed by the TNEC. . . . Nothing less will stem the merger movement."[44]

In order to reduce a large backlog of antitrust cases dating to the years of World War II, and to speed up internal procedures, the Antitrust Division revived the use of "prefiling conferences." Under this policy, after having investigated a particular situation and having made the decision to proceed with the case, the Antitrust Division would notify the prospective defendant and offer to negotiate a consent decree. The division also gave increased emphasis to the consent decree, a product of negotiation and compromise between the government and the defendant. Although it carries the force of a litigated judgment, the decree usually avoids a certain amount of unfavorable publicity for the corporation, and saves the time, manpower, and money of a long trial.[45]

The Justice Department also encouraged the use of premerger clearance, also called prior notification or advanced approval. Under this procedure, the companies involved in a proposed merger would submit all pertinent information to the Attorney General. Based upon the data presented, the Antitrust Division would issue a letter "clearing" or denying the merger. This preclearance, if granted, was considered an assurance that the government would not initiate proceedings against the merger at that time. Nevertheless, the clearance letter specifically reserved the right of the Attorney General to take action at a later date should additional information become available or other evidence warrant such action. The request for premerger clearance, however, was voluntary on the part of the corporations concerned, and in the absence of such voluntary submission, the antitrust agencies had to rely on newspapers and trade journals to find out about impending mergers. As noted above, both the Committee to Study the Antitrust Laws and the TNEC recognized the need for legislation requiring organizations contemplating merger to submit relevant information to the Department of Justice. Finally acknowledging this need, bills were introduced in the House and Senate at various times beginning in 1956, but premerger notification did not become law during the Eisenhower or Kennedy-Johnson Administrations.[46]

Until the 1950s, antitrust hearings had been conducted on an ad hoc basis by various Senate committees. As the concern over mergers and concentration increased, especially during congressional discussion concerning the Celler-Kefauver Act, it became evident that this sporadic attention was insufficient. Thus, in 1953, Senator William Langer established the Subcommittee on Antitrust and Monopoly of the Committee on the Judiciary, which he chaired. The new subcommittee was officially recognized by the Senate Rules Committee on March 18, 1955. In January of 1957, Senator Estes Kefauver became chairman of the subcommittee, and in July of that year began hearings into administered prices. The steel, automobile, drug, and other industries were investigated in hearings that lasted until 1963 and filled over 18,000 pages of testimony. However, no antitrust legislation resulted.[47]

On July 11, 1949, the Judiciary Committee of the House of Representatives, chaired by Emanuel Celler, established Subcommittee No. 5, the Subcommittee on the Study of Monopoly Practices. During the following year, the new subcommittee, also chaired by Representative Celler, began hearings into concentration and monopoly power in the steel industry, to be followed by inquiries into the newspaper and aluminum industries. Although four bills became law during the late 1950s, no major antitrust legislation was enacted.[48]

The House Subcommittee's hearings into antitrust enforcement resulted in a report, issued in late 1955, that criticized the "token gesture" made to enforce Section 7 during the years since the Celler-Kefauver Amendment. The report also accused the Antitrust Division of inertia and the FTC of a "disdain" for the intent of Congress. Beneficial effects, however, were an increase in the number of complaints filed by the FTC and an additional appropriation to that agency for antitrust enforcement. In May 1959, the subcommittee issued a report, based on two years of investigation and 4,500 pages of testimony, which denounced the consent decree process of the Department of Justice as weak and lacking in effective follow-up procedures.[49] In addition, Chairman Celler actively promoted stronger antitrust enforcement in his public speeches during this period.

Finally, both Celler and Kefauver supported premerger notification, but, as previously noted, they were unable to secure passage of such a law during their remaining years in Congress.

Two landmark cases regarding market concentration reached the Supreme Court during the 1950s, both involving the DuPont Corporation. In December 1947, the Justice Department initiated the "cellophane" case, charging DuPont with monopolizing the cellophane market. At this time the DuPont Corporation itself produced 75 to 80 percent of the output of this product, while its licensee, Sylvania, produced the remainder. DuPont, however, claimed that the market was not cellophane, but flexible packaging materials—wax paper, aluminum foil, and so forth—and that its share of this broad market was less than 20 percent. DuPont prevailed in the District Court and the government appealed to the Supreme Court. In June 1956, Justice Reed, writing for the majority, concurred with the lower court and found for the DuPont Corporation. The Court accepted DuPont's interpretation of a broad market within which cellophane was but one of several fungible products. The court then acknowledged DuPont's monopoly position in cellophane, but noted that the corporation's position had been attained through business expertise and patent protection. It concluded that monopoly "was thrust upon DuPont."[50] Thus, it appeared that the courts would continue to define the relevant market and that the rule of reason had been resurrected to define monopoly power.

In June 1949, the Justice Department filed suit to require DuPont to divest itself of its 23 percent holding in the stock of General Motors (GM). At the time, GM purchased 68 percent of its finishes and 38 percent of its fabrics from DuPont. The government charged that DuPont's position as the major supplier of finishes and fabrics to GM was based on the close relation between the firms rather than on competition. The government further asserted that this constituted a vertical merger, restraint of trade, and foreclosure of a large portion of the market for these products to other potential suppliers. DuPont argued that the stock was held solely as an investment, that Section 7 did not apply to vertical mergers, that the anticompetitive effect of a merger must be measured at the time the stock was acquired, not 30 years later,[51] and that its sales of automobile finishes and fabrics were less than 5 percent of its sales of all types of finishes and fabrics. When the District Court found for the defendant, the government appealed to the Supreme Court.

On June 3, 1957, the Supreme Court decided in favor of the government. The Court found that an investment would become unlawful if it brought about, or attempted to bring about, a substantial lessening of competition; that Section 7 applied to vertical mergers; and that the concept of "incipiency" in the Clayton Act denotes not the time of acquisition of stock, but any time at which the acquisition may lead to prohibited effects. The Court therefore ordered DuPont to divest itself of its GM stock. Of particular interest, the Court found that the relevant market was not finishes and fabrics, but automotive finishes and automotive fabrics, thereby recognizing DuPont's substantial position in those markets and that GM alone constituted a substantial market for the purchase of these products. Thus, the Court's definition of the relevant market had been narrowed from its position in the previous year's cellophane case.[52]

Because several early cases under the amended Section 7 had ended in consent decrees,[53] which do not provide legal precedent, the antitrust agencies had to wait until the landmark 1958 *Bethlehem Steel* case for their first adjudicated decision. In December 1956, Bethlehem Steel Corporation, the nation's second-largest steel producer with 16.3 percent of industry capacity, had announced its proposed merger with Youngstown Sheet and Tube Company, the sixth-largest producer, with 4.6 percent. The merger, if consummated, would have increased the top four firms' share, or market concentration, to 64 percent of national capacity, with the top two, U. S. Steel and the enlarged Bethlehem, representing 50 percent. The Justice Department challenged and the District Court enjoined the proposed merger. The defendants argued that the merger would enable Bethlehem-Youngstown to more effectively challenge the dominant position of U. S. Steel, and that the Chicago area, where Youngstown produced but Bethlehem did not, lacked sufficient capacity and the combined firms would have the resources to expand in that area. Judge Weinfeld rejected these arguments and found the proposed merger to be in violation of Section 7. He reasoned that if the combined firm could more effectively challenge the industry leader, approval would invite the remaining steel firms to merge in opposition to the big two and head the industry toward a triopoly. Weinfeld further stated that Bethlehem was a potential entrant into the Chicago area and that each had the "ability to undertake, on its own, a program to meet the existing and anticipated demand" in that region. He also noted that a merger would eliminate competition in Pennsylvania, Ohio, and other areas where the two did compete. As if to justify Judge Weinfeld's findings, Bethlehem announced in December 1962 that it would construct a steel plant 30 miles east of Chicago and by 1964 was producing at that location.[54]

Thus, the courts had again given notice that in the absence of specific legislation, they would be the interpreters of the relevant market and concentration within it.

The years following the enactment of the Celler-Kefauver Amendment witnessed the third and greatest merger movement in United States history. Between 1951 and the beginning of the Kennedy Administration in January 1961, over 5,400 formerly independent manufacturing firms disappeared by merger (Table 1.1) and the conglomerate form of merger, which represented 37.5 percent of mergers in 1951, increased to approximately 60 percent by 1961 (Figure 2.3). In addition, during this period, the 200 largest corporations increased their share of national manufacturing assets from 47.7 percent to 56.3 percent (Table 2.2). Despite congressional hearings into concentration and monopoly power, no legislation was passed to retard this merger wave, and no conglomerate merger case reached the Supreme Court. The incoming Kennedy Administration would have to weigh this increasing concentration of economic power against America's historical commitment to antitrust.[55]

3

The Response: The Executive

THE WHITE HOUSE: THE GOVERNMENT-BUSINESS ENVIRONMENT

The Business Community

The previous chapter detailed the growth of business concentration in the United States, especially during the Kennedy-Johnson years—the years of the Third Great Merger Movement. In order to examine the national government's response to that movement, it is necessary to identify the business community with which the branches and agencies of government had to interact and the political atmosphere within which that interaction took place.

During these years, the Federal Trade Commission estimated that there were approximately 370,000 manufacturing firms in the United States, with 195,000 chartered as corporations and the remainder identified as proprietorships and partnerships. Jim Heath, in *John F. Kennedy and the Business Community*, estimated that there were approximately 50 million white-collar individuals who considered themselves to be "businessmen." Blue-collar workers and farmers also considered themselves to be businessmen. Thus, the business "community" was not a single interest group, but a gigantic mixture of diverse interests, supported by over 13,000 national, state, and local organizations and over 5,000 local chambers of commerce, each seeking to affect government policy at all levels.[1]

Obviously these individuals and organizations were not equally influential nor could they command equal attention from government. However, just 200 of these manufacturing firms, less than 0.1 percent, controlled over 60 percent of the assets and received over 60 percent of the annual profits of the entire 370,000.[2] Although political leaders praised and encouraged small business development, reality required them to recognize that the health and growth of the national economy depended upon the decisions and activities of the largest firms. Therefore it was the leaders of these firms that constituted the most significant segment of the business community, the big businessmen with which the government had to interact.

Although these individuals belonged to numerous associations and were represented by public relations personnel, their direct link with the federal government was through the Business Advisory Council (BAC), the most prestigious, yet possibly least known, voice of big business. The BAC was established in 1933 as a "business cabinet" to provide corporate expertise to the Roosevelt Administration in addressing the problems of the Great Depression. Consisting of 60 primary and approximately 100 associate members, all board chairmen or executives of the largest corporations, this exclusive, self-governing, and self-perpetuating group had access to the highest levels of the executive branch. The Administration's point of contact with this elite group was the Secretary of Commerce, although the council members prepared their own agendas and conducted their own meetings. During World War II and the Cold War period, BAC members held various posts in the national government, including the positions of Secretary of the Treasury, Defense, and Army in the Eisenhower Cabinet. Toward the end of the Eisenhower years, council members were pressing for reductions in the federal debt, nonmilitary government spending, and personal and corporate taxes.[3]

President Kennedy's Secretary of Commerce, Luther Hodges, a successful textile manufacturer and former Governor of North Carolina, was disturbed about the special status of the BAC. Since this group was supposed to advise the Administration through him, as Secretary of Commerce, he believed that he should have authority over it. Hodges wished to broaden the council to include executives of small and medium-sized businesses, approve the selection of members, establish dates and agendas for meetings, open some or part of these meetings to the media, and have the meetings chaired by government as well as business officials.[4] Hodges's views were not well received. Election to the BAC was the ultimate recognition accorded corporate executives by one another, and they had long enjoyed their secret meetings with or without invited government officials. IBM's Thomas Watson, Jr. spoke the thoughts of many BAC members when he stated that Hodges projected an anti-big business impression. The BAC Chairman, U. S. Steel's Roger Blough, anxious to maintain the connection with the Administration, tried to convince the members to accommodate Hodges's requests. He failed. On July 5, 1961, Blough headed a delegation that informed the President that the Business Advisory Council was disaffiliating itself from the federal government, but would operate as a private group ready to assist any government agency seeking its help. Shortly thereafter, the group changed its name to the Business Council.[5]

Kennedy realized he needed business support in order to achieve economic growth at home and maintain America's position in world affairs. He therefore directed Cabinet officials to cooperate with the Business Council, and sent White House aides Ralph Dungan and Myer Feldman to patch up relations with council members. Cabinet members began to attend council meetings, and council members were invited to White House meetings. Chairman Blough was instrumental in the establishment of council "liaison committees" with the Departments of Treasury, Commerce, Defense, and Labor, and with the Council of Economic Advisors.[6]

Following the "steel crisis" of April 1962, briefly described below, Kennedy began to advocate a tax cut as a means not only of stimulating the economy, but also of improving government-business relations. Council members Henry Ford II and Stuart T. Saunders, President of the Norfolk and Western Railroad, took the lead in backing this effort by forming the Business Committee for Tax Reduction, which eventually enlisted almost 3,000 corporate leaders to pressure Congress for the reduction. By November 1963, the tax reduction effort was well underway.[7]

President Johnson, anxious for big business support, met with 89 members of the Business Council just 12 days after Kennedy's death. In this and subsequent meetings, Johnson, aware of the members' concerns, promised to work with Congress to hold or reduce government spending. By the following summer, council members were expressing confidence in the President and in the prospects for continued business growth. Their concern over antitrust was moderated by suggestions from presidential intimates such as Abe Fortas that these matters could be handled through "sensible administration" of existing laws. Council members and big businessmen in general supported Johnson against Goldwater in the 1964 presidential election. Shortly thereafter, Attorney General Nicholas Katzenbach assured council members that no vigorous antitrust activity was planned and that there would be no antimerger campaign initiated.[8]

By 1966, however, Johnson's "guns and butter" approach to the Vietnam War effort began to take its toll on the economy. The inflation rate, which had held at 1.5 percent per year during the early 1960s, rose to over 2 percent, and Administration officials unsuccessfully urged business executives to restrain price increases. Council members overwhelmingly supported the war effort, but also believed that unless spending for Great Society programs was curtailed a serious inflation would result. By mid-1967, war costs were exceeding estimates, inflation had reached an annual rate of 3.5 percent, and business leaders were restless. Business Council members continued to advise Johnson to cut nonmilitary spending. To alleviate the situation, Gardner Ackley, Chairman of the Council of Economic Advisors, recommended a one-year, 6 percent tax surcharge on both individuals and corporations. Johnson knew that Congress was not interested in a tax increase, and that big business would not accept a tax increase without a reduction in federal spending. Meeting in August with members of the Business Council, as well as the presidents of the National Association of Manufacturers and the U.S. Chamber of Commerce, the President proposed a temporary 10 percent tax surcharge, accompanied by a $7.5 billion spending cut. The businessmen were willing to support the tax surcharge, but they insisted on reductions in nonmilitary spending. Ford and Saunders again took the lead in securing support for the President, and within a few months had enlisted 500 corporate executives to put pressure on members of Congress. Johnson, however, was hesitant about cutting Great Society programs. When Congress demanded a minimum $6 billion cut in nondefense spending, council members insisted that Johnson comply. Needing business support, the President reluctantly agreed. In June 1968, the tax surcharge bill was passed.[9]

By mid-1968, inflation had reached an annual rate of 5 percent, war costs continued to exceed estimates, domestic unrest had increased, and Johnson had announced that he would not seek renomination. Council members generally supported the war effort, but had no desire to support a political party divided over the war abroad and its idealistic goals at home. Given a choice between a great society and an orderly one, big business looked again toward the Republican Party as 1968 came to a close.[10] Thus, as it had since 1933, the Business Council, as the primary representative of big business in its dealings with the federal government, established the political-economic setting in which the Kennedy-Johnson Administrations would attempt to balance their attitudes toward antitrust against their need for business support.

The Kennedy Years

In the 1960 presidential election campaign, both major parties had inserted antitrust planks in their platforms. The Republicans had but one phrase, pledging continued active enforcement of the antitrust laws. On the other hand, the Democrats, stating their opposition to monopoly, pledged vigorous enforcement of the antitrust laws, favored a requirement that corporations file advance notice of merger with the antitrust agencies, and pledged a more equitable share of federal contracts to small business.[11]

In his campaign, John F. Kennedy emphasized the theme of growth, which was to be the overriding objective of his presidency. He wanted to get America moving again.[12] On the domestic side, only growth could overcome the unemployment, idle industrial capacity, and economic recessions of the previous decade. On the international side, in the Cold War atmosphere of the time, only a strong growing economy could restore American prestige and combat Soviet military and industrial expansion.

Indeed, continued U.S.-Soviet hostility had brought about a level of defense spending unprecedented in peacetime American history. Moreover, the technological requirements of the nuclear battlefield had resulted in a demand for special-purpose equipment produced in special-purpose facilities, and an interweaving of political bargaining and shared power between big business and government.[13] In addition, the exceptional performance of the national economy since the beginning of World War II, and U.S. industrial leadership since that time, had made big business palatable to the American public. Kennedy could expect little or no public support for a crusade against monopoly power. The President also knew that business had largely favored the Republican Party and that he was not the first choice of the business community.[14] Thus, he would seek to establish a partnership between government and business in order to work toward the attainment of his goal of national economic growth. But he would also seek to attack this concentration of economic power through support for increased authority for the Antitrust Division and Federal Trade Commission, and indirectly through increased assistance to small business.

Kennedy began immediately to pursue his theme of economic growth and his plan to build a partnership with big business. In his first State of the Union message, he repeatedly emphasized the need for growth and offered tax incentives to business to spur investment in plant and facilities. On February 13, 1961, in an address to the National Industrial Conference Board, he stressed the need for growth and claimed a "kinship" with his audience, emphasizing that business and government are necessary partners and that their success is intertwined. Nevertheless, he wished to be precise in regard to the position of his Administration: "We are vigorously opposed to corruption and monopoly and human exploitation—but we are not opposed to business." Within the following month, Kennedy announced plans to award additional contracts to small business for defense and for research and development, and in April announced the establishment of a White House Committee on Small Business.[15]

Later in that same month, Congressman Celler had sought the President's support for legislation requiring corporations contemplating merger to provide prior notification to the Department of Justice. Such notification would have enabled the government to evaluate the competitive effects of a merger and indicate its objections, if any; reduce the difficulty of restoring merged companies to their original status; and prevent the merging companies from secretly gaining advantage over their law-abiding competitors.[16] Taking up this proposal in a special message to Congress on March 15, 1962, Kennedy stated "I strongly recommend enactment of legislation to require reasonable advance notice to the Department of Justice and to the appropriate Commission or Board of any merger expected to result in a firm of substantial size."[17] Although such legislation had been previously proposed by the Temporary National Economic Committee and the Attorney General's National Committee to Study the Antitrust Laws, premerger notification did not become law during the Kennedy-Johnson years.

As the autumn of 1961 approached, the President recognized a growing loss of rapport with big business. The clash between Commerce Secretary Hodges and the Business Council had created obvious strains. Lee Loevinger, Assistant Attorney General for Antitrust, had frightened the business community by threatening to investigate and/or dismember General Electric, General Motors, General Mills, U. S. Steel, and American Telephone and Telegraph, and by filing 42 suits in his first nine months. Moreover, in a November speech, Attorney General Robert F. Kennedy seemed to support Loevinger and further offended businessmen by emphasizing that although the Administration was not antibusiness, it would vigorously prosecute violators of the antitrust laws.[18]

Meanwhile, in reply to a reporter's question, the President stated that if "we're supposed to cease enforcing the antitrust law" in order for business to stop considering his Administration to be antibusiness, "I suppose the cause is lost." On December 6, in a major address before the National Association of Manufacturers, Kennedy hammered again on his twin themes of economic growth and business-government partnership. "For every reason, government and business are completely interdependent and completely involved. And while we may differ on the policies which may bring this country prosperity, there is no disagreement about the tremendous importance of . . . the growth of this country."[19]

Then came the widely publicized "steel crisis" of April 1962, when the major steel executives, who had previously agreed with labor and the government to restrain wage and price increases, announced an across-the-board increase in their steel prices. Kennedy, feeling betrayed, used the Office of the President to exert public pressure and forced the companies to roll back their increases.[20] This victory marked a new low in Kennedy's relation with business,[21] and corporate America braced itself for a dramatic increase in antitrust activity. The President, however, mindful of his goal of economic growth and the need for a healthy business climate, chose not to increase antitrust pressure. Instead, he sought to improve business-government relations.[22]

Addressing the U.S. Chamber of Commerce on April 30, Kennedy remarked that it was easy to charge an administration with being antibusiness, but it is more difficult to demonstrate how a nation can survive without business-government cooperation. Further, a private enterprise economy must be truly competitive if it is to realize its true potential. He then pointed out that nearly every action taken by his and previous administrations in the area of antitrust had been in response to complaints brought by businessmen. The antitrust laws, therefore, are not antibusiness, but are in the best interest of business and the general public. Returning to his theme of growth, Kennedy concluded by stating that "our primary challenge is not how to divide the economic pie, but how to enlarge it."[23]

In another attempt to "mend fences" the President delivered what came to be considered his best speech on economics at the Yale University Commencement, June 11, 1962. He again spoke of a business-government partnership but apparently didn't sway big business. According to Harvard Business School's Theodore Levitt, businessmen viewed the speech as one in which they were placed in the role of students, with Kennedy the teacher, talking down to them. They believed that they were made to appear unreasonable for opposing the Administration, and they resented the academic setting for so important a business speech. Consequently, many businessmen viewed the speech as another attack on them.[24]

In 1955, the Attorney General's National Committee to Study the Antitrust Laws, recognizing that the Department of Justice was handicapped in a civil antitrust investigation because it could not compel the submission of documents or other evidence, recommended that the Attorney General be empowered to issue a Civil Investigative Demand, which would require the corporation or party under investigation to submit pertinent documents to it. Presidents Eisenhower and Kennedy supported the measure and Loevinger convinced Senator Kefauver and Congressman Celler that such legislation was needed. Kennedy signed the authorization into law on September 19, 1962.[25] This would be the only significant antitrust legislation during the Kennedy-Johnson years, and the only one since the Celler-Kefauver Act of 1950.

The President also supported authorization for the Federal Trade Commission to issue temporary cease-and-desist orders against the continuance of unfair business practices while the cases concerned were pending. In the absence of such a law, and with the FTC powerless to halt such unfair or illegal practices, small competitors could be severely harmed, driven into bankruptcy, or forced into merger on adverse terms. The Administration, however, was unable to secure passage of this legislation.[26]

One week after signing into law the Civil Investigative Demand, President Kennedy held a special news conference with business editors and publishers. He discussed the free market as the best "regulator of our economic system" and stressed the need for safeguarding competition. Finally, he spoke of the need for "as close an understanding as possible" between business and government.[27] Business had benefited from the Kennedy Administration—new depreciation allowances, an investment tax credit, increased defense spending, legislation favorable to the drug industry, tax revision, a foreign trade bill, and most importantly for this study, no attack on the increasing concentration of industrial power. But his appeasement attempts were in vain; the business community responded to the President's efforts with continued hostility.[28]

As the new year began, the Kennedy Administration acknowledged its inability to establish the business-government partnership that the President had so doggedly pursued. As the Attorney General stated, "I don't know that businessmen, the big ones, anyway, no matter what we do, will ever be in love with us."[29]

The Kennedy-Johnson Administrations continued their pursuit of business support, but domestic and world affairs intervened to reduce the attention that might have been given to antitrust. In 1966, Loevinger commented that "by 1963, civil rights had become the showcase of the Department of Justice and antitrust had been, not entirely, but to a large extent, eclipsed."[30]

The Johnson Years

Like his predecessor, President Johnson was interested in promoting economic growth. Unlike his predecessor, he was able to gain the support of business to a degree unmatched by any Democratic President in this century.[31] In effecting the transition from the Kennedy Administration, Johnson unashamedly appealed to business. "I'm the only President you have. . . . I need your cooperation, I need it now. I need it tomorrow, next week, next month." And, mindful of the antibusiness charges hurled against the previous Administration, he continued: "We are not pro-labor; we are not pro-business. . . . We are pro-what-is-best for our country."[32]

Johnson impressed his position on the regulatory agencies. If they had to take action against an organization, they were instructed to do so. "But there is no reason to go out and get them worried about what you're going to do or pass out any new philosophy, telling businessmen what they ought to be thinking and doing."[33] Paul Rand Dixon, Chairman of the Federal Trade Commission during the Kennedy-Johnson years, reflected upon Johnson's position. "I remember shortly after Kennedy died—at one of the first meetings with President Johnson when he had us all down there and said he wanted to make it plain that he didn't want just meddling around with business for the sake of meddling. I think he was addressing himself to me principally."[34]

The President had a similar message for the Justice Department's Antitrust Division: Do your work as you should, but don't go around talking about it.[35] Following the assassination of President Kennedy, his brother, the Attorney General, remained in the Johnson Administration until the following September. However, he largely left the management of the Justice Department to his politically sensitive Deputy, Nicholas Katzenbach, who eventually succeeded him as Attorney General. Katzenbach had practically no interest in antitrust, nor did Johnson.[36] William H. Orrick, who had succeeded Loevinger as Assistant Attorney General in charge of the Antitrust Division, believed that "President Johnson thought of the antitrust laws as a means of negotiation with businessmen rather than having any regard for them as laws. There were a good many cases that should have been brought but just weren't brought."[37]

Johnson's first love, of course, was his Great Society program. He was well aware that the success of his many programs was dependent upon a strong and growing economy, which in turn was dependent upon business optimism and confidence in his administration. Thus, he kept massaging the business community with on-the-record meetings, off-the-record meetings, and personal invitations to the White House and the LBJ Ranch. He was successful to an amazing degree. By the summer of 1964 large segments of the business community, including prominent leaders such as Henry Ford II and Stuart T. Saunders, were actively supporting the President.[38] As U.S. involvement in the Vietnam War increased, economic growth and business support became even more important.

In March 1961, the American economy began an expansion that was to continue throughout the Kennedy-Johnson years and into the first ten months of the Nixon Administration. Although marred by war-related inflation, this 102-month expansion was the longest period of sustained economic growth in the history of the United States.[39] Despite Senate hearings, and the concern of individual supporters of antitrust, the Third Great Merger Movement and the conglomerate movement within it rushed forward.

THE JUSTICE DEPARTMENT

Economic growth, and the business support essential to it, had been established as the dominant theme of the Kennedy-Johnson Administration. Thus, the tone of antitrust policy, especially in the Department of Justice, would reflect that theme. During these years, three Attorneys General and four Assistant Attorneys General for Antitrust would influence the antitrust activities of that department.

In one of his earliest interviews as Attorney General, Robert Kennedy expressed his concern about concentration. "Too much power scares me, whether we find it in a trade union or in a corporation."[40] This concern, coupled with the selection of Lee Loevinger as Assistant Attorney General for Antitrust, suggested a forthcoming assault on mergers.

Loevinger, previously a judge on the Minnesota Supreme Court, earlier had been an attorney in the Antitrust Division and had a reputation as pro-antitrust. Robert Kennedy had told him that he expected antitrust to be a crucial program in the Justice Department and that he (Kennedy) wanted "an expert who would give direction and have a progressive and energetic anti-trust program." Loevinger replied that he believed that antitrust was "indispensable to the maintenance of a free enterprise system" and that antitrust was a kind of "secular religion" with him.[41]

Loevinger lost no time in displaying his zeal for antitrust. In April 1961, in his initial speech as Assistant Attorney General, before the American Bar Association, Loevinger stated that violators of the antitrust laws are guilty of "economic racketeering" and should be subject to as severe a punishment as "we can persuade the courts to impose." In interviews and in appearances before Congress he threatened to dismember some of the nation's largest corporations. Business became alarmed, referring to him as "wild" and "out of control." In November, in an attempt to ease business anxieties, the Attorney General presented an address before the Economic Club of New York entitled "Vigorous Anti-Trust Enforcement Assists Business." The attempt at conciliation failed, however, as Robert Kennedy seemed to support Loevinger and pledged prosecution of antitrust violators.[42]

Businessmen continued to distrust the Kennedy Administration and to expect an increase in antitrust activity, especially following the 1962 "steel crisis." However, according to Loevinger, "antitrust was played down" at that time. Prior to the April confrontation, the Antitrust Division had been preparing price-fixing charges against the major steel companies. Nevertheless, in the discussion of action to be taken in response to this incident, it was decided that the filing of these charges would be delayed several weeks in order to avoid the impression that they were the result of the "crisis." Despite the shock that had been given to the business-government environment, the President and his advisors were anxious to improve that environment and chose not to press for increased antitrust activity.[43]

Loevinger responded to his critics in the August 1962 issue of *Fortune*, by stating that over two-thirds of the 1,200 complaints annually received by the

Antitrust Division were from businessmen seeking antitrust protection from other businessmen. He further pointed out that since it was impossible to fully investigate all these complaints, cases were selected on the basis of potential contribution to the achievement of antitrust objectives. He scolded those businessmen who considered the antitrust laws to be too indefinite and uncertain, and those who considered them too rigid and inflexible. He attempted to assure them that his office was probusiness, but antimonopoly; that it did not seek to win cases or impose penalties, but sought only compliance with the law.[44] Though intended to reconcile, the article was too aloof, too didactic. Business suspicions were not allayed.

During Loevinger's two and a half years as Assistant Attorney General, 32 challenges to corporate mergers were filed by the Antitrust Division. Of these, only three involved the 25 most active acquiring firms (Table 2.4); two of these three involved a conglomerate.[45]

The first, filed on May 16, 1961, was against the acquisition of Malco Refineries of New Mexico by Continental Oil Company (CONOCO). In 1968, the District Court, on remand from the Supreme Court, held that the acquisition violated Section 7 and ordered divestiture.[46]

The second, filed on August 16, 1961, opposed the merger of Ling-Temco Electronics, Inc. and the Chance Vought Corporation, leading firms in electronics and aerospace products. The Antitrust Division charged that competition between the two companies would be eliminated and that Chance Vought would be removed as an individual producer in the design and development of aerospace equipment. In November 1961, the District Court ignored the conglomerate aspect, found that only insubstantial competition existed between the two firms, that the evidence did not show that the aerospace industry was a separate line of commerce, and that it considered the merger to be a diversification by Ling-Temco. The Justice Department did not appeal the case to the Supreme Court and thus gave up an opportunity to bring a conglomerate merger case before that Court.[47]

In the third, filed on June 5, 1963, the Justice Department sought a preliminary injunction to block the acquisition of American Viscose Corporation (Avisco), producer of industrial chemicals, by Food Machinery Corporation (FMC), a large producer of packaging machinery. Avisco produced over 55 percent of the viscose and approximately 35 percent of the rayon and acetate fibers consumed in 1962. The Justice Department claimed that the merger would substantially lessen competition in the manufacture and sale of packaging machinery, carbon bisulfide, caustic soda, and other industrial chemicals, and in rayon. The District Court found that the two corporations were not and never had been competitors in the manufacture or sale of any product, Avisco had sold no products to FMC, and FMC had sold only two products of any value to Avisco. Once the court had found that the merger was neither horizontal nor vertical, it denied the injunction, noting that the government had not cited a single instance in which an injunction had been granted to prevent a conglomerate merger. Thus, the District Court refused to consider the conglomerate aspect of the case. After the Justice Department's appeal was rejected, the case was dismissed in October 1963, upon motion of the government. Thus, by not appealing to the Supreme Court, the Justice Department gave up another opportunity to bring a conglomerate merger case before that Court.[48]

The Antitrust Division successfully challenged three mergers in the aluminum industry, two involving Kaiser Aluminum and Chemical Corporation and the third, ALCOA. It also successfully challenged Ford's acquisition of Electric Autolite Company, maker of automotive parts, and Kimberly-Clark's acquisition of Blake, Moffit and Towne, a western paper wholesaler. Although these suits involved horizontal and vertical mergers rather than conglomerates, they did serve to level the merger movement during 1962, 1963, and 1964 (Table 1.1).[49] Nevertheless, Loevinger was aware, as were his pro-antitrust critics, that the great majority of the antitrust cases filed during his stewardship were concerned with price fixing, not with the overall structural issues of merger and concentration.[50]

During the Loevinger years, the Supreme Court handed down its opinion in the *Brown Shoe* case, the first merger under the new Section 7 to reach that Court. The Justices found that the merger between Brown and Kinney Shoe Companies tended substantially to lessen competition at the horizontal level and the vertical aspects threatened to foreclose other manufacturers from effectively competing for retail outlets, eventually resulting in their demise. Divestiture of Kinney was ordered. The Justices further stated that the congressional intent of Section 7 was "that tendencies toward concentration in industry are to be curbed in their incipiency."[51]

Reviewing the *Brown Shoe* case in the Spring 1963 issue of the *Kentucky Law Journal*, Loevinger wrote that the dominant purpose of Section 7 was "to arrest the increase in economic concentration in the American economy. Any merger which substantially contributes to such an increase in any significant market or submarket is prohibited." If such an increase is disclosed by the evidence, all other issues are irrelevant. Loevinger evidently felt inhibited by the Administration's concern over business confidence.[52]

Robert Kennedy, however, had a good appreciation of the political and social consequences of antitrust, of the wider implications of antitrust enforcement.[53] In a March 1963 article, he stated that the aim of antitrust "is the same as that of business in general: to maintain and nourish the strength of our nation's free economy. The burden of accomplishing this aim, however, is not that of Government, in the last analysis. It is up to business itself."[54]

Although Loevinger had been selected to give direction to the antitrust program, he proved to be a poor administrator. There appeared to be little or no sense of priority or purpose, planning, or policy development in the Antitrust Division during his tenure. Moreover, the President and the Attorney General were sensitive to the strained relations between Loevinger and business leaders. Therefore, in June 1963, Loevinger was appointed a Commissioner of the Federal Communications Commission.[55]

William H. Orrick, Jr., replaced Loevinger as Assistant Attorney General for

Antitrust. Orrick had displayed considerable administrative ability as a Kennedy campaign member, Chief of the Justice Department's Civil Division, and Undersecretary of State for Administration. Attempting to familiarize himself with Antitrust Division policy, he found that there was none—that historically most of its cases began with a complaint from outside. Furthermore, 70 percent of the pending matters concerned price fixing, while only 30 percent concerned structural problems. In order "that we may direct our efforts to those areas in which they are most needed, and so that these efforts may be better coordinated and more purposefully controlled," Orrick established a Policy Planning Group to review the utilization of the Antitrust Division's resources and to conduct an in-depth study of heavily concentrated industries. This study was "not intended to be the basis for a short-run program of antitrust indictments . . . [but] an attempt to lengthen our vision."[56]

In a speech on April 17, 1964, before the Antitrust Section of the American Bar Association, Orrick announced that the possible application of the *DuPont-General Motors* case "to the problem of concentration is certainly an important part of our current thought and is, indeed, a major product under study by our Policy Planning Group." An acquisition which at first may appear neutral may be in the long run destructive of competition or could form part of an industry-wide trend toward concentration. Orrick went on to state that the Supreme Court opinion in this case has provided a tool to help restore to an over-concentrated industry the competitive vigor it has lost. "Although we are planning no broad-gauge inquiry into past transactions, in appropriate hard-core cases of economic concentration we will give serious consideration to its use."[57] Despite the threat, no action was taken to unravel mergers previously consummated by America's industrial giants.

As Orrick viewed it, the purpose of his office was not to regulate or manage business, but to keep business and the economy free.[58] His public speeches, therefore, seem to indicate that he was on a crusade, or campaign, to encourage big business to be concerned with the effects of concentration, to police itself, and to cooperate with government in maintaining a competitive economy. Orrick was concerned that each merger removed one of the competing alternatives to the consumer, and brought more of society's economic power into the hands of fewer individuals who bore no political responsibility to the public. He expressed his opinion that if concentration continued to increase, the economy would pass into private socialism and the public would respond by demanding increased regulation or even public ownership.[59] He noted that the antitrust laws, the Antitrust Division, and the courts exist to prevent industry from becoming regulated; without the enforcement of the antitrust laws, the extension of regulation would be inevitable.[60]

As an alternative to merger, Orrick urged internal expansion through new investment in additional productive facilities, which would result in additional employment and general economic growth. He pointed out that Congress and the courts also considered internal growth more desirable than merger. And in those cases where a merger had been successfully challenged and divestiture ordered, he suggested that the company and the public would have been better served had the time, money, and effort expended in litigation been put into internal development.[61]

Appearing before the Senate Subcommittee on Antitrust and Monopoly on April 21, 1965, Orrick posed the question, "What degree of overall concentration of economic power should the antitrust laws, as presently written, prohibit?" He asserted that for 75 years the national economy has been threatened by a concentration of control in the hands of a few large corporations, but the antitrust laws do not clearly define the degree of concentration that Congress should regard as intolerable. He continued that Section 7 of the Clayton Act defines the mergers it prohibits by reference to anticompetitive effects in any section of the country in any line of commerce. But this should not obscure the fact that some mergers— those referred to as conglomerate—which may have only a slight anticompetitive effect in a specific line of business or geographical location may diminish nationwide competition. He asked, "Can we say that such concentration of national economic power is not what Congress intended to prevent?" His own view, Orrick continued, is that even though the antitrust laws do not provide specific limits as to the acceptable extent of concentration, the Antitrust Division and the courts must consider the nationwide economic impact of any merger. The test of illegality under the antitrust laws is the anticompetitive effect. Therefore, if there is an anticompetitive effect, the antitrust laws can reach the conglomerate merger.[62]

During Orrick's two years as Assistant Attorney General, 26 challenges to corporate mergers were filed. Of these, only one involved the 25 most active acquiring firms, although the merger itself was not conglomerate (Table 2.4). On June 19, 1964, the Justice Department filed suit against General Telephone and Electronics (GTE), charging violation of Section 7. The complaint charged that GTE's acquisition of Western Utilities Corporation and its three subsidiary companies would substantially lessen competition in the manufacture, distribution, and sale of telephone equipment. The complaint also charged that manufacturers who compete with GTE would be foreclosed from the telephone equipment market represented by the previously independent companies.[63]

Significant mergers during this period that were successfully challenged by the Justice Department were the Humble Oil (Standard Oil of New Jersey subsidiary) acquisition of the western operations of Tidewater Oil Company, the Allied Chemical acquisition of General Foam, the agreement by Chrysler to acquire Mack Trucks, and the acquisition by Champion Papers of three smaller manufacturers of paper products.[64]

Orrick had hoped to accomplish more. He found a bottleneck, however, in Nicholas Katzenbach, who had succeeded Robert Kennedy as Attorney General. Katzenbach wasn't interested in antitrust and was influenced by political considerations. Thus, he frequently refused to file cases recommended by the Antitrust Division. As Orrick stated, Katzenbach didn't want "to become a vigorous antitruster and he wasn't and didn't."[65] An opportunity to challenge a conglomerate merger was lost when Katzenbach refused to file a complaint against the acquisition of the New York Yankees baseball team by the Columbia Broadcasting System. Orrick also opposed the merger of the Pennsylvania and New York Central Railroad, but Katzenbach refused to file a complaint because of the Administration's support of the merger. In addition, a monopoly case against AT&T, seeking the divestiture of Western Electric, was not filed.[66]

Both Loevinger and Orrick have claimed that there were no White House attempts to influence antitrust efforts. Moreover, Katzenbach has stated, "Both Presidents were insistent in all matters in the Department of Justice that political considerations be given no weight whatsoever. The best politics were no politics at all."[67] Nevertheless, the Antitrust Division was not without its political pressure. A brief sample of Orrick's *Daily Report* to the Attorney General will give the reader an indication of these pressures.

> August 1, 1963: "Senator Moss called about the consent decree in the Falstaff Beer merger case which limits Falstaff to 39 percent of the Utah market.... We advised that the decree provided for either a sale or a production limitation and that we are now awaiting a report of whether a sale can be made." (Daily reports for August 6 and August 16 also list calls from Senator Moss seeking to have the consent decree changed to increase Falstaff's production allowance.)
>
> October 4, 1963: "Governor Barron. The Governor of West Virginia called me to urge the importance of our settling the Ingersoll-Rand case on a basis which would permit the Company to buy Galis, a West Virginia company. The Governor asserts that this solution would mean 1500 jobs in West Virginia. . . . Senator Robert Byrd has also expressed an interest to me."[68]

In a letter dated September 1, 1964, to Attorney General Kennedy, Senator Robert Byrd of West Virginia requested that since Hazel-Atlas plants in Clarksburg and Wheeling manufactured stamped glass products and caps, not containers, they not be included in the Continental divestiture ordered by the Supreme Court. In a letter to Katzenbach dated 16 days later, Senator William Jennings of West Virginia made the same request regarding the Hazel-Atlas plants. However, in a letter to Orrick, dated August 12, 1964, Lee W. Minton, International President of the Glass Bottle Blowers Association of U.S. and Canada, recommended that the Justice Department approve the sale of Hazel-Atlas plants to the Brockway Glass Company.[69]

Landers, Frary, and Clark, a manufacturer of household electrical appliances, with plants in New Britain, Connecticut, and Fort Smith, Arkansas, had been purchased in 1961 by J. B. Williams Company, a manufacturer of shaving cream and other toiletries for men. The appliance operation, however, lost up to $12 million in the next few years and was offered for sale. On March 13, 1965, Landers laid off 500 employees and its demise appeared imminent. General Electric was the only interested purchaser, but the Antitrust Division opposed the acquisition because of GE's leading position in the electrical appliance industry. In letters to President Johnson, Senators Ribicoff and McClellan stressed the Great Society's concern with unemployment and economic hardship and recommended the consummation of the merger. No case was filed .[70]

Of course there were many instances when political pressure was not successful, and 26 antimerger cases were filed during the Orrick years.[71] Such pressure, however, combined with continuing differences with Attorney General Katzenbach, contributed to Orrick's decision to leave the Justice Department in June 1965.

By June 1965, when Donald F. Turner, a Harvard Law professor with a doctorate in economics and a reputation as an antitrust scholar, succeeded Orrick as head of the Antitrust Division, the Tonkin Gulf Resolution (August 1964) and the attack on the U.S. air base at Pleiku (February 1965) had already propelled the Johnson Administration down the slippery road that led to increased military involvement in Vietnam. During the three years in which Turner was to serve as Assistant Attorney General, racial violence, characterized by riots in Watts, Newark, Detroit, and elsewhere, and climaxed by the assassination of Martin Luther King, Jr., threatened to dismantle Johnson's social programs. More than ever, on both the war front and the domestic front, the Administration needed the strong support of business. Business leaders, however, though more comfortable with the Johnson White House than the Kennedy, had become increasingly concerned with recent Supreme Court rulings regarding potential competition, joint ventures, reciprocity, and protection of small competitors. They realized that these rulings could provide the impetus for an increase in antitrust activity and especially antimerger efforts. Johnson and Katzenbach were acutely aware of these needs and concerns. Turner, therefore, was appointed to rationalize antitrust policy and articulate it so as to reassure the business community.[72]

In his first major address, on August 10, 1965, before the Antitrust Section of the American Bar Association, Turner stated that "It is the duty of the Department of Justice, not to bring a case simply on the basis that it thinks it *can* win, but to bring only those cases that it thinks it *should* win." It is our duty to assist the courts in creating a rational body of antitrust law. Antitrust law is not static. We must be willing at all times to examine past judicial decisions. On the other hand, when a merger we are investigating could be found unlawful on a theory not yet established by the courts, it is our duty to provide the courts with the opportunity to consider that theory by bringing an appropriate case.[73]

Turner saw antitrust enforcement as a source of cues to business concerning what would be considered legal or not by the Antitrust Division. The Division "must decide whether a case is worth taking to court, either for its intrinsic impact on some aspect of the economy, its value as a warning to other businessmen, or for the opportunity it offers to clarify some murky legal question. Antitrust is largely a self-policing affair, and we must rely on business to police themselves [*sic*] by giving them warnings via selected prosecutions."[74]

Nevertheless, Turner was already on record as doubting that Section 7 applied to conglomerate mergers. In a much-quoted article in the May 1965 issue of the *Harvard Law Review*, he questioned their anticompetitive impact, and urged caution in proceeding against them unless there was a clearly anticompetitive issue. He asserted that one cannot support an attack on conglomerates "without trenching on significant economic and other values, and therefore, without an unprecedented reliance on judgments of an essentially political nature." According to Turner, it may be appropriate to consider whether the courts and the antitrust agencies, or the Congress, should make these judgments.

I do not believe Congress has given the courts and the FTC a mandate to campaign against "super-concentration" in the absence of any harm to competition. In light of the bitterly disputed issues involved, I believe that the courts should demand of Congress that it translate any further directive into something more formidable than sonorous phrases in the pages of the Congressional Record.[75]

Acknowledging that this article had been widely read by the private bar, Turner stated, "We should not attack a merger simply because the companies are large in the absolute sense, and we should not attack aggressive but fair competitive conduct simply on the basis that some competitors are hurt." It is not a function of the Department of Justice to attempt to make judgments that are within the province of the Congress.[76]

Appearing before the Senate Committee on Small Business on April 6, 1967, Turner stated that he believed "that the concentration of assets into fewer and fewer hands—even when not accompanied by probable anticompetitive consequences ... is something to worry about." He then proposed a legislative solution: "Congress could pass a statute that would say to the top fifty or a hundred companies, 'Any time you make an acquisition in excess of a certain size you must peel off assets of comparable magnitude.'" Such a requirement, he argued, would force companies to evaluate more carefully their contemplated acquisitions and the profitability of their present holdings. It would force them to reevaluate continually their operations and even to sell those that could be better conducted by others. Such a law would bring considerable economic benefit and would deal with concentration much more effectively than case-by-case antitrust enforcement.[77]

Statements such as those noted above offered a green light to corporations seeking rapid growth through merger. Above all, they signaled that conglomerate merger was the preferred route to take—the route least likely to be attacked.

Turner's three years as Assistant Attorney General witnessed the peak years of the Third Great Merger Movement (Table 1.1). The disappearance of large firms, by number and by total assets, more than doubled and tripled, respectively, during this period (Table 2.1). In order to impose a consistent rationale on antitrust actions, Turner assigned a case review function to the Policy Planning Office and staffed it with recent law school graduates. Unfortunately, this proved not only to be a waste of resources, but a source of irritation to the trial attorneys. The trial attorneys conducted the investigations, wrote the briefs, and tried the cases. They had earned their credentials, and they reported to a section chief who usually had ten or more years' experience. Both the trial attorneys and the section chiefs resented having their cases reviewed by such comparatively inexperienced lawyers. A decline in both morale and productivity resulted. Moreover, the Policy Planning Office became so consumed with its review function that policy planning practically disappeared.[78]

Writing in the *Journal of Law and Economics*, Richard Posner, a university professor and specialist in the field, concluded that the antitrust agencies were ignoring the statistical prerequisites of serious planning. They did not view antitrust enforcement as a business whose outputs were reductions in monopoly power and whose inputs were the legal and statistical activities necessary to bring about such reductions.

The Department of Justice makes little effort to identify those markets in which serious problems of monopoly are likely to arise; makes no systematic effort to see whether its decrees are being complied with; keeps few worthwhile statistics on its own activities . . . and is, in short, inappropriately run as a law firm . . . where the social product of the legal services undertaken is not measured.[79]

During Turner's three years as Division Chief, 41 antimerger cases were filed. Of these, only two involved the 25 most active acquiring firms, and only one of which was a conglomerate (Table 2.4). On July 13, 1966, the Justice Department filed suit against the acquisition of Tidewater Oil Company by Phillips Petroleum Company, and on July 25, 1967, the department successfully challenged the acquisition of Desilu Productions by Gulf and Western.[80] Since Gulf and Western's 1966 acquisition of Paramount Pictures was not challenged, it must be assumed that even though Gulf and Western was an active conglomerate, the acquisition of Desilu was considered a horizontal merger building upon the previously acquired Paramount. Although he doubted the application of the antitrust laws to conglomerate mergers, Turner could be aggressive against horizontal mergers.

Also during this period, the Justice Department successfully challenged Cities Service Company's acquisition of Jenny Manufacturing Company, the largest independent service station chain in Massachusetts and New Hampshire; Wilson Sporting Goods' proposed acquisition of the Nisson Corporation, the largest manufacturer of gymnastic equipment; and Bethlehem Steel Corporation's proposed acquisition of Cerro Corporation, an important producer of copper tubing.[81]

Nevertheless, Turner was not an aggressive Assistant Attorney General. In a rapidly expanding economy, characterized by an increasing merger movement, antitrust enforcement called for a dynamic leader, willing to probe and push the frontiers of antitrust law. Instead, Turner acquiesced in the economic realpolitik of the Great Society and Vietnam War effort. Although strongly opposed to horizontal mergers that would increase concentration, he did not oppose the merger of either Union and Pure Oil Companies or Atlantic and Richfield Oil Companies, nor did he oppose the conglomerate acquisition of Consolidation Coal by Continental Oil Company. Union, Atlantic, and Continental were among the 25 most active acquiring firms during the 1960s (Table 2.5). Turner also moved to dismiss the case against General Motors' monopoly of the American railroad locomotive market due to insufficient evidence. Both Loevinger, during whose tenure the case was filed, and his Eisenhower Administration predecessor, Robert Bicks, believed that there was sufficient evidence to prove that General Motors' 80 percent share of this market was due to reciprocity (railroads buying General Motors locomotives in order to get its huge shipping business, especially the transportation of new automobiles). Thus, the courts were not given the opportunity to decide these major cases, which could have resulted in structural changes in their industries and slowed the trend toward greater concentration.[82]

In a June 1966 speech, Turner had stated his belief, supported by an Antitrust Division study, that heavy advertising was anticompetitive since it raised entry barriers and entrenched existing oligopolists, led to monopoly profits, and denied consumers sufficient information to make intelligent choices among competing goods. Business braced itself for an antitrust attack against advertising. Aware of the disturbance caused, Turner delivered an address during the following February entitled "Advertising and Competition: Restatement and Amplification." In this speech he again affirmed the contribution of advertising to monopoly profits, and further stated that in some instances heavy advertising had made a substantial contribution to market concentration. However, he assured the business community that he intended no antitrust campaign against advertising, but sought only better means of providing increased information to consumers, such as consumer information programs and publications, sponsored by both government and private groups. Thus, Turner squelched an opportunity to more thoroughly investigate, and possibly take some corrective action against, an area that continued to affect competition and contribute to concentration.[83]

Like his predecessors, Turner was subject to various political pressures. In a letter to Attorney General Katzenbach dated July 16, 1966, Congressman Jerome R. Waldie requested the Department of Justice to reconsider its opposition to the acquisition of Tidewater Oil Company by Phillips Petroleum. Waldie expressed his concern that Tidewater's Avon, California facility might be closed if the acquisition was not consummated. And on July 29, 1966, Turner sent to Katzenbach, for approval and filing, a suit against AT&T charging monopolization of telephone equipment. Katzenbach took no action.[84]

In 1966, ITT, one of the largest and most active conglomerates, announced its intention to acquire the American Broadcasting Corporation. The Antitrust Division had investigated, but Turner had declined to oppose the merger and Katzenbach remained silent. Katzenbach, however, resigned in October 1966, to take a position with IBM, and was replaced by his Deputy, Ramsey Clark. Since the merger needed the approval of the Federal Communications Commission (FCC), Clark directed Turner to try to prevent the FCC from approving the merger. The latter, while pointing out the possibility of anticompetitive consequences, advised the FCC that the Department of Justice was not contemplating antitrust action. The FCC approved the merger on December 21. Dissatisfied, Clark pressured the FCC for a rehearing, using such Section 7 theories as potential competition (ITT as a potential entrant into television and radio broadcasting) and reciprocity (ITT would induce its suppliers to advertise on ABC). The FCC again approved the merger in June 1967. Clark vowed to take the FCC decision to the Federal Appeals Court. Gardner Ackley, Chairman of the Council of Economic Advisors (CEA), in a memorandum to President Johnson dated June 29, 1967, indicated the CEA's support for the Attorney General in his opposition to the merger. After indicating several reasons for opposing the merger, Ackley stated, "This merger is just one example of the recent tidal wave of 'conglomerate mergers.' The resulting increase in the number of industrial giants poses *threats to price and product competition, and of undue corporate influence on public policy.*"[85] It appeared that Clark was determined to push this merger to the Supreme Court if necessary, and ITT, along with other conglomerates, was anxious to keep conglomerate merger cases out of the highest court. Therefore, in January 1968, ITT announced that it was abandoning the proposed merger.[86] Clark had scored a highly visible victory against both conglomeration and concentration.

Nevertheless, Clark was unable to institute an aggressive antitrust policy against conglomerate mergers, due largely to Turner's conviction that, in the absence of new legislation put forth by Congress, the present antitrust laws did not extend to conglomerate mergers, except in cases of obvious anticompetitive results.

In addition to the case review process, Turner's plan for rationalizing the antitrust activity of the Justice Department included the development of merger guidelines. In his first speech as Assistant Attorney General, in August 1965, Turner spoke of the need for the establishment and publication of rules to assist both the Antitrust Division attorneys and the private bar in merger issues.[87] The Merger Guidelines were eventually promulgated on May 30, 1968. They contain sections on horizontal, vertical, and conglomerate mergers, as well as an introductory section pertaining to underlying terms and issues. The guidelines were intended to promote compliance by businessmen, consistency in the Justice Department's enforcement actions, and general discussions and study of issues relevant to antitrust policy in the area of mergers.[88]

The guidelines listed permissible percentages of market share, held by both the acquiring and acquired firms, above which the Justice Department would probably sue for divestiture. In regard to conglomerate mergers, the guidelines acknowledged that these mergers have not been subjected to as extensive or sustained analysis as the other types, but indicated that potential entry, reciprocity, and mergers that entrench market power would result in Justice Department investigation and possible suit. (See Appendix A.) The guidelines were generally considered to contain nothing new; the percentages could have been approximated and the rules culled from recent Supreme Court decisions, which is what corporation lawyers already had been doing. On the negative side, the guidelines encouraged merger-minded businessmen to choose the conglomerate route, thereby accelerating that movement within the Third Great Merger Movement.[89]

The guidelines were the final product of Turner's years as Assistant Attorney

General. Coinciding with their release, he announced his resignation and returned to Harvard Law School. He was succeeded by his Deputy, Edwin Zimmerman, a former Stanford Law School Professor.

In his initial speech as Assistant Attorney General, on August 7, 1968, before the Antitrust Section of the American Bar Association, Zimmerman noted the unusually high number of corporate mergers, especially of the conglomerate variety, and the prevalence of high concentration in many important industries.[90] Four months later, speaking before the New York City Bar Association, he repeated these observations. "The most startling development in recent years—the enormous merger movement—shows no sign of diminution. . . . But its dramatic nature should not detract from the other major problem—the continued pervasiveness of concentrated markets."[91] He acknowledged that antitrust enforcement was not yet fully developed for the purpose of attacking concentration, as distinguished from monopoly. He put forth the possibility that additional legislation might be needed, which could be framed in such a way as to minimize the costs and difficulties usually associated with divestiture. An example of such legislation, previously suggested by Turner, would be a requirement that firms above a certain size could not make new acquisitions without divesting an equivalent amount of assets.

He reiterated his predecessor's belief that the Justice Department should bring cases based on doctrinal and economic justification, not because the prospect of judicial success was high. But he also believed that the Justice Department should accept the challenge to go beyond existing court decisions to expand the frontiers of antitrust law. Finally, he supported internal growth as the preferred method of corporate expansion: "Antitrust must keep all possible pressure on the economic entities to create and expand into new fields, rather than simply assume, through merger, the market positions of other, erstwhile, major firms."[92] During Zimmerman's seven and a half months as Assistant Attorney General, 16 antimerger cases were filed, only one of which involved one of the 25 most active acquiring firms (Table 2.4). This was the horizontal acquisition of Sinclair Oil Company by Atlantic Richfield. The Justice Department filed suit on January 15, 1969, and the Supreme Court ordered divestiture on April 28, 1971.[93]

Of the thousands of mergers consummated during the Kennedy-Johnson Years, only 115 were challenged by the Antitrust Division of the Department of Justice (Figure 3.1).

THE FEDERAL TRADE COMMISSION

The other federal agency charged with enforcing the antitrust laws is the Federal Trade Commission (FTC). During the Kennedy-Johnson years, the FTC was dominated by Paul Rand Dixon, a former FTC attorney who had been serving as Staff Director and Chief Counsel of the Senate Subcommittee on Antitrust and Monopoly. Appointed FTC Chairman by President Kennedy, Dixon assumed his duties on March 21, 1961, and held that position through the first year of the Nixon Administration.[94]

While the Antitrust Division is headed by a single individual, authority at the FTC is shared by five Commissioners, appointed by the President, serving staggered seven-year terms. By law, not more than three members may be of the same political party. Although the Commissioners are supposedly equal in authority, the Chairman does in fact wield extensive influence as the point of contact for the executive and legislative branches, through his/her appointment authority to certain positions within the Federal Trade Commission, and as general administrator of the agency. During the Dixon years, there was considerable dissension among the Commissioners.[95]

The intellectual leadership of the FTC during this period was provided by Philip Elman, former Assistant Solicitor General of the United States. Scholarly and outspoken, his legal views generally prevailed. He authored the FTC's position in the *Clorox* case, upheld by the Supreme Court, and the *Bendix-Fram* case, which, though ending in a consent agreement, extended the logic of *Clorox*. A political independent, he served from April 1961 until September 1970.[96]

The third Kennedy appointee, Alfonso Everett MacIntyre, a strong supporter of small business, served from September 1961 to September 1975. Mary Gardiner Jones, appointed by President Johnson in October 1964, remained into the Nixon years. The only Republican during the 1960s, she reputedly sought the Chairmanship. The position of fifth Commissioner was held by four different individuals during the Kennedy-Johnson years.[97]

Following the Kennedy-Johnson theme of economic growth fueled by strong business support, Dixon placed improvement of business relations at the top of the FTC's goals. He favored industry guidelines and voluntary compliance, with limited litigation. Thus, the FTC turned from a case-by-case view to one favoring consent agreements, formal advisory opinions, and merger guidelines. During Dixon's first two years as Chairman, only one merger was challenged, and only 54 were challenged during the entire Kennedy-Johnson Administration.[98]

Dixon was aware of the increasing concentration in American industry and looked upon it as a potential threat to the U.S. economy and to small business in particular. In speeches titled "Antitrust and Economic Freedom," "Antitrust Compliance: The 'Will' to be Free," and "Conglomerate Merger Fever: The 1967 Virus," and in an appearance before the House Select Committee on Small Business, he stressed the FTC's inability to protect the millions of small businesses, and emphasized that it was the antitrust laws that protected American freedom. He recognized conglomerate mergers as "another way to lose freedom by just letting concentration keep going unabated."[99] Nevertheless, of the 54 mergers challenged by the FTC during the Kennedy-Johnson years (Figure 3.2), only four involved the 25 most active acquiring firms, and each was settled without litigation. On June 4, 1964, the Federal Trade Commission's challenge of the acquisition of the Crossett Company by Georgia-Pacific Corporation, a leading manufacturer of coarse paper and bags, was settled by consent decree. Although divestiture was not ordered, Georgia-Pacific was prohibited from specific acquisitions for up to ten years and was required to make coarse paper available to independent jobbers for a five-year period.[100]

On August 2, 1966, the FTC challenged the joint ventures between National Distillers & Chemical Corporation and Phillips Petroleum Company, which established two corporations engaged in the manufacture of plastic products made from polyethylene and polypropylene resins. The consent order required dissolution of all joint ventures between Phillips and National and divestiture of certain facilities acquired by the joint ventures. It further banned future acquisitions in certain segments of the synthetic resins industry for up to 20 years.[101]

In accordance with a consent order dated November 21, 1967, Continental Oil Company and Stauffer Chemical Company agreed to terminate a joint venture that established three corporations in the vinyl chloride monomer industry, which is engaged in the manufacture of plastics and resins from chemical compounds. The order also required Continental to sell two acquired producers of polyvinyl chloride, required Continental and Stauffer each to assist a new firm to enter the vinyl chloride monomer industry, and prohibited future acquisitions and joint ventures by either company in that field without FTC approval.[102]

By consent order dated November 7, 1968, Occidental Petroleum Corporation was required to sell the ammonium phosphate and blended fertilizer operations obtained through its acquisition of Hooker Chemical Corporation. In addition, Occidental was forbidden to acquire any domestic producer in any line of business for the next five years.[103]

On April 28, 1965, the Supreme Court handed down its decision in the *Consolidated Foods* case, previously discussed. This was the first FTC merger case to be decided by the highest court since the passage of the 1950 Celler-Kefauver Act. Consolidated was ordered to divest itself of the Gentry Corporation.

Among other significant mergers challenged during this period was the 1957 conglomerate-product extension acquisition by General Foods Corporation of S.O.S., the nation's third-largest manufacturer of household steel wool. By 1962, S.O.S. had achieved 56 percent of this market, due primarily to General Foods advertising and other marketing techniques (e.g., discounts on other General Foods products). The FTC filed for divestiture on September 30, 1963. The Court of Appeals, on November 9, 1967, upheld the FTC finding that the merger had an adverse impact upon competition and reduced the number of potential entrants. The Supreme Court denied certiorari on May 20, 1968. Divestiture was accomplished.[104]

On October 27, 1965, the FTC successfully challenged the vertical acquisition of Nobil Shoe Company, then the ninth-ranking independent retailer in the United States, by Endicott-Johnson Corporation, the nation's fourth-largest shoe manufacturer. Although divestiture was not directed, the consent order prohibited Endicott-Johnson from making any acquisitions for 20 years without prior FTC approval.[105]

In 1963, Proctor & Gamble (P&G), then the 28th-largest U.S. corporation and leading marketer of household consumer products, acquired Folger & Company, the largest independent coffee retailer, with 26 percent of grocery coffee sales. On February 9, 1965, the FTC filed a complaint charging this conglomerate-product extension merger with violation of Section 7. However, two years later, on February 9, 1967, the commission agreed to a consent decree requiring P&G to divest itself of only one of Folger's five largest coffee plants, and prohibiting P&G from accepting discounts or reduction in media advertising rates on its coffee products until February 1972. P&G was permitted to retain the Folger brand name and all other Folger properties. The FTC did not explain its action, or how this action would remedy the anticompetitive effects that led to the initial FTC challenge. Dissenting, Commissioner John R. Reilly exclaimed, "the Commission thundered in the complaint and cheeped in the order." Thus, the FTC surrendered an opportunity to pursue a case that might have resulted in a significant extension of antitrust law.[106]

On April 13, however, the Supreme Court handed down the landmark *Clorox* decision. The Justices found that because P&G was the largest producer of soaps and other household products, it was a likely potential competitor in the liquid bleach industry. The Court also noted that because P&G was the nation's largest advertiser, it could so increase the advertising expenditure on Clorox as to harm its competitors and raise entry barriers; or, through cross-subsidization, could lower the market price of Clorox to harm competitors. P&G was directed to divest itself of the Clorox Chemical Company.[107]

On June 29, 1967, the FTC challenged the acquisition of Fram Corporation, the third-ranking producer of automotive filters, by the Bendix Corporation. At that time, Bendix was the 61st-largest company in the United States and a major producer of automobile parts. Although this conglomerate-product extension case did not reach the Supreme Court, it expanded the *Clorox* decision, giving greater scope to the potential competition doctrine by setting forth the "toehold" theory. Whereas Clorox had been the leader in household liquid bleach, with over 50 percent of the market, Fram was the third-ranking producer of automotive filters, with approximately 17 percent of the market. Moreover, the leading firm was the AC Division of General Motors, a company able to combat any advertising or cross-subsidization activity by Bendix. Nevertheless, the FTC had adopted a 10 percent market share of the acquired company as a rough dividing line in assessing the effect on competition. Below 10 percent would be a generally permitted toehold acquisition; above that would be unacceptable. Since Fram's share exceeded 10 percent, the FTC was prepared to litigate. By consent agreement of November 12, 1974, Bendix was required to divest Fram.[108]

During this period, the courts and antitrust agencies indicated a preference for internal over external growth, the latter being potentially more injurious to competition. However, the toehold theory was a recognition that acquisition was generally faster and less costly than new development or internal growth. Nevertheless, if the acquired firm was dominant or a leading producer in its field, the merger would further entrench it and further harm small competitors. Thus, the toehold theory was adopted. This concept merely states that if a company wishes to expand into a new market, it is less anticompetitive for that firm to acquire one of the smaller producers, one with less than 10 percent of market share. Moreover, a toehold acquisition could actually promote competition in a concentrated market by providing increased competition to the leading firms.[109]

Chairman Dixon steadfastly denied that he had ever been subjected to White House pressure on any FTC decision or facet of internal operations, or that the executive branch had directed the commission to get into or keep out of any problem area. Nevertheless, the FTC was not without its external pressures. Since it receives its appropriations and operational responsibilities from Congress, the commission is sensitive to the needs of that body, and to specific committees and influential Congressmen. This latter point was made clear in September 1969, when Commissioner Elman told a Senate group that congressional pressure "corrupts the atmosphere" in which the FTC works. He charged that Congressmen make private, unrecorded calls on behalf of companies seeking FTC approval of mergers. He called this a "subtle, insidious, and destructive" intrusion on the regulatory process.[110]

Samuel Richardson Reid, discussing some reasons for the failure of antitrust law to curb mergers, elaborated upon Elman's comments by reminding us of the great power of affluent special interest groups, especially those representing business, and their intensive lobbying efforts. "Some Congresspeople willingly cooperate and actively help these vested interests. The pressures that special interest groups can apply and the temptations that they dangle before public officials . . . are not to be underestimated or taken lightly." And Dixon, speaking before a Senate subcommittee, stated that Congress may pass laws, but at the same time it satisfies "the demand of special industry groups for freedom from real regulation by the simple expedient of appropriating only token amounts of money for the actual enforcement of the law."[111]

Perhaps the most outstanding example of political pressure during the 1960s was that exerted by Congress to prevent the FTC from conducting a study of the 1,000 leading American industrial firms. The study, proposed in 1962 by Willard Mueller, head of the Federal Trade Commission's Bureau of Economics, was to investigate, through questionnaires, the merger activity and corporate relations among the 1,000 companies. Funds for the study, which Dixon said would have better equipped the FTC to deal with the merger movement that "threatens to engulf us," were approved by the Bureau of the Budget (now the Office of Management and Budget). However, the Bureau's Business Advisory Council on Federal Reports, a private association composed of executives of those 1,000 corporations, apparently leaked information to the Chamber of Commerce, which in turn sought congressional support to prevent the study. Consequently, when representatives of the FTC appeared before the House Appropriations Committee, they were accused of harassing the business community. For three consecutive years, Congress not only refused to approve funds for the study, but attached a rider to the FTC's appropriations bill prohibiting the commission from spending any of its money on such an inquiry.[112] In Dixon's own words: "The Budget Bureau approved it and when I got up to the Congress, they were standing in line to disapprove it. They put a whippersnapper in my appropriations that I couldn't use any of the money for such purposes."[113] Although the Council of Economic Advisors was in favor of the study, the council did not take an official position in the matter.[114] And since the support of the business community was essential to the Kennedy-Johnson program for economic growth, no Administration efforts were made to undertake the proposed study.

Another example of pressure exerted upon the FTC concerned ex parte communications. These are contacts made by individuals outside the FTC (that is, business) with the purpose of converting a commissioner's point of view on a particular matter. Though not illegal, these contacts, in the words of Commissioner Elman, "provide a fertile breeding ground for dark rumors and ugly suspicions. At the very least they permit the appearance of impropriety . . . and to this extent reduce public confidence in . . . the Commission's action." Elman provoked much antagonism among his fellow Commissioners by trying to enact a ban on ex parte contact. Unsuccessful, he voluntarily imposed such a ban on himself.[115]

Aside from the various pressures accompanying case-by-case litigation, Elman believed that litigation itself was an "intolerably slow, costly, clumsy, fragmentary and inadequate process . . . especially unsuited for dealing with industry-wide" problems. He believed, instead, that the FTC staff should utilize various data, including past experience and expert opinion, to devise a comprehensive picture of the industrial and market setting in which a wave of mergers may be impending or occurring, and from which probable competitive effects could be gauged. These findings could provide a framework within which guidelines could be established to determine the probable legality of prospective mergers. In such manner, the commission could assist business by clarifying and simplifying the application of Section 7.[116] Chairman Dixon, anxious to support the Administration's position on government-business relations, concurred in the concept of industry guidelines. The first of these guidelines was promulgated as part of the *Beatrice Foods* decision in 1965.

Between 1951 and 1956, the four largest dairy companies in the United States had acquired several hundred dairies, both direct competitors and those operating in different geographic markets (market extension mergers). Beatrice Foods alone had acquired 174. The FTC challenged these acquisitions in 1956, and issued its first divestiture order, against Foremost Dairies, in 1962. Cases against Borden and National Diary were settled by consent decrees in 1963 and 1964. In each case, the corporation was directed to divest a certain amount of its acquisitions and to refrain from further mergers for 10 years.[117]

In the *Beatrice* decision of April 1965, in addition to divestiture and a 10-year prohibition on mergers, the FTC intended to put forth "clear and concrete legal standards for mergers for the guidance of businessmen." The FTC recognized that economic and technical changes in the dairy industry made inevitable the demise of the smallest firms. Thus, actual and potential competition would be best served by channeling mergers away from the leading firms, which already had achieved economies of scale, and toward medium and small producers. These, in turn, would be able to grow and compete more effectively with the larger firms. Therefore the commission put forth guidelines for future mergers. Henceforth the FTC would consider acquisitions by large dairies as "highly suspect." Medium-size dairies could acquire smaller firms, but they could not merge with smaller firms that were significant horizontal competitors, nor with other medium or larger companies. Mergers between small firms to achieve economic and/or technical efficiencies would be considered lawful. The FTC's strong stance regarding mergers in the dairy industry significantly curtailed the rate of acquisitions during the following decade. In addition, the market share of the top four producers declined to their 1950 level while medium and small producers grew.[118]

During the next three years, the FTC issued guidelines in the cement and grocery manufacturing industries.[119] In each of these situations, a rapid increase in merger activity threatened to restructure the industry, entrenching the leading producers, forestalling potential competition, and harming the small competitors.

Between 1960 and 1966, the FTC issued 10 complaints challenging 17 vertical acquisitions in the cement industry. Despite these complaints, the forward integration of cement manufacturers into cement purchasers, especially ready-mix concrete producers, continued unabated. In response to this merger wave, in 1966 the Federal Trade Commission's Bureau of Economics produced a study on mergers in the cement industry, and in that same year the commission opened a formal inquiry with public hearings on the matter. Based on the accumulated evidence, the FTC issued its merger guidelines, *Enforcement Policy with Respect to Vertical Mergers in the Cement Industry*, on January 3, 1967. The commission thus announced its intention to challenge any mergers in excess of certain specified limits, and required all cement producers to notify it at least 60 days in advance of any intended acquisitions. Following the publication of the guidelines, the annual number of mergers decreased dramatically, and the market share of the four leading producers declined to pre-1950 levels.[120]

On May 15, 1968, the FTC published its *Enforcement Policy with Respect to Product Extension Mergers in Grocery Products Manufacturing*. These guidelines dealt with the product extension type of conglomerate merger, wherein the merging companies are not direct competitors, but are functionally related. (Proctor & Gamble's acquisition of Clorox and Consolidated Foods' acquisition of Gentry are examples of this type of merger.) Grocery products include food and non-food consumer products customarily sold in grocery stores. Grocery product manufacturing was characterized by a relatively few large manufacturers operating across many product lines. Advertising and other sales promotion created a major barrier to entry. Based on the commission's own accumulated experience, including its own staff studies, and a 1966 report by the National Commission on Food Marketing, the FTC decided to issue merger guidelines. As with the guidelines in the cement industry, the commission announced its intent to challenge any mergers exceeding certain specified limits. For example, if the acquired firm was one of the top eight producers of a grocery product, or had more than a 5 percent share of the relevant market, the merger would probably be challenged. The commission also announced that its guidelines would apply to mergers between grocery product and nongrocery product manufacturers. Unlike the dairy and cement industries, the acquisitions of large food product companies rose modestly after the announcement of the merger guidelines. However, the FTC challenged only two grocery product mergers between 1968 and 1976. In December 1976, the commission withdrew the guidelines without prior announcement, explanation, or a period of public comment.[121]

Discussion of the above guidelines indicates that merger activity in a particular industry may respond quickly to an antitrust agency's announcement of its enforcement intentions. Nevertheless, the success of such guidelines requires vigorous enforcement action.

Economic growth was the dominant theme of the Kennedy-Johnson Administrations. Both Presidents knew that the success of their domestic social programs, and the military involvement in Vietnam, were dependent upon a strong and growing economy, which in turn was dependent upon business optimism and support. This realpolitik view of government-business relations had its effect on the antitrust activities of the Justice Department and the Federal Trade Commission. Faced with a shortage of resources, and the lack of a White House commitment to antitrust, only 170 of the thousands of mergers during these years were challenged by the two agencies. And of these, only 11 acquisitions of the 25 most active acquiring firms were challenged. Yet those years witnessed the disappearance by merger of over 9,400 firms in the greatest merger movement in the history of our country up to that time—the Third Great Merger Movement.

TOWARD THE LEGISLATIVE PROCESS

By the end of 1967, the Third Great Merger Movement had reached such proportions that it could no longer be ignored by the Administration and Congress. In that year alone, 1,496 firms had disappeared into mergers, a 50 percent increase over the previous year. And 1968 was to witness the disappearance of 2,442 firms, a two-thirds increase over 1967 (Table 1.1).

On October 6, 1967, White House aide Ernest Goldstein prepared a Memorandum for the President. In the memo, Goldstein informed President Johnson that after a series of meetings, Chairman Dixon and Assistant Attorney General Turner recommended the establishment of a task force to study:

- New merger patterns which are apparently beyond the reach of existing legislation, and
- "Bigness," which as such has never been the subject of direct Antitrust Legislation.[122]

The President approved, and Phil C. Neal, Dean of the University of Chicago Law School, was selected to be Chairman of the White House Task Force on Antitrust Policy. The Task Force, composed of distinguished nongovernment attorneys, began its work in December.

On November 16, 1967, Senator Javits, on behalf of himself and Senators Brewster, Cooper, and Hartke introduced a bill to establish a Commission on Revision of the Antitrust Laws of the United States.[123]

Continuing concern over the changing structure of the economy and its impact on inflation led the President to establish the Cabinet Committee on Price Stability. The President sought advice concerning the strengthening of "free market institutions," and directed the Cabinet Committee to prepare in-depth studies and make recommendations concerning government policy in these areas. The Secretaries of Treasury, Commerce, and Labor, the Director of the Bureau of the Budget, and the Chairman of the Council of Economic Advisors were members of the Cabinet Committee. Willard F. Mueller was appointed Executive Director of the Committee.[124]

Meanwhile, since July 1964, Senator Philip A. Hart, Chairman of the Senate Subcommittee on Antitrust and Monopoly, had been holding hearings on the increasing economic concentration resulting from the current merger movement. In a letter to Chairman Dixon, dated May 17, 1968, Hart suggested that the FTC conduct an investigation into concentration, mergers, and conglomerates. "The importance to Congress of such an investigation for a full understanding of the issues and problems involved cannot be overstated." Hart indicated that the Senate Antitrust Subcommittee had been told on the one hand that bigness is "inevitable and desirable, that the antitrust laws are an anachronism," but on the other hand Congress has been told to "enact new legislation to curb further growth by mergers of large firms."[125]

Concerned over the significant increase in mergers during 1967, and prompted by Hart's letter, the FTC announced on July 2 that it would conduct an investigation of the merger movement, "particularly in regard to the growth of conglomerate corporations." In addition, on October 9, Congressman Celler announced that the House Antitrust Subcommittee would "undertake a comprehensive study into the economic and political significance of conglomerate mergers." And in a press release on December 2, Senator Hart suggested legislation that would restrict the largest corporations to growth by internal means only. Growth by merger would be specifically prohibited. He also suggested that corporations engaged in interstate activity should have federal charters.[126]

The Report of the Cabinet Committee was submitted to the President on December 28. It noted that aggregate concentration increased more sharply in 1967 than in any other year in modern industrial history. There appeared to be a link between growing aggregate concentration and market concentration. "Not only do the largest companies operate in numerous industries, but they increasingly occupy the leading positions in these industries." In addition, many of these large conglomerate firms are "partially integrated through a vast network of jointly owned subsidiary companies" and an extensive pattern of management interlocks. "Further merger-achieved centralization of economic power and decision-making may seriously impair the proper functioning of our competitive, free enterprise economy, as well as threaten the social and political values associated with a decentralized economic system." It appears that the Celler-Kefauver Act is "inadequate to cope with the massive industrial restructuring resulting from current conglomerate merger activity."[127]

The annual *Economic Report of the President*, submitted to Congress in January 1969, noted the "gargantuan" proportions of the current merger wave, and that 83 percent of the large mergers in 1967 were conglomerate. The report spoke of the need to reduce concentration and channel merger activity in directions that would increase competition. Finally, it stated that "An effective program to deal with the high levels of concentration may require new legislation."[128]

New legislation was at the heart of the White House Task Force Report, which was submitted to the President on July 5, 1968. The report recommended a "Concentrated Industries Act," which proposed specific legislation regarding concentration in particular oligopolistic markets, and a "Merger Act," which would prohibit mergers in which a very large firm acquires one of the leading firms in a concentrated industry. The report noted that new legislation was required because the history of antitrust enforcement did not justify reliance on existing laws. The report also recommended that steps be taken to improve the quality and availability of economic and financial data relevant to the formulation and enforcement of antitrust laws, and that further study be given to a requirement for advance notification of mergers. (Appendix B.)[129]

Thus, as the Third Great Merger Movement, and the conglomerate movement within it, raced through the 1960s, concerned eyes began to look toward Congress for legislation to curtail the wave of acquisitions that threatened to reshape the industrial economy.

Figure 3.1
Acquisitions Challenged by the Antitrust Division, Kennedy-Johnson Administrations (calendar year)

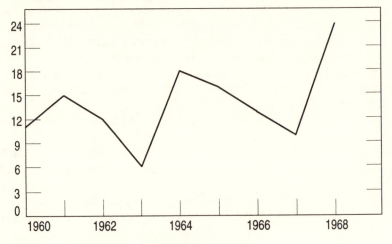

Note: Two challenges were made in January 1969.

Figure 3.2
Acquisitions Challenged by the Federal Trade Commission, Kennedy-Johnson Administrations (calendar year)

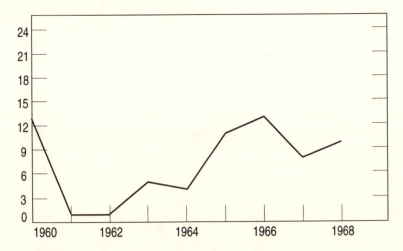

Note: One challenge was made in January 1969.

Source: Adapted from Willard F. Mueller, *The Celler-Kefauver Act: The First 27 Years* (Washington: U. S. Government Printing Office, 1979), 129–171.

4

The Response: The Congress

THE LEGISLATIVE BRANCH:
THE GOVERNMENT-BUSINESS ENVIRONMENT

In a speech to the Democratic Policy Council on February 25, 1970, Senator Philip A. Hart, Chairman of the Senate Subcommittee on Antitrust and Monopoly, made the following comments:

Perhaps the greatest bill of goods sold in this country today is that we have a free competitive economy. In fact, there may be no more competition today than . . . when Congress was so shocked by the action of the trusts that it passed the Sherman Act to break them up. . . . Increasing economic concentration—spurred in large part by the growth of the multi-tentacled conglomerate—now gives the majority of all manufacturing assets to 200 corporations. With this comes the immunities to marketplace demands that giantism endows.[1]

Although specific industries may have been more or less concentrated in the 1960s than in the early 1900s, some industries that were vibrant at the turn of the century had declined by the Kennedy-Johnson years (e.g., anthracite coal mining), and others had not existed in the earlier period (e.g., aircraft engines), many center firms in industries that were established in the early 1900s were still among the most powerful in the Kennedy-Johnson years. Thomas K. McCraw, referring to data developed by Alfred D. Chandler, Jr., pointed out that in 1917, 103 of the 200 largest corporations in the United States were in petroleum, rubber, machinery, food products, and transportation equipment. In 1973, 87 were still among the 200 and the others had been absorbed by the 87 or had become units of conglomerates. He also noted that 36 of the largest 100 corporations in 1909 were still among the top 100 in 1958.[2] These figures indicate the stability of the large center firms over five decades and reflect the degree of market concentration in their respective industries.

It is important to distinguish between market concentration—the share of industry output provided by the four leading firms—and aggregate concentration, measured by the amount of assets held by corporations, especially the 200 largest manufacturing and mining corporations. According to Census Bureau figures, market concentration increased slightly between 1954 and 1966. Nevertheless, by 1966, 33 percent of all manufacturing in the United States took place in industries in which four companies produced 50 percent or more of the total output (Figure 2.2). However, of greater significance is the increase in aggregate concentration from the passage of the Celler-Kefauver Act in December 1950. The amount of assets held by the 200 largest firms increased from 47.7 percent of the national total in 1951 to 60.9 percent in 1968, an increase of 30 percent in 18 years (Table 2.2). Put another way, by the end of 1968, just 87 gigantic corporations held 46 percent of all manufacturing assets and received 50 percent of all annual profits in the United States (Figure 2.1). Most of these asset-powerful companies also were among the four leading firms (in terms of market concentration) in their industries (Table 2.3).[3]

Spurring the rapid increase in aggregate concentration was the conglomerate form of merger, which represented 88.5 percent of all large mergers from 1948 to 1963 (Figure 2.3). It was this form of merger that seemed to have the potential for reciprocity, cross-subsidization, and other anticompetitive practices.[4] And, as indicated below, such economic power gives rise to political power.

It was this increase in aggregate concentration that prompted Senator Hart to make the statement presented above. By the time his words were uttered, the Third Great Merger Movement had eliminated over 9,400 firms during the Kennedy-Johnson years. Eighteen thousand pages of testimony before the Senate Subcommittee on Antitrust and Monopoly had confirmed immunity to the market forces of demand and supply resulting from administered prices.[5] In a speech in January 1967, Senator Hart pointed out that after-tax corporate profits had increased 88 percent over the previous ten years while manufacturing labor costs had increased only 2.5 percent. He also noted that corporations were setting prices to meet target profits even in industries operating below capacity.[6] In addition, in each of the 16 post-Celler-Kefauver merger cases that came before it during the Kennedy-Johnson years, the Supreme Court had found an actual or potential threat to competition, and decided against the merger.[7] And in 1969, the Attorney General and the Assistant Attorney General for Antitrust in the Nixon Administration had expressed alarm over the increased concentration resulting from the Third Great Merger Movement, and had initiated action against five conglomerate mergers.[8]

Increasing concentration, and the need for legislative action to combat it, had been recognized in the report of the Cabinet Committee on Price Stability, the 1969 *Economic Report of the President*, and the recommendations of the White House Task Force on Antitrust Policy. Moreover, Hart's own subcommittee had concluded almost six years of periodic hearings into increasing economic concentration, which would total over 5,300 tightly printed pages. Yet none of these findings, or the mergers that precipitated them, induced any legislative action on the part of the United States Congress.

Why was this unrestrained merger activity and increasing concentration allowed to develop and continue? The main reason that Congress did not move aggressively in the antitrust arena is that it perceived little or no interest in the subject on the part of its constituents. Although there may have been some individual distrust of big business, an increasing variety of consumer goods and a generally rising standard of living mitigated against a mobilization of voter concern over economic concentration. In addition, advertising, especially on television, presented large corporations in a positive light. And the voice of big business was forcefully and repeatedly heard on Capitol Hill. As politicians, legislators are usually interested in being reelected.

In April 1967, Senator Russell Long, in a speech on the chamber floor, estimated that "about 95 percent of campaign funds at the congressional level are derived from businessmen." Moreover, the *Washington Post* reported in its editions of May 7 and 8, 1969, that approximately two-thirds of the 435 members of the House of Representatives had significant interests in private business. Further, there were numerous instances in which they had interests in enterprises that could be subject to laws written by the committees on which these Representatives served. In addition, corporations frequently invited Congressmen to be guest speakers at various functions, for which they would be given an honorarium of $5,000 or more. As Senator Hart remarked, "When a major corporation from a state wants to discuss something with its political representatives, you can be sure it will be heard. When that same company operates in 30 states, it will be heard by 30 times as many representatives."[9]

Whereas corporations did not want Congress to interfere with their activities, and their views were constantly being communicated to their Senators and Representatives, there was no special interest group pushing for stronger legislation regarding mergers and antitrust policy, no special interest group demanding a Congressional clarification pertaining to permissible/impermissible concentration in various segments of the economy.[10] Thus, economic concentration led not only to a less than competitive market structure, but to a more pliable political structure as well.

THE SENATE

Estes Kefauver, the Senate's most persistent and well-known antitrust voice during the late 1950s and early 1960s, was greatly concerned with the effect of economic concentration on America's political structure. His objection to the concentration of economic power lay in the resulting exploitation of the many by the few—an economic exploitation that he believed would lead eventually to political exploitation. Thus, Kefauver equated a society providing free competition between many producers as a prerequisite for a democratic political system. A recurring theme in his speeches was that "it is only a step from the loss of economic freedom to the loss of political freedom." He was not antibusiness. Although many businessmen, large and small, saw them as unsettling or destabilizing, Kefauver believed that the antitrust laws were the businessman's best friend because, properly enforced, they could prevent anticompetitive practices that affect not only consumers and small businessmen, but even large corporations threatened by predatory practices. He also believed that corporate adherence to the antitrust laws would protect all business from increased government regulation that would reduce their economic freedom. Thus Henry Ford II, in 1961, warned his fellow businessmen that if they did not keep their own house in order, the responsibility could be taken from them.[11]

As far back as the congressional hearings that led to the Celler-Kefauver Act, Kefauver expressed his concern over mergers that resulted in the control of corporations being shifted from local communities to often distant central headquarters. He feared that through such action, local people would lose control over some degree of their economic freedom. Moreover, Kefauver's reputation as a champion of the small businessman had been established in 1946 when, as a Representative, he had chaired a subcommittee of the House Select Small Business Committee, which held hearings on the trend toward economic concentration.[12]

As previously noted, it was not until 1953 that the Senate Subcommittee on Antitrust and Monopoly was established, and not until 1955 that it was officially recognized by the Senate Rules Committee. Kefauver was one of the original members of the subcommittee. In 1955, he drew the wrath of Federal Trade Commission Chairman Edward Howery, who accused Kefauver and Congressman Celler of "standing over our shoulders and attempting to dominate our opinions." Kefauver also labeled the report of the Attorney General's National Committee to study the Antitrust Laws "a gigantic brief for the non-enforcement of the anti-trust laws." In his criticism of the National Committee Report, Kefauver was joined by other congressional figures. Senator John Sparkman, Chairman of the Senate Small Business Committee, stated that the report seemed to ignore the needs of small business and to contain recommendations that could undermine the government's antitrust program. Representative Henry Reuss said the report failed to recognize that the federal government had fostered a trend toward monopoly by giving defense contracts to big companies. Senator Paul Douglas urged a "fresh study" of business to strengthen the antitrust laws and to require businesses planning a merger to prove to the Justice Department that the proposed "mergers would actively promote competition and not restrict it."[13]

In January 1957, Kefauver became Chairman of the Senate Antitrust Subcommittee and announced plans to investigate concentration, industry by industry, to determine its effect on free enterprise and especially on small business. On July 9 of that year, the subcommittee began hearings into administered prices, that is, prices set and maintained by the leading firms regardless of a decline in demand, cost reductions, or other market changes. During the next six years, the hearings studied the steel, automobile, drug, and bread industries. The subcommittee was interested in the extent to which the concentration of economic power had enabled the relatively few producers in these industries to overcome the normal price-determining forces of demand and supply. After the studies Kefauver concluded, in May 1963, that "perhaps the most important finding of these investigations is that in these industries price competition which, under our system of free enterprise, is assumed to be the protector of the public interest, tends to be conspicuous by its absence."[14]

Thus, by the time of his death on August 10, 1963, the subcommittee had confirmed the reality of administered prices in concentrated industries, denounced by Gardiner Means, members of the Temporary National Economic Committee, and others, beginning in 1934. Although the printed transcripts of the hearings filled over 18,000 pages, no legislation resulted.[15] The Senate (and the House) was not interested in pursuing a vigorous antitrust policy.[16]

Another indication of the Senate's general lack of interest in antitrust during this period could be found in the appointments to the subcommittee. When vacancies occur on subcommittees, committee chairmen are usually responsive to the recommendations for replacement made by their subcommittee chairmen. However, Senator James Eastland, chairman of the subcommittee's parent Judiciary Committee, had generally ignored Kefauver's requests. Thus, by 1962, Kefauver had become outnumbered six to three on his own subcommittee. He could count on antitrust support only from Senators Thomas Dodd and Edward Kennedy. Such was the antitrust sentiment when Senator Philip A. Hart assumed the Chairmanship on August 19, 1963.[17]

In a letter to Senator Eastland, dated January 14, 1964, Hart discussed the projected activities of his subcommittee. Acknowledging the findings on administered prices, he stated that the most important problem in the field of antitrust was the concentration of economic power. "That those noncompetitive factors which may result through centralization of economic power be searchingly examined is essential to the continued vigor of our free competitive structure." Within the purview of such an examination would also be the growing trend toward conglomerate merger. "The nature of the conglomerate organization, [and] the special problems which it poses to competition raise issues which are both more complex and more serious than many of the other problems with which the antitrust laws traditionally have been concerned." He also noted that with the exception of the *Clorox* case, "both the Justice Department and the Federal Trade Commission have seemed reluctant to undertake any action in this area."[18]

Thus, on July 1, 1964, the Senate Antitrust Subcommittee began hearings on economic concentration. Senator Hart opened the hearings with a brief statement noting that our economic system is based on the concept of competition and freedom of action among competitors. Nevertheless, many small and medium-sized manufacturers had complained about the difficulties of competing in markets with a high degree of concentration. He emphasized that "we are not opposed to bigness as such. We are concerned instead with concentration and its economic effect. . . . Our goal is a free-enterprise economy which is, in fact, free." He stated his hope that evidence would be gained from the hearings to do whatever was necessary "to guarantee that the American economy maintains the competitive vigor which has made it a model for the world."[19]

The initial hearings, during July and September of that year, witnessed a parade of distinguished economists attesting to the increase in concentration and conglomeration, and the potential impact on competition. When the hearings reopened on March 16, 1965, Senator Hart exclaimed: "For too long we have kept our heads in the sand and refused to recognize what I think most responsible businessmen have long known, that our economy is becoming increasingly concentrated."[20]

On April 14 of the following year, addressing a meeting of the Antitrust Section of the American Bar Association, Hart attacked the timidity of the antitrust agencies. "The public trust-busters are showing little evidence of concern over the greatest merger tide in our history. . . . The general public is tranquilized by prosperity. And antitrust agencies . . . are adopting a tentative—if not timid—attitude toward anything but hard-core violations." He also attacked inflationary "industry-wide lock-step pricing [administered prices] which are virtually ignored by the antitrust agencies." The American economy, he continued, is still dynamic, but it requires a "tough, stringent, and vigorous" antitrust policy to keep it that way, not a laissez-faire approach.[21]

Hart again attacked administered prices in a speech in January 1967, stating that higher prices had little relationship to costs and demand. "Competition in many of the nation's basic industries has diminished to the point where one corporation sets prices to meet a target profit and others follow along." This lock-step pricing means that competition is not at work to bring lower prices to consumers. Prices go up in "industries that are operating far below productive capacities," indicating that price increases are not in response to overwhelming demand exceeding insufficient supply.[22]

By the end of 1967, the Third Great Merger Movement had reached such proportions that it could no longer be ignored. As indicated above, in October of that year President Johnson established the White House Task Force on Antitrust Policy, and in November Senators Javits, Brewster, Cooper, and Hartke sought to establish a commission to revise the antitrust laws. In 1968, Congressman Celler announced that the House Antitrust Committee would investigate conglomerate mergers.[23] Meanwhile, the Senate Subcommittee on Antitrust and Monopoly continued its hearings, and Senator Hart increased his attacks on concentration.

In a speech before the Antitrust Section of the American Bar Association on April 7, 1968, Hart exclaimed that "antitrust today is sick and nobody seems greatly concerned." He reminded his audience that corporate executives seek not competition, but power—economic and political power. "Local economic

independence cannot be preserved in the face of consolidation such as we have
had in the last few years." According to Hart, control of American business was
moving from local communities to a few large cities where central managers decide
the policies of far-flung business empires. "What antitrust needs is a constituency
and this is precisely what it lacks. We are called a consumer Congress. Yet the
basic economic concerns—price and quality—can be protected only by vigorous
antitrust."[24]

On October 1, Hart's sentiments were echoed by the subcommittee's chief
counsel, Jerry S. Cohen. In a speech before the American Management Association,
he stated that Congress was not in favor of tightening or enforcing the antitrust
laws. "The mind of Congress to restrict mergers is absolutely nothing. . . . We
couldn't get ten or twelve votes. Congress has been sold a bill that antitrust is
interfering with business." Cohen also commented that companies hurt by the
growing power of the conglomerates should not expect any help from Congress.[25]

Hart, like Kefauver before him, had found that his fellow Senators and
Representatives were not interested in antitrust, that indeed antitrust had no
constituency. "The only time you get action on antitrust," he said, "is if—pray God
we avoid it—there is economic collapse."[26] In a speech to the Law Forum at Duke
University on November 19, 1968, he stated: "Competition is an empty concept
unless accompanied by the most alert and tough kind of antitrust enforcement.
Such enforcement has been forthcoming from the administrations of neither political
parties." And he accused Congress, because of its relation with big business, of
discouraging vigorous antitrust enforcement. But he also said that part of the blame
must be attributed to public apathy, and a lack of recognition of the extent to which
big business impacts upon the life of each citizen.[27]

As the last days of the Johnson Administration wound down, Hart called for
restricting the growth of the largest corporations to internal expansion,[28] a position
shared by the antitrust agencies and the Supreme Court.[29] And in speeches delivered
on December 2 and 13, he strongly advocated federal chartering of corporations
engaged in interstate and international commerce.[30] "I envision Federal Charters
primarily as a means of achieving a competitive structure and of controlling undue
conglomeration." Then the focus would be shifted from federal enforcement to
market structure, and competition, rather than regulation, would determine the
direction of our economy. Federal chartering "can provide the answer we need in
controlling growing concentration and the corporate excesses which threaten
competition."[31] Despite the fact that federal incorporation had been considered as
early as 1899 by businessmen seeking nationwide uniformity, and as early as 1902
by President Theodore Roosevelt, Hart could find no support for federal chartering.[32]

After three and a half years of hearings and numerous speeches, Hart was still
fighting Congressional indifference and public apathy toward antitrust. Of the nine
subcommittee members, only Senators Hart and Roman L. Hruska were usually in
attendance, the latter being unabashedly pro-big business.[33] Hart was unable to
develop an antitrust constituency. Nevertheless, the subcommittee's hearings, on

administered prices and economic concentration, provide an excellent assessment of America's industrial economy taking up where the Temporary National Economic Committee left off almost two decades before.[34]

THE HOUSE

In the House of Representatives, the leading antitrust voice during the late 1950s and into the early 1960s was Emanuel Celler, coauthor of the Celler-Kefauver Act. On July 11, 1949, the Judiciary Committee of the House, chaired by Celler, established a subcommittee on the study of Monopoly Practices, later renamed the Antitrust Subcommittee. During the following year, the subcommittee, also chaired by Celler, began hearings into concentration and monopoly power in the steel industry, to be followed by inquiries into the newspaper and aluminum industries. In late 1955 the subcommittee issued a report that criticized the "token gesture" made to enforce Section 7 of the Clayton Act during the years since the Celler-Kefauver Amendment. The report also accused the Antitrust Division of inertia and the FTC of a "disdain" for the intent of Congress. In May 1959 the subcommittee denounced the consent decree process of the Department of Justice as weak and lacking in effective follow-up procedures.[35] In addition, Celler actively promoted stronger antitrust enforcement in his public speeches. In a letter to President Kennedy dated April 28, 1961, the Congressman sought the President's support for legislation requiring corporations contemplating a merger to provide prior notification to the Department of Justice.[36] In a letter dated April 17, 1962, to Myer Feldman, Deputy Special Assistant to President Kennedy, Celler announced that he was planning to introduce two bills to strengthen Section 7, provided they met with Administration approval. "These bills have been prompted . . . by the concentration of economic power in a number of basic industries. While the Celler-Kefauver Act prevents mergers which would create greater concentration in industry, it often tends to protect the entrenched position of the industry leader." The first bill would make it unlawful for a group of corporations to exercise dominant economic power in any line of commerce where its effect would be to lessen competition substantially or create or maintain a monopoly. The second would establish a presumption that such power exists when four or fewer firms possess 50 percent of the assets or capacity, or make 50 percent of the sales, and one of such firms possesses 25 percent of the assets or capacity, or makes 25 percent of the sales in a specific product line. The government would still have to prove a lessening of competition or tendency toward monopoly. Celler concluded: "Assuming that Administration approval is forthcoming, early hearings on this [proposed] legislation are contemplated."[37] No positive action was taken by the Executive or the Congress.

During the remainder of the Kennedy-Johnson years, the vigor and activity of the subcommittee, and its Chairman's interest in antitrust, practically disappeared. Between 1963 and 1968, the subcommittee held only eleven days of hearings (the

Senate Antitrust Subcommittee held 237).[38] "There were months when we had absolutely nothing to do," grumbled a former subcommittee staff member. "For some reason, Celler went backwards on antitrust."[39] Several reasons can be found. Receiving no support for antitrust from the Administration or his fellow Congressmen, he turned his attention to civil rights, an issue rapidly growing in political significance. In addition, his obvious conflicts of interest had become widely known, since his law firm handled many large corporations which were involved with the federal government. He had a "two door" arrangement with his law firm. Clients whose business concerned the government entered through one door, without Celler's name on it; other clients entered through a door with his name on it. No one was fooled, although the *New York Times Magazine* called it one of the most notorious embarrassments to Congress.[40] Finally, his age most certainly had affected his energy and the number of issues he wished to pursue. Celler was 74 in 1963, yet he refused to relinquish the chairmanship of the subcommittee.

By 1968, the Third Great Merger Movement, and the conglomerate movement within it, had reached such proportions that other government agencies initiated studies to investigate the phenomenon.[41] In response to the FTC's July announcement that it would study conglomerate mergers, Representative Henry S. Reuss asked the FTC to investigate the extent to which mergers that concentrated economic power also concentrated political power. In a letter to FTC Chairman Dixon dated September 16, 1968, Reuss asked if "a conglomerate (or any large corporation) has significant holdings in a majority of the congressional districts in this country, is it likely to have an inordinate influence over congressional action?" He suggested that the FTC find out how many corporations had significant holdings in more than 35 or 40 percent of the congressional districts, and then determine the correlation between a Congressman's vote on certain issues and the corporation's interest in them. Chairman Dixon, while acknowledging that increasing concentration of economic power may lead to a concentration of political power, said his agency did not have the resources to conduct such a study.[42] Dixon must have reasoned that if Congress had previously denied funds to study America's 1,000 largest firms and the relations between them,[43] Congress certainly would have rejected such a study with its potentially explosive political fallout.

On October 9, 1968, Celler announced that his subcommittee would undertake a comprehensive study into the significance of conglomerate mergers. "It may be that the traditional standards of the antitrust laws . . . need reevaluation in the light of [the] economic and political effects of conglomerate mergers. . . . The Antitrust Subcommittee's study will be [a] comprehensive evaluation of the multiple forces that operate in conglomerate mergers . . . in order to gauge their relation to current antitrust standards to preserve a competitively oriented economy." Hearings, conducted between July 30, 1969 and May 15, 1970, resulted in no recommendations for legislation to broaden or strengthen the antitrust laws.[44] Antitrust simply had no constituency.

TOWARD THE SUPREME COURT

Writing in 1963, Joseph S. Clark, Senator from Pennsylvania and former Mayor of Philadelphia, stated: "It is the third branch of government, the legislative, where things have gone awry. . . . This is the area where democratic government is breaking down. This is where the vested-interest lobbies tend to run riot, where conflict of interest is concealed from the public, where demagoguery, sophisticated or primitive, knows few bounds . . . where the lust for patronage and favors for the faithful do the greatest damage to the public interest."[45] Or, as Professor John Flynn of the Utah School of Law explained: If a "company can hire the best lawyers, the best public relations firm, and the best economists, and can invest thousands of dollars in explaining its case . . . then I think we can fairly say that it has bought political power."[46]

Edwin H. Sutherland, in his classic *White Collar Crime*, originally published in 1949, pointed out that while businessmen pay lip service to competition and free enterprise, they are not willing to let the economic system respond to the laws of supply and demand. Unfortunately, he continued, businessmen who violate the laws designed to regulate business do not customarily lose status among their associates, and they do not think of themselves as criminals or violators of the law. Nor does the public usually think of them as criminals, except in extreme cases. Even though the businessman may be given a low rating as to probable honesty, he is rendered a high social status. If he is convicted, the white-collar criminal generally receives a relatively light sentence.[47]

Senator Hart summed up the business-government relationship when he noted that Congress, being a political body, had been more receptive to the needs of powerful business interests than to those of consumers. Companies that deplore "big brotherism," he said, have no hesitation in asking for special legislative treatment. But the basic consumer concerns can be protected only by vigorous antitrust enforcement. "And Congress has shown no stomach for demanding action in this field."[48]

Congress is generally propelled by pressure, not principle. Until enough people tell it that antitrust is important, until a political coalition develops to actively lobby for antitrust, Congress will continue its indifference. But it was not Congress alone that contributed to the erosion of antitrust enforcement during the Kennedy-Johnson years. The executive branch consistently requested far too little funds for antitrust, and the agencies, therefore, lacked resources for vigorous enforcement. Big business supported the status quo, and the public remained indifferent. An Administration committed to economic growth, the increasing needs of the Vietnam War, civil rights, and the Great Society; and the Congress, committed to its own self-interest, called for a business-government partnership. It remained for the Supreme Court to combat the tidal wave of mergers that alarmed a number of people in and out of Congress.

5

The Response: The Supreme Court

THE JUDICIAL-BUSINESS ENVIRONMENT

The Supreme Court is an active participant in a continuous policy-making process that establishes the judicial-business environment in which contemplated mergers are abandoned, consummated, and even torn asunder. Just as the Court may frame far-reaching and unpredictable social policy when it decides upon the constitutionality of a particular action such as school segregation, so too in its interpretation of statutory law, such as Section 7, it may establish an environment that influences subsequent actions of the Congress, the antitrust agencies, and the business community. Moreover, the Supreme Court is a political body, which in its interpretations and decisions puts forth its own political and economic preferences.[1]

The Court may narrowly or broadly interpret statutes, close loopholes or leave them open, change previous Court decisions, or take a position that would require new legislation to alter. By its grant or denial of certiorari, it chooses those cases it wishes to hear, and refuses to hear those it does not. (For example, it can refuse to hear an appeal of a case won by an antitrust agency in a lower court.) On the other hand, the Supreme Court, like every other court, must wait until cases are brought to it. The antitrust agencies, because of their severely limited personnel resources, can only investigate a small fraction of the total number of mergers in a given period, and then challenge only a small percentage of that number.[2] Therefore the agencies must carefully select those cases that are considered worth the expenditure of time and effort—those that are considered necessary in order to test a legal principle or establish a legal precedent, thereby expanding or contracting the legal environment of business. Further, they must challenge only those mergers that they have a reasonable chance of winning, lest they encourage a disregard of their very existence by corporate executives and Congressmen frequently intimidated by big business.

The acquiring company must weigh the possibility of challenge against the advantages to be gained by the acquisition. Although many contemplated mergers are abandoned, the possibility of challenge is so low that the firms may decide to consummate the merger. Then, even if challenged, the corporation continues to earn the profits from the acquired company until and if divestiture is ordered. Moreover, most challenges are settled by consent decree, often with a relatively small penalty to the corporation.

Because Congress, in authoring the antitrust laws, posited broad charters to insure that competition was preserved, the specific meaning and application of these laws, at a given time, is what the courts, and especially the Supreme Court, say it is. As will be noted below, during the Kennedy-Johnson years the Supreme Court decided what constituted a relevant product market, a relevant geographic market, a "substantial" lessening of competition, and a tendency toward monopoly. It also determined what constituted potential competition, condemned a joint venture, and gave some quantitative guidelines regarding nonpermissible concentration. In these years, the Supreme Court was a very active policy maker in its concern over the increasing concentration resulting from the Third Great Merger Movement.

SIGNIFICANT ANTITRUST CASES OF THE 1960s

The first merger case to reach the Supreme Court following the passage of the Celler-Kefauver Act was the *Brown Shoe* case,[3] handed down by the Court on June 25, 1962. The Justices, concerned with increasing concentration and recognizing the precedents they were about to set, reviewed in detail the intent of Congress in passing the 1950 Amendment, and put forth eight factors as pertinent to the validity of any specific merger. These points are summarized below so that the reader may note how the Justices adhered to them when delivering their merger opinions in this and subsequent cases during the Kennedy-Johnson years.

First, Congress did wish to include the acquisition of assets within the coverage of the Act.

Second, it hoped to make plain that Section 7 applied not only to mergers between actual competitors but also to vertical and conglomerate mergers whose effect may tend to lessen competition in any line of commerce in any section of the country.

Third, Congress was concerned with arresting mergers at a time when the trend to a lessening of competition was still in its incipiency.

Fourth, Congress rejected the use of Sherman Act standards, which may have been applied to some early cases arising under original Section 7.

Fifth, Congress recognized the stimulation to competition that might flow from particular mergers. It would not impede, for example, a merger between two small companies to enable the combination to compete more effectively with larger corporations dominating the relevant market, nor a merger between a corporation that is financially healthy and a failing one that no longer can be a vital competitive factor in the market. The legislative history illuminates congressional concern with the protection of competition, not competitors, and its desire to restrain mergers only to the extent that such combinations may tend to lessen competition.

Sixth, Congress neither adopted nor rejected any particular tests for measuring the relevant product or geographic markets within which the anticompetitive effects of a merger were to be judged. Nor did it adopt a definition of the word "substantially," either in quantitative terms of sales, assets, or market shares, or in qualitative terms, by which a merger's effects on competition were to be measured.

Seventh, while providing no definite quantitative or qualitative tests by which enforcement agencies could gauge the effects of a given merger to determine whether it may substantially lessen competition or tend toward monopoly, Congress indicated plainly that a merger had to be functionally viewed, in the context of its particular industry. That is, a merger should be gauged by whether the consolidation was to take place in an industry that was fragmented or concentrated, that had seen a recent trend toward domination by a few leaders or had remained fairly consistent in its distribution of market shares among the participating companies, that had easy access to markets by suppliers and buyers or had experienced foreclosure, or that had witnessed the ready entry of new competition or the erection of barriers to prospective entrants.

Eighth, Congress used the words "may be" substantially to lessen competition to indicate that its concern was with probabilities, not certainties. Mergers with a probably anticompetitive effect were to be proscribed by this act.[4]

Following the listing of these points, the Supreme Court, in a 6–1 decision, written by Chief Justice Warren, affirmed the District Court's finding that the 1956 merger of Brown and G. R. Kinney Shoe Companies violated Section 7 of the Clayton Act.

Although domestic shoe production was scattered among a large number of manufacturers, the top four—International, Endicott-Johnson, Brown (including Kinney) and General Shoe—produced approximately 23 percent of the nation's shoes. The District Court found a definite trend among shoe manufacturers to acquire retail outlets. Brown itself had acquired 845 such outlets by 1956. Moreover, between 1950 and 1956 nine independent shoe store chains, operating 1,114 retail shoe stores, had become subsidiaries of large firms and had ceased their independent operations. And once the manufacturers acquired retail outlets, there was a definite trend for the parent-manufacturers to supply an ever-increasing percentage of the retail outlets' needs, thereby foreclosing other manufacturers from effectively competing for the retail accounts.

Another trend found to exist in the shoe industry was a decrease in the number of firms manufacturing shoes. In 1947, there were 1,077 independent manufacturers, but by 1954 their number had decreased 10 percent to 970. During the same period of time, Brown had acquired seven companies engaged solely in shoe manufacturing. As a result, in 1955, Brown was the fourth-largest shoe manufacturer in the country, producing about 25.6 million pairs of shoes or about 4 percent of the nation's total footwear production.

Kinney was principally engaged in operating the largest family-style shoe store chain in the United States, operating over 400 such stores in more than 270 cities. These stores made about 1.2 percent of all national retail shoe sales by dollar volume in 1955. In addition, Kinney owned and operated four plants that manufactured men's, women's, and children's shoes and whose combined output was 0.5 percent of the national shoe production in 1955, making Kinney the twelfth-largest manufacturer in the United States. Kinney stores obtained about 20 percent of their shoes from Kinney's own manufacturing plants. At the time of the merger, Kinney bought no shoes from Brown. However, in line with Brown's admitted reasons for acquiring Kinney, Brown, by 1957, had become the largest outside supplier of Kinney, supplying 7.9 percent of Kinney's shoes.[5]

The Justices agreed with the parties and the District Court's finding that for both vertical and horizontal purposes the relevant product markets were men's, women's, and children's shoes, and that the geographic market was the entire United States.[6]

The Court then addressed the vertical aspects of the merger. The diminution of the vigor of competition that may stem from a vertical arrangement results primarily from a foreclosure of a share of the market otherwise open to competitors. This is an important consideration in determining whether the effect of a vertical arrangement may be substantially to lessen competition, or to tend to create a monopoly. The Justices then stated that the facts in this case:

[We are convinced] that the shoe industry is being subjected to just such a cumulative series of vertical mergers which, if left unchecked, will be likely "substantially to lessen competition."
We reach this conclusion because the trend toward vertical integration in the shoe industry, when combined with Brown's avowed policy of forcing its own shoes upon its retail subsidiaries, may foreclose competition from a substantial share of the market without producing any countervailing competitive, economic, or social advantages.[7]

Addressing the horizontal aspects, the Justices reviewed the sales volume in 118 cities of varying sizes ranging from "Topeka, Kansas, to Batavia, New York, and Hobbs, New Mexico," and noted that the combined Brown and Kinney sales ranged from 5 percent to 57 percent share in one, two, or all three of the men's, women's, and children's shoe markets. They noted the tendency toward concentration in the industry, and that as a result of the merger Brown "moved into second place nationally in terms of retail stores directly owned," and in combination with those contracted, controlled 1,600 shoe outlets.[8] They concluded:

We cannot avoid the mandate of Congress that tendencies toward concentration in industry are to be curbed in their incipiency, particularly when those tendencies are being accelerated through giant steps striding across a hundred cities at a time. In the light of the trends in this industry we agree with the Government and the court below that this is an appropriate place at which to call a halt.[9]

Thus, the Supreme Court, noting the decrease in small competing units in the economy, condemned both the vertical and horizontal aspects of the merger. It placed particular emphasis on the trend toward concentration in the industry and declared that such trends are to be curbed in their incipiency.

The second merger case to reach the Supreme Court following the Celler-Kefauver Act was the *Philadelphia National Bank* case.[10] Although banks and financial institutions, and the financial aspects of mergers, have not been included in this study, this case will be mentioned briefly because the quantitative guideline—30 percent market share—enunciated by the Court was to be considered the maximum allowable in subsequent merger cases before the Supreme Court during the 1960s.

The proposed merger would have joined the Philadelphia National Bank (PNB), the second-largest bank in the Philadelphia metropolitan area (Philadelphia county, and three contiguous Pennsylvania counties), with the Girard Trust Corn Exchange Bank (Girard), the third-largest bank in that area. The Department of Justice sued to prevent the merger, but the District Court found for the banks. The government then appealed to the Supreme Court, and the banks postponed consummation pending that Court's decision.

Justice Brennan delivered the 6–2 opinion on June 17, 1963. He noted that were the merger effected, the resulting bank would be the largest in the area, with approximately 36 percent of the area banks' total assets, 36 percent of deposits, and 34 percent of loans. It and the second largest (the First Pennsylvania Bank and Trust Company, then the largest) would have 59 percent of the assets, 58 percent of deposits, and 58 percent of the loans, with the four largest having over 77 percent of the assets, deposits, and loans. He further noted that PNB and Girard respectively had acquired nine and six formerly independent area banks since 1950, and the total number of independent banks in the area had declined from 108 in 1947 to 42 in 1963—a noticeable trend toward concentration.[11]

Specifically, we think that a merger which produces a firm controlling an undue percentage share of the relevant market, and results in a significant increase in the concentration of firms in that market, is so inherently likely to lessen competition substantially that it must be enjoined in the absence of evidence clearly showing that the merger is not likely to have such anticompetitive effects. . . .

The merger of appellees will result in a single bank's controlling at least 30% of the commercial banking business in the . . . area. Without attempting to specify the smallest market share which would still be considered to threaten undue concentration, we are clear that 30% presents that threat. Further, whereas presently the two largest banks in the area (First Pennsylvania and PNB) control between them approximately 44% of the area's commercial banking business, the two largest after the merger (PNB-Girard and First Pennsylvania) will control 59%. Plainly, we think, this increase of more than 33% in concentration must be regarded as significant.[12]

The opinion also noted that there was nothing in the record to rebut the anticompetitive tendency indicated by these percentages and directed the lower court to enjoin the merger.

In this second case, the Court strongly indicated its concern over increasing concentration, specifically in the relevant geographic market of metropolitan Philadelphia. It also appeared to give notice to the business community that 30 percent would be the maximum tolerable share of the relevant product market permissible through merger.

In the first of four significant 1964 cases, the *El Paso Natural Gas* case,[13] the Justices elaborated on their belief that Section 7 was concerned with the role of probable, or potential, competitors in maintaining competition.

During the 1950s, Pacific Northwest Pipeline Corporation (Pacific Northwest) was a major supplier of natural gas in the area west of the Rockies, but did not sell in California. Although it had sought to enter the California market, it had not been successful. In 1956, it had entered into negotiations to supply gas to Southern California Edison Company (Edison), the largest user in Southern California. In response, however, El Paso, the major state supplier with over 50 percent of that market, offered Edison a firm supply at substantially reduced prices. Later in that year, Pacific Northwest agreed to be acquired by El Paso. In July 1957, the Justice Department filed suit to block the merger. Nevertheless, the merger was completed in December 1959, after approval had been received from the Federal Power Commission earlier in that month.[14]

The 7–1 decision of the Court, delivered on April 6, 1964, was written by Justice Douglas. Referring to *Brown Shoe*, he noted that Congress had used the words "may be substantially to lessen competition" to indicate its concern with probabilities, not certainties. Mergers with a probable anticompetitive effect were prohibited.[15]

Pacific Northwest's position as a competitive factor in California was not disproved by the fact that it had never sold gas there. Nor is it conclusive that Pacific Northwest's attempt to sell to Edison failed. That might be weighty if a market presently saturated showed signs of petering out. But it is irrelevant in a market like California, where incremental needs are booming. . . . Unsuccessful bidders are no less competitors than the successful one. . . . Pacific Northwest . . . had adequate reserves and managerial skill. It was so strong and militant that it was viewed with concern, and coveted by El Paso.[16]

Justice Douglas also stated that had Pacific Northwest remained independent there could be no doubt that it would have continued its efforts to penetrate the California market. The Court found the merger in violation of Section 7 and ordered divestiture. By its decision, it also served notice that in future cases it would carefully consider potential competitors.

Following the 1959 acquisition of Rome Cable Corporation (Rome) by Aluminum Company of America (ALCOA), the Justice Department filed suit claiming that the merger violated Section 7. The District Court held that there was no violation and the government appealed to the Supreme Court. Justice Douglas delivered the 6–3 opinion on June 1, 1964.[17]

In 1958, the year before the merger, ALCOA was the leading producer of aluminum conductor cable with 27.8 percent of the market, but produced no copper conductor. Rome produced both copper and aluminum conductor, with its share of the latter market at 1.3 percent. The Court found that the two products were separable for the purpose of analyzing the competitive effects of the merger. It therefore directed its attention to aluminum conductor as the relevant product market.[18]

The Court noted that in addition to its 27.8 percent, ALCOA with its three leading competitors controlled more than 76 percent of the market, and only nine producers, including Rome, accounted for 95.7 percent. In other words, the market was dominated by four competitors, but also was served by a small group of independents. Although the acquisition of Rome added only 1.3 percent to ALCOA's share, "that seems to us reasonably likely to produce a substantial lessening of competition." Further, "Rome seems to us the prototype of the small independent that Congress aimed to preserve by Section 7."[19] The judgment of the lower Court was reversed and divestiture was directed.

By its findings in this case, the Court indicated that if it felt it necessary to preserve competition and halt further concentration, it would not hesitate to decide what constituted the relevant product market. It also indicated that an increase in concentration as small as 1.3 percent would be considered a "substantial lessening of competition." Finally, the Court also seemed to warn business that a 29.1 percent market share resulting from merger (ALCOA and Rome) was too close to its 30 percent guideline in *Philadelphia Bank* to be tolerated.

In 1960, Pennsalt and Olin-Mathieson, both chemical corporations, jointly formed the Penn-Olin Chemical Company to produce and sell sodium chlorate in the Southeastern United States. Prior to the formation of Penn-Olin, two companies, Hooker Chemical and American Potash, held over 90 percent of the relevant geographic market. Nevertheless, the Justice Department considered the joint venture to be a violation of Section 7 and sought dissolution. The District Court found no violation and the government appealed to the Supreme Court.[20]

Justice Clark delivered the 5–4 opinion on June 22, 1964.[21] The opinion noted that "this is the first case reaching this Court . . . that directly involves the validity under Section 7 of the joint participation of two corporations in the creation of a third as a new domestic producing organization. We are, therefore, plowing new ground."[22] The Court noted that both corporations could have entered the geographic market, and each had evidenced a long sustained and strong interest in so doing. Thus, the joint venture foreclosed them from the market, since the parents would not compete with their progeny. In addition, the joint venture eliminated potential competition between the two in the sodium chlorate market, which might have existed had the joint venture not taken place. Finally, the Court noted that even if it was probable that only one of the parents would have entered the market, the joint venture eliminated the potential competitor "that might have remained at the edge of the market." The requirements of Section 7 are met when a "reasonable likelihood" of a substantial lessening of competition in the relevant market is shown. The judgment of the lower court was vacated and the case remanded to it for further investigation into the relationship between the joint venturers, and their impact as individual competitors/potential competitors in the relevant market.[23] Thus, the Court reiterated its concern with potential competition previously put forth in *El Paso*, and also indicated its belief that joint ventures were prohibited by Section 7.[24]

In a similar case, three weeks after the *ALCOA-Rome* decision, the highest court again warned the business community that it would determine the relevant product market if it considered such action necessary and that mergers approaching 30 percent would not be tolerated. Justice White delivered the 7–2 opinion in the *Continental Can* case on June 22, 1964.[25]

In 1956, Continental Can Company, the nation's second-largest producer of metal containers, acquired Hazel-Atlas Glass Company, the third largest producer of glass containers in the United States. At the time of the merger, Continental and American Can Company, the largest producer, accounted for 71 percent of the metal container business, while Hazel-Atlas, with 9.6 percent of the glass container industry, combined with Owens-Illinois and Anchor-Hocking to produce over 55 percent of that market.

The Court found that competition between metal and glass containers for the same end uses had been "insistent, continuous, effective, and quantitywise very substantial."[26] Justice White then stated that, since the purpose of determining a relevant product market is to measure the effect of a specific acquisition, that market must conform to competitive reality. He continued:

We hold that the interindustry competition between glass and metal containers is sufficient to warrant treating as a relevant product market the combined glass and metal container industries and all end uses for which they compete.[27]

Having combined metal and glass containers into one product market, the Court then noted that the combination of Hazel-Atlas's 3.1 percent share, and Continental's 21.9 percent, now totaled 25 percent of this relevant product market.

Where a merger is of such size as to be inherently suspect, elaborate proof of market structure, market behavior and probable anticompetitive effects may be dispensed with in view of Section 7's design to prevent undue concentration. . . .[28]
We think our holding is consonant with the purpose of Section 7 to arrest anticompetitive arrangements in their incipiency.[29]

The decision of the District Court, upholding the merger, was reversed. Once again, the Court had indicated its determination to oppose mergers resulting in a market share approaching 30 percent, and to so mold the relative market as to assist it in preventing further concentration in that market.

The *Consolidated Foods* case, decided in 1965, was the first conglomerate merger-product extension case to come before the Supreme Court. The issue was reciprocity. On April 28, Justice Douglas delivered the unanimous opinion that such behavior by Consolidated had violated Section 7.[30]

In 1951, Consolidated Foods Corporation, a large food processor, wholesaler, and retailer, had acquired Gentry, Inc., a manufacturer of dehydrated onion and garlic. After acquisition, Consolidated had attempted to use its market position to induce its suppliers and processors to buy Gentry's products. The Federal Trade Commission held that the acquisition violated Section 7 because it gave Consolidated the threat of foreclosure to Gentry's competitors and to its (Consolidated's) suppliers who did not buy from Gentry. In addition, it gave Consolidated the lure of reciprocal buying from those who did buy from Gentry. Thus, the FTC claimed that the effect of the acquisition may have been to substantially lessen competition, and ordered divestiture. The Court of Appeals, however, noted that Gentry's share of the market had increased only 3 percent, from 32 to 35 percent in ten years, and therefore held that the FTC had failed to show that the acquisition had substantially lessened competition.[31]

The Supreme Court's opinion noted that during the postacquisition period Gentry was able to increase its share of onion sales by 7 percent and hold its losses in garlic to 12 percent, while increasing its market share by 3 percent. Moreover, this increase was accomplished in spite of having products inferior to those of the market leader, Basic Vegetable Products, as admitted by Gentry's President. As a result, the Court concluded that there was substantial evidence to indicate reciprocity, reversed the finding of the Appeals Court, and therefore sustained the FTC's divestiture order. Reciprocity, the Court noted, is one of the anticompetitive practices at which the antitrust laws are aimed.[32]

Almost three years after *Philadelphia Bank*, in the *Von's Grocery* case, the Supreme Court severely lowered the geographic market share it would accept. Von's had acquired Shopping Bag Food Stores in 1960. Before the merger, Von's was the third-largest retail grocer and Shopping Bag the sixth largest in the Los Angeles area. Their combined share was 7.5 percent of that market. Thus, the District Court concluded that the government had failed to prove a violation of Section 7.

In delivering the 6–2 opinion on May 31, 1966, Justice Black stated that from 1948 to 1958 the number of Von's stores increased from 14 to 27, while Shopping Bag increased from 15 to 34, and their merger created the second-largest grocery chain in the Los Angeles area. He further noted that from 1950 to 1963, the number of single store operators had decreased from 5,365 to 3,590. "These facts alone are enough to cause us to conclude contrary to the District Court that the Von's-Shopping Bag merger did violate Section 7." The opinion again indicated that Congress's intention in passing the Celler-Kefauver Act was to preserve competition among many small businesses by arresting a trend toward concentration in its incipiency.[33]

The Court thus reaffirmed its concern with preservation of small independent businesses that it had enunciated in the *ALCOA-Rome* case, and gave notice to business that it would go below the 30 percent geographic market share guideline of the *Philadelphia Bank* case if it considered such action necessary to restrict further concentration.

The final case included in this chapter is the 1967 *Clorox* case, in which the high court found Proctor & Gamble (P&G) in violation of Section 7 as a result of its 1957 acquisition of Clorox Chemical Company, the largest producer of household liquid bleach. Justice Douglas delivered the 7–0 opinion on April 11, 1967. This was the second conglomerate-product extension case to come before the Supreme Court.

At the time of the merger, Clorox accounted for 48.8 percent of the liquid bleach market, with its nearest competitor, Purex, having 15.7 percent. The remainder of the market was scattered among more than 200 producers. P&G was a huge manufacturer of diverse household products, primarily soaps and detergents. It held 54.4 percent of the latter market. P&G was also the largest advertiser in the United States, with 1957 expenditures exceeding $127 million.[34] The FTC sued to dissolve the merger, but the Court of Appeals upheld P&G.

The Supreme Court, however, found that this merger was anticompetitive for several reasons. It noted that the acquisition by such a powerful company of the firm already dominant in the liquid bleach industry would dissuade the many smaller firms from aggressively competing with it. It would further raise entry barriers because of the reluctance of potential entrants to compete with the giant P&G. Moreover, since P&G was considered the most likely entrant into the liquid bleach field, the merger eliminated it as a potential competitor. In addition, because all brands of liquid bleach are chemically identical, advertising is vital to sales, and appeared to be the primary reason for Clorox's leadership position. P&G, already the nation's leading advertiser, could further discourage potential entrants and could pressure retailers to increase shelf space for Clorox. Finally, through cross-subsidization, P&G could lower the market price of Clorox and harm competitors.[35] Thus, the Supreme Court reaffirmed its view on potential competition and its continuing concern with the preservation of small competitors. It also gave notice that it would carefully consider the possibility of cross-subsidization resulting from merger.

In the above cases, the Supreme Court repeatedly voiced its concern with the preservation of competition and its determination to halt trends toward further concentration. It indicated its suspicion of joint ventures, its concern with potential competitors, and its regard for the small, independent producer. In addition, the Court gave warning to businessmen that, if it deemed it necessary, it would decide the relevant product and geographic markets, and that it would not tolerate the possibility of reciprocity or cross-subsidization. Indeed, during the Kennedy-Johnson years, the Supreme Court played a major role in attempting to slow the pace of the Third Great Merger Movement.

TOWARD THE NIXON YEARS

Sixteen merger cases, initiated after the passage of the Celler-Kefauver Act, reached the Supreme Court during the Kennedy-Johnson years. Each time the Court found for the government.[36]

A review of the High Court's opinions in the 16 cases indicates that Chief Justice Warren, and Justices Brennan and Clark, voted in the majority in every case in which they participated. Justices Douglas and Black dissented only in *Penn-Olin*, while Justice White dissented in only three of the 16.[37] Thus, the political philosophy of the Warren Court was procompetition, pro-antitrust, and strongly opposed to further economic concentration. As the above cases indicate, it did not hesitate to mold the circumstances presented to it in order to support its procompetitive philosophy. As previously noted, however, the Supreme Court is a political body whose composition and outlook change over time. As the Johnson Administration drew to a close, the merger views of the Court during the Nixon years remained to be seen.

By 1969, the Court had given notice that it could interpret Section 7 to strike down any horizontal, vertical, or conglomerate product extension merger that it so wished. However, no pure conglomerate merger case had yet come before it. Whether this Court, so demonstrably procompetition, would have the opportunity during the Nixon years to put its stamp on the conglomerate movement also remained to be seen.

6

Conclusions

The Kennedy-Johnson years witnessed the third and greatest merger movement up to that time in U.S. history. During these years, over 9,400 firms disappeared into merger, increasing from 954 in 1961 to 2,442 in the peak year of 1968 (Table 1.1). In addition, an overwhelming number of the large mergers were of the conglomerate variety (Figure 2.3).

Despite America's historical (both idealistic and statutory) commitment to competition and opposition to monopoly, President Kennedy knew he could expect little public support for a crusade against the increasing concentration of economic power. The generally remarkable performance of the national economy since the beginning of World War II, and the United States' industrial leadership since that time, had made big business palatable to the American public. Moreover, Kennedy's campaign theme, which was to remain the goal of his Presidency, was economic growth. He needed business support for that growth. President Johnson, too, knew the importance of business support. The success of his Great Society's many programs was dependent upon a strong and growing economy, which in turn was dependent upon business optimism and confidence in his administration. As U.S. involvement in the Vietnam War increased, economic growth and business support became even more important.

This realpolitik view of the government-business environment had its effect on the Antitrust Division and the Federal Trade Commission. Faced with a shortage of resources and the lack of a White House commitment to antitrust, only 170 mergers were challenged by the two antitrust agencies during the Kennedy-Johnson years. And of these, only 11 acquisitions of the 25 most active acquiring firms were challenged.

During these years, the Congress was generally indifferent to antitrust. Senator Hart, like Senator Kefauver before him, found that, despite numerous speeches and years of hearings into administered prices and economic concentration, their fellow Senators were not interested in antitrust. In the House, Representative Celler, former champion of antitrust, having received no support from the probusiness Administration or his Congressional colleagues, turned his attention to Civil Rights, a more politically significant issue. Antitrust simply had no constituency to push for Congressional attention.

Only the Supreme Court was consistently procompetition and anticoncentration during these years. In each of the 16 merger cases that came before it, the Court interpreted revised Section 7 to strike down every actual or potential threat to competition and to prevent further concentration.

During the Kennedy-Johnson years, both the Executive and the Congress, reflecting the largely apathetic outlook of the electorate, generally ignored its historical commitment to the preservation of competition. Thus the Third Great Merger Movement rushed forward.

If we will not endure a king as a political power, we should not endure a king over the production, transportation and sale of any of the necessaries of life. If we would not submit to an emperor, we should not submit to an autocrat of trade, with power to prevent competition and to fix the price of any commodity.

Senator John Sherman[1]

7

Epilogue

A major problem of antitrust is the lack of consistent agreement among economists, and among legislators and judges, as to the acceptability of corporate bigness and economic concentration. Thus, since the passage of the Sherman Act, the Supreme Court struggled with changing economic conditions, seeking to preserve the small competitor, and to clarify such concepts as substantial lessening of competition and trends toward concentration. Then, the great merger wave of the 1950s and 1960s resulted in a concentration of economic power and potential threat to competition greater than previously experienced in American history. The Supreme Court, through its findings in the 16 merger cases that came before it during the Kennedy-Johnson years, established 30 percent as the maximum acceptable market share resulting from merger, stated that it would not tolerate reciprocity or cross-subsidization, and gave notice that it would consider the elimination of potential entrants, including that accomplished by joint venture, to be anticompetitive. In addition, although no pure conglomerate merger case had come before it, the Court also indicated in the *Brown Shoe* case that it considered the provisions of Section 7 to be applicable to conglomerate mergers. Thus, in the absence of a strong Executive and Congressional commitment to antitrust, the Supreme Court forged a firm foundation for aggressive legal and legislative action against further concentration.

President-elect Richard Nixon appointed a study group, the Task Force on Productivity and Competition, chaired by University of Chicago Professor George J. Stigler, to advise him on antitrust, mergers, and the conglomerate phenomenon. Whereas the group appointed by President Johnson had expressed its concern with the increasing number of mergers and concentration in the economy, and had recommended corrective legislation,[1] the Stigler Report saw little or no threat to competition in these events. The Task Force announced its opposition to new legislation to deconcentrate highly concentrated oligopolistic industries. It also recommended that the Department of Justice take no action against existing conglomerates or conglomerate mergers pending a conference to gather information on their competitive effects (Appendix C).[2] Thus, the business community anticipated continued laxity in antitrust enforcement under the Nixon Administration. Moreover, the appointment of John Mitchell, Nixon's Wall Street law partner, as Attorney General, and Richard McLaren, a Chicago antitrust lawyer and former Chairman of the Antitrust Section of the American Bar Association, as Assistant Attorney General for Antitrust, further assured corporate leaders of a probusiness White House.

McLaren, however, was especially concerned with conglomerates, and recognized that the country was undergoing a massive merger trend that could result in a potentially harmful restructuring of the economy. He could have accepted the Stigler Report and done nothing, or could have established another study group to investigate economic conditions. Instead, he decided that a more intensive enforcement policy against mergers was needed.[3]

In an appearance before the House Ways and Means Committee, on March 12, 1969, McLaren expressed his deep concern over the current merger movement and promised to use his statutory antitrust authority to meet threats to competition posed by the conglomerate phenomenon. "The complexity and relative novelty of the conglomerate merger trend makes our task a challenging one; the magnitude of that trend makes it an urgent necessity." Unlike Turner, McLaren believed that present legislation was sufficient to attack conglomerates. "We are willing to risk losing some cases to find out how far [antitrust legislation] will take us in halting the current accelerated trend toward concentration by merger."[4]

Accordingly, during the next five months, the Justice Department challenged the following conglomerate mergers:

—April 14. LTV's acquisition of Jones & Laughlin Steel Corporation. LTV had become the nation's fourteenth-largest industrial corporation and Jones & Laughlin was the sixth-largest steel producer.

—April 28. ITT's acquisition of Canteen Corporation. ITT had become the eleventh-largest industrial concern and Canteen was one of the leading nationwide vending companies.

—May 21. Northwest Industries' contested acquisition of B.F. Goodrich. Northwest, a diversified holding company, built on the Chicago and Northwestern Railroad, was one hundred-thirtieth in national sales among industrial firms. B.F. Goodrich, also diversified and a leader in tire production, was eighty-third in the nation. Combined they would have ranked thirty-eighth. (Northwest failed in its attempt to acquire Goodrich, and the government dropped its case on May 3, 1974.)

—August 1. ITT's acquisition of Hartford Fire Insurance Company. Hartford was the fourth-largest property and liability insurance company.

—August 1. ITT's acquisition of Grinnell Corporation. Grinnell was a leading firm in the manufacture and sale of automatic sprinkler systems.[5]

On August 6, 1969, Attorney General Mitchell, speaking before the Georgia Bar Association, also attacked conglomerates and the increased concentration resulting from the mergers of the 1960s:

Concentration of this magnitude is likely to eliminate existing and potential competition. It increases the possibility for reciprocity and . . . pose[s] substantial barriers to firms wishing to participate in a competitive market.[6]

He also noted that such concentration creates a "community of interest" among corporations who meet in various markets, and this tends to reduce competition. Finally, he listed three instances when the Justice Department would probably file suit:

The Department of Justice may very well oppose any merger among the top 200 manufacturing firms or firms of comparable size in other industries. . . . The Department of Justice will probably oppose any merger by one of the top 200 manufacturing firms of any leading producer in any concentrated industry. . . . The Department will continue to challenge mergers which substantially lessen potential competition or develop a substantial potential for reciprocity.[7]

By mid-1969, it appeared as though the Nixon Administration would take a tough attitude toward mergers, especially of the conglomerate variety. As the year continued, however, a sluggish economy and a declining stock market resulted in a slowdown in merger activity, and the beginning of an unravelling of some of the conglomerates. In addition, the Nixon Administration, though wary of the "upstart" conglomerates, was essentially probusiness, and unwilling to disturb the entrenched old-line oligopolists. Congress continued to show little to no interest in antitrust. Vietnam and civil rights continued to hold the public attention.

LTV's Jones & Laughlin, Braniff Airways, and Okonite Cable units were less profitable than expected, other subsidiaries were in financial difficulties, and the conglomerate was having a cash flow problem. On June 10, 1970, LTV agreed to a consent decree that permitted the retention of Jones & Laughlin but required the divestiture of Braniff and Okonite.[8]

Meanwhile, ITT was having organizational problems digesting its recent acquisitions, had tired of lobbying to drive a wedge between Mitchell-McLaren and Nixon, and was embarrassed by the revelation of its contribution to the city of San Diego in what appeared to be a bribe to bring the 1972 Republican National Convention to that city. On September 24, 1971, ITT entered into consent decrees that permitted the retention of Hartford but required the divestiture of Canteen and Grinnell.[9]

By the negotiation of these consent decrees, the Supreme Court was denied the opportunity to rule on the status of pure conglomerate mergers under Section 7 of the Clayton Act.

The 1980s would witness another great merger frenzy, encouraged by a laissez-faire attitude on the part of the Reagan Administration and congressional indifference toward antitrust legislation. By 1971, however, the Third Great Merger Movement had ended (Figure 7.1).

Figure 7.1
Disappearance by Merger of Manufacturing and Mining Firms, 1948–1972

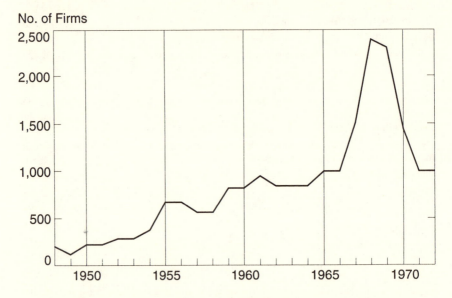

Source: Adapted from Federal Trade Commission, Bureau of Economics, *Current Trends in Merger Activity, 1971,* Statistical Report No. 10 (Washington, D. C., May 1972), 6.

Appendix A:
Merger Guidelines, U. S. Department of Justice

1. *Purpose.* The purpose of these guidelines is to acquaint the business community, the legal profession, and other interested groups and individuals with the standards currently being applied by the Department of Justice in determining whether to challenge corporate acquisitions and mergers under Section 7 of the Clayton Act. (Although mergers or acquisitions may also be challenged under the Sherman Act, commonly the challenge will be made under Section 7 of the Clayton Act and, accordingly, it is to this provision of law that the guidelines are directed.) The responsibilities of the Department of Justice under Section 7 are those of an enforcement agency, and these guidelines are announced solely as a statement of current Department policy, subject to change at any time without prior notice, for whatever assistance such statement may be in enabling interested persons to anticipate in a general way Department enforcement action under Section 7. Because the statements of enforcement policy contained in these guidelines must necessarily be framed in rather general terms, and because the critical factors in any particular guideline formulation may be evaluated differently by the Department than by the parties, the guidelines should not be treated as a substitute for the Department's business review procedures, which make available statements of the Department's present enforcement intentions with regard to particular proposed mergers or acquisitions.

2. *General Enforcement Policy.* Within the overall scheme of the Department's antitrust enforcement activity, the primary role of Section 7 enforcement is to preserve and promote market structures conducive to competition. Market structure is the focus of the Department's merger policy chiefly because the conduct of the individual firms in a market tends to be controlled by the structure of that market, i.e., by those market conditions which are fairly permanent or subject only to slow

Source: Press Release, U.S. Department of Justice, May 30, 1968.

change (such as, principally, the number of substantial firms selling in the market, the relative sizes of their respective market shares, and the substantiality of barriers to the entry of new firms into the market). Thus, for example, a concentrated market structure, where a few firms account for a large share of the sales, tends to discourage vigorous price competition by the firms in the market and to encourage other kinds of conduct, such as use of inefficient methods of production or excessive promotional expenditures, of an economically undesirable nature. Moreover, not only does emphasis on market structure generally produce economic predictions that are fully adequate for the purposes of a statute that requires only a showing that the effect of a merger "may be substantially to lessen competition, or to tend to create a monopoly," but an enforcement policy emphasizing a limited number of structural factors also facilitates both enforcement decision-making and business planning which involves anticipation of the Department's enforcement intent. Accordingly, the Department's enforcement activity under Section 7 is directed primarily toward the identification and prevention of those mergers which alter market structure in ways likely now or eventually to encourage or permit non-competitive conduct.

In certain exceptional circumstances, however, the structural factors used in these guidelines will not alone be conclusive, and the Department's enforcement activity will necessarily be based on a more complex and inclusive evaluation. This is sometimes the case, for example, where basic technological changes are creating new industries, or are significantly transforming older industries, in such fashion as to make current market boundaries and market structure of uncertain significance. In such unusual transitional situations application of the normal guideline standards may be inappropriate; and on assessing probable future developments, the Department may not sue despite nominal application of a particular guideline, or it may sue even though the guidelines, as normally applied, do not require the Department to challenge the merger. Similarly, in the area of conglomerate merger activity, the present incomplete state of knowledge concerning structure-conduct relationships may preclude sole reliance on the structural criteria used in these guidelines, as explained in paragraphs 17 and 20 below.

3. *Market Definition.* A rational appraisal of the probable competitive effects of a merger normally requires definition of one or more relevant markets. A market is any grouping of sales (or other commercial transactions) in which each of the firms whose sales are included enjoys some advantage in competing with those firms whose sales are not included. The advantage need not be great, for so long as it is significant it defines an area of effective competition among the included sellers in which the competition of the excluded sellers is, *ex hypothesi,* less effective. The process of market definition may result in identification of several appropriate markets in which to test the probable competitive effects of a particular merger.

A market is defined both in terms of its product dimension ("line of commerce") and its geographic dimension ("section of the country").

(i) *Line of Commerce.* The sales of any product or service which is distinguishable as a matter of commercial practice from other products or services will ordinarily constitute a relevant product market, even though, from the standpoint of most purchasers, other products may be reasonably, but not perfectly, interchangeable with it in terms of price, quality, and use. On the other hand, the sales of two distinct products to a particular group of purchasers can also appropriately be grouped into a single market where the two products are reasonably interchangeable for that group in terms of price, quality, and use. In this latter case, however, it may be necessary also to include in that market the sales of one or more other products which are equally interchangeable with the two products in terms of price, quality, and use from the standpoint of that group of purchasers for whom the two products are interchangeable.

The reasons for employing the foregoing definitions may be stated as follows. In enforcing Section 7 the Department seeks primarily to prevent mergers which change market structure in a direction likely to create a power to behave non-competitively in the production and sale of any particular product, even though that power will ultimately be limited, though not nullified, by the presence of other similar products that, while reasonably interchangeable, are less than perfect substitutes. It is in no way inconsistent with this effort also to pursue a policy designed to prohibit mergers between firms selling distinct products where the result of the merger may be to create or enhance the companies' market power due to the fact that the products, though not perfectly substitutable by purchasers, are significant enough alternatives to constitute substantial competitive influences on the production, development or sale of each.

(ii) *Section of the Country.* The total sales of a product or service in any commercially significant section of the country (even as small as a single community), or aggregate of such sections, will ordinarily constitute a geographic market if firms engaged in selling the product make significant sales of the product to purchasers in the section or sections. The market need not be enlarged beyond any section meeting the foregoing test unless it clearly appears that there is no economic barrier (e.g., significant transportation costs, lack of distribution facilities, customer inconvenience, or established consumer preference for existing products) that hinders the sale from outside the section to purchasers within the section; nor need the market be contracted to exclude some portion of the product sales made inside any section meeting the foregoing test unless it clearly appears that the portion of sales in question is made to a group of purchasers separated by a substantial economic barrier from the purchasers to whom the rest of the sales are made.

Because data limitations or other intrinsic difficulties will often make precise delineation of geographic markets impossible, there may often be two or more groupings of sales which may reasonably be treated as constituting a relevant geographic market. In such circumstances, the Department believes it to be ordinarily most consistent with the purposes of Section 7 to challenge any merger which appears to be illegal in any reasonable geographic market, even though in another reasonable market it would not appear to be illegal.

The market is ordinarily measured primarily by the dollar value of the sales or other transactions (e.g., shipments, leases) for the most recent twelve month period for which the necessary figures for the merging firms and their competitors are generally available. Where such figures are clearly unrepresentative, a different period will be used. In some markets, such as commercial banking, it is more appropriate to measure the market by other indicia, such as total deposits.

I. HORIZONTAL MERGERS

4. *Enforcement Policy.* With respect to mergers between direct competitors (i.e., horizontal mergers), the Department's enforcement activity under Section 7 of the Clayton Act has the following interrelated purposes: (i) preventing elimination as an independent business entity of any company likely to have been a substantial competitive influence in a market; (ii) preventing any company or small group of companies from obtaining a position of dominance in a market; (iii) preventing significant increases in concentration in a market; and (iv) preserving significant possibilities for eventual deconcentration in a concentrated market.

In enforcing Section 7 against horizontal mergers, the Department accords primary significance to the size of the market share held by both the acquiring and the acquired firms. ("Acquiring firm" and "acquired firm" are used herein, in the case of horizontal mergers, simply as convenient designations of the firm with the larger market share and the firm with the smaller share, respectively, and do not refer to the legal form of the merger transaction.) The larger the market share held by the acquired firm, the more likely it is that the firm has been a substantial competitive influence in the market or that concentration in the market will be significantly increased. The larger the market share held by the acquiring firm, the more likely it is that an acquisition will move it toward, or further entrench it in, a position of dominance or of shared market power. Accordingly, the standards most often applied by the Department in determining whether to challenge horizontal mergers can be stated in terms of the sizes of the merging firms' market shares.

5. *Market Highly Concentrated.* In a market in which the shares of the four largest firms amount to approximately 75 percent or more, the Department will ordinarily challenge the mergers between firms accounting for, approximately, the following percentages of the market:

Acquiring Firm	Acquired Firm
4%	4% or more
10%	2% or more
15%	1% or more

(Percentages not shown in the above table should be interpolated proportionately to the percentages that are shown.)

6. *Market Less Highly Concentrated.* In a market in which the shares of the four largest firms amount to less than approximately 75 percent, the Department will ordinarily challenge mergers between firms accounting for, approximately, the following percentages of the market:

Acquiring Firm	Acquired Firm
5%	5% or more
10%	4% or more
15%	3% or more
20%	2% or more
25% or more	1% or more

(Percentages not shown in the above table should be interpolated proportionately to the percentages that are shown.)

7. *Market with Trend Toward Concentration.* The Department applies an additional, stricter standard in determining whether to challenge mergers occurring in any market, not wholly unconcentrated, in which there is a significant trend toward increased concentration. Such a trend is considered to be present when the aggregate market share of any grouping of the largest firms in the market from the two largest to the eight largest has increased by approximately seven percent or more of the market over a period of time extending from any base year 5-10 years prior to the merger (excluding any year in which some abnormal fluctuation in market shares occurred) up to the time of the merger. The Department will ordinarily challenge any acquisition, by any firm in a grouping of such largest firms showing the requisite increase in market share, of any firm whose market share amounts to approximately two percent or more.

8. *Non-Market Share Standards.* Although in enforcing Section 7 against horizontal mergers the Department attaches primary importance to the market shares of the merging firms, achievement of the purposes of Section 7 occasionally requires the Department to challenge mergers which would not be challenged under the market share standards of Paragraphs 5, 6, and 7. The following are the two most common instances of this kind in which a challenge by the Department can ordinarily be anticipated:

(a) acquisition of a competitor which is a particularly "disturbing," "disruptive," or otherwise unusually competitive factor in the market; and

(b) a merger involving a substantial firm and a firm which, despite an insubstantial market share, possesses an unusual competitive potential or has an asset that confers an unusual competitive advantage (for example, the acquisition by a leading firm of a newcomer having a patent on a significantly improved product or production process).

There may also be certain horizontal mergers between makers of distinct products regarded as in the same line of commerce for reasons expressed in Paragraph 3(i) where some modification in the minimum market shares subject to challenge may be appropriate to reflect the imperfect substitutability of the two products.

9. *Failing Company.* A merger which the Department would otherwise challenge will ordinarily not be challenged if (i) the resources of one of the merging firms are so depleted and its prospects for rehabilitation so remote that the firm faces the clear probability of a business failure, and (ii) good faith efforts by the failing firm have failed to elicit a reasonable offer of acquisition more consistent with the purposes of Section 7 by a firm which intends to keep the failing firm in the market. The Department regards as failing only those firms with no reasonable prospect of remaining viable; it does not regard a firm as failing merely because the firm has been unprofitable for a period of time, has lost market position or failed to maintain its competitive position in some other respect, has poor management, or has not fully explored the possibility of overcoming its difficulties through self-help.

In determining the applicability of the above standard to the acquisition of a failing division of a multi-market company, such factors as the difficulty in assessing the viability of a portion of a company, the possibility of arbitrary accounting practices, and the likelihood that an otherwise healthy company can rehabilitate one of its parts, will lead the Department to apply this standard only in the clearest of circumstances.

10. *Economies.* Unless there are exceptional circumstances, the Department will not accept as a justification for an acquisition normally subject to challenge under its horizontal merger standards the claim that the merger will produce economies (i.e., improvements in efficiency) because, among other reasons, (i) the Department's adherence to the standards will usually result in no challenge being made to mergers of the kind most likely to involve companies operating significantly below the size necessary to achieve significant economies of scale; (ii) where substantial economies are potentially available to a firm, they can normally be realized through internal expansion; and (iii) there usually are severe difficulties in accurately establishing the existence and magnitude of economies claimed for a merger.

II. VERTICAL MERGERS

11. *Enforcement Policy.* With respect to vertical mergers (i.e., acquisitions "backward" into a supplying market or "forward" into a purchasing market), the Department's enforcement activity under Section 7 of the Clayton Act, as in the merger field generally, is intended to prevent changes in market structure that are likely to lead over the course of time to significant anticompetitive consequences. In general, the Department believes that such consequences can be expected to occur whenever a particular vertical acquisition, or series of acquisitions, by one or more of the firms in a supplying or purchasing market, tends significantly to raise barriers to entry in either market or to disadvantage existing non-integrated or partly integrated firms in either market in ways unrelated to economic efficiency.

(Barriers to entry are relatively stable market conditions which tend to increase the difficulty of potential competitors' entering the market as new sellers and which thus tend to limit the effectiveness of the potential competitors both as a restraint upon the behavior of firms in the market and as a source of additional actual competition.)

Barriers to entry resting on such factors as economies of scale in production and distribution are not questionable as such. But vertical mergers tend to raise barriers to entry in undesirable ways, particularly the following: (i) by foreclosing equal access to potential customers, thus reducing the ability of non-integrated firms to capture competitively the market share needed to achieve an efficient level of production, or imposing the burden of entry on an integrated basis (i.e., at both the supplying and purchasing levels) even though entry at a single level would permit efficient operation; (ii) by foreclosing equal access to potential suppliers, thus either increasing the risk of a price or supply squeeze on the new entrant or imposing the additional burden of entry as an integrated firm; or (iii) by facilitating promotional product differentiation, when the merger involves a manufacturing firm's acquisition of firms at the retail level. Besides impeding the entry of new sellers, the foregoing consequences of vertical mergers, if present, also artificially inhibit the expansion of presently competing sellers by conferring on the merged firm competitive advantages, unrelated to real economies of production or distribution, over non-integrated or partly integrated firms. While it is true that in some instances vertical integration may raise barriers to entry or disadvantage existing competitors only as the result of the achievement of significant economies of production or distribution (as, for example, where the increase in barriers is due to achievement of economies of integrated production through an alteration of the structure of the plant as well as of the firm), integration accomplished by a large vertical merger will usually raise entry barriers or disadvantage competitors to an extent not accounted for by, and wholly disproportionate to, such economies as may result from the merger.

It is, of course, difficult to identify with precision all circumstances in which vertical mergers are likely to have adverse effects on market structure of the kinds indicated in the previous paragraph. The Department believes, however, that the most important aims of its enforcement policy on vertical mergers can be satisfactorily stated by guidelines framed primarily in terms of the market shares of the merging firms and the conditions of entry which already exist in the relevant markets. These factors will ordinarily serve to identify most of the situations in which any of the various possible adverse effects of vertical mergers may occur and be of substantial competitive significance. With all vertical mergers it is necessary to consider the probably competitive consequences of the merger in both the market in which the supplying firm sells and the market in which the purchasing firm sells, although a significant adverse effect in either market will ordinarily result in a challenge by the Department. ("Supplying firm" and "purchasing firm," as used herein, refer to the two parties to the vertical merger transaction, the former of which sells a product in a market in which the latter buys that product.)

12. *Supplying Firm's Market.* In determining whether to challenge a vertical merger on the ground that it may significantly lessen existing or potential competition in the supplying firm's market, the Department attaches primary significance to (i) the market share of the supplying firm, (ii) the market share of the purchasing firm or firms, and (iii) the conditions of entry in the purchasing firm's market. Accordingly, the Department will ordinarily challenge a merger or series of mergers between a supplying firm, accounting for approximately ten percent or more of the sales in its market, and one or more purchasing firms, accounting *in toto* for approximately six percent or more of the total purchases in that market, unless it clearly appears that there are no significant barriers to entry into the business of the purchasing firm or firms.

13. *Purchasing Firm's Market.* Although the standard of paragraph 12 is designed to identify vertical mergers having likely anticompetitive effects in the supplying firm's market, adherence by the Department to that standard will also normally result in challenges being made to most of the vertical mergers which may have adverse effects in the purchasing firm's market (i.e., that market comprised of the purchasing firm and its competitors engaged in resale of the supplying firm's product or in the sale of a product whose manufacture requires the supplying firm's product) since adverse effects in the purchasing firm's market will normally occur only as the result of significant vertical mergers involving supplying firms with market shares in excess of ten percent. There remain, however, some important situations in which vertical mergers which are not subject to challenge under paragraph 12 (ordinarily because the purchasing firm accounts for less than six percent of the purchases in the supplying firm's market) will nonetheless be challenged by the Department on the ground that they raise entry barriers in the purchasing firm's market, or disadvantage the purchasing firm's competitors, by conferring upon the purchasing firm a significant supply advantage over unintegrated or partly integrated existing competitors or over potential competitors. The following paragraph sets forth the enforcement standard governing the most common of these situations.

If the product sold by the supplying firm and its competitors is either a complex one in which innovating changes by the various suppliers have been taking place, or is a scarce raw material or other product whose supply cannot be readily expanded to meet increased demand, the merged firm may have the power to use any temporary superiority, or any shortage, in the product of the supplying firm to put competitors of the purchasing firm at a disadvantage by refusing to sell the product to them (supply squeeze) or by narrowing the margin between the price at which it sells the product to the purchasing firm's competitors and the price at which the end-product is sold by the purchasing firm (price squeeze). Even where the merged firm has sufficient market power to impose a squeeze, it may well not always be economically rational for it actually to do so; but the Department believes that the increase in barriers to entry in the purchasing firm's market arising simply from the increased risk of a possible squeeze is sufficient to warrant prohibition of any merger between a supplier possessing significant market power and a substantial purchaser of any product meeting the above description. Accordingly, where such a product is a significant feature or ingredient of the end-product manufactured by the purchasing firm and its competitors, the Department will ordinarily challenge a merger or series of mergers between a supplying firm, accounting for approximately 20 percent or more of the sales in its market, and a purchasing firm or firms, accounting *in toto* for approximately ten percent or more of the sales in the market in which it sells the product whose manufacture requires the supplying firm's product.

14. *Non-Market Share Standards.*

(a) Although in enforcing Section 7 against vertical mergers the Department attaches primary importance to the market shares of the merging firms and the conditions of entry in the relevant markets, achievement of the purposes of Section 7 occasionally requires the Department to challenge mergers which would not be challenged under the market share standards of paragraphs 12 and 13. Clearly the most common instances in which challenge by the Department can ordinarily be anticipated are acquisitions of suppliers or customers by major firms in an industry in which (i) there has been, or is developing, a significant trend toward vertical integration by merger such that the trend, if unchallenged, would probably raise barriers to entry or impose a competitive disadvantage on unintegrated or partly integrated firms, and (ii) it does not clearly appear that the particular acquisition will result in significant economies of production or distribution unrelated to advertising or other promotional economies.

(b) A less common special situation in which a challenge by the Department can ordinarily be anticipated is the acquisition by a firm of a customer or supplier for the purpose of increasing the difficulty of potential competitors in entering the market of either the acquiring or acquired firm, or for the purpose of putting competitors of either the acquiring or acquired firm at an unwarranted disadvantage.

15. *Failing Company.* The standards set forth in paragraph 9 are applied by the Department in determining whether to challenge a vertical merger.

16. *Economies.* Unless there are exceptional circumstances, and except as noted in paragraph 14(a), the Department will not accept as a justification for an acquisition normally subject to challenge under its vertical merger standards the claim that the merger will produce economies, because, among other reasons, (i) where substantial economies of vertical integration are potentially available to a firm, they can normally be realized through internal expansion into the supplying or purchasing market, and (ii) where barriers prevent entry into the supplying or purchasing market by internal expansion, the Department's adherence to the vertical merger standards will in any event usually result in no challenge being made to the acquisition of a firm or firms of sufficient size to overcome or adequately minimize the barriers to entry.

III. CONGLOMERATE MERGERS

17. *Enforcement Policy.* Conglomerate mergers are mergers that are neither horizontal nor vertical as those terms are used in sections I and II, respectively, of these guidelines. (It should be noted that a market extension merger, i.e., one involving two firms selling the same product, but in different geographic markets, is classified as a conglomerate merger.) As with other kinds of mergers, the purpose of the Department's enforcement activity regarding conglomerate mergers is to prevent changes in market structure that appear likely over the course of time to cause a substantial lessening of the competition that would otherwise exist or to create a tendency toward monopoly.

At the present time, the Department regards two categories of conglomerate mergers as having sufficiently identifiable anticompetitive effects as to be the subject of relatively specific structural guidelines: mergers involving potential entrants (Paragraph 18) and mergers creating a danger of reciprocal buying (Paragraph 19).

Another important category of conglomerate mergers that will frequently be the subject of enforcement action—mergers which for one or more of several reasons threaten to entrench or enhance the market power of the acquired firm—is described generally in Paragraph 20.

As Paragraph 20 makes clear, enforcement action will also be taken against still other types of conglomerate mergers that on specific analysis appear anticompetitive. The fact that, as yet, the Department does not believe it useful to describe such other types of mergers in terms of a few major elements of market structure should in no sense be regarded as indicating that enforcement action will not be taken. Nor is it to be assumed that mergers of the type described in Paragraphs 18 and 19, but not covered by the specific rules thereof, may not be the subject of enforcement action if specific analysis indicates that they appear anticompetitive.

18. *Mergers Involving Potential Entrants.*

(a) Since potential competition (i.e., the threat of entry, either through internal expansion or through acquisition and expansion of a small firm, by firms not already or only marginally in the market) may often be the most significant competitive limitation on the exercise of market power by leading firms, as well as the most likely source of additional actual competition, the Department will ordinarily challenge any merger between one of the most likely entrants into the market and:

(i)   any firm with approximately 25 percent or more of the market;

(ii)   one of the two largest firms in a market in which the shares of the two largest firms amount to approximately 50 percent or more;

(iii)   one of the four largest firms in a market in which the shares of the eight largest firms amount to approximately 75% or more, providing the merging firm's share of the market amounts to approximately 10% or more; or

(iv)   one of the eight largest firms in a market in which the shares of these firms amount to approximately 75 percent or more, provided either (A) the merging firm's share of the market is not insubstantial and there are no more than one or two likely entrants into the market; or (B) the merging firm is a rapidly growing firm.

In determining whether a firm is one of the most likely potential entrants into a market, the Department accords primary significance to the firm's capability of entering on a competitively significant scale relative to the capability of other firms (i.e., the technological and financial resources available to it) and to the firm's economic incentive to enter (evidenced by, for example, the general attractiveness of the market in terms of risk and profit; or any special relationship of the firm to the market; or the firm's manifested interest in entry; or the natural expansion pattern of the firm; or the like).

(b) The Department will also ordinarily challenge a merger between an existing competitor in a market and a likely entrant, undertaken for the purpose of preventing the competitive "disturbance" or "disruption" that such entry might cause.

(c) Unless there are exceptional circumstances, the Department will not accept as a justification for a merger inconsistent with the standards of this paragraph 18 the claim that the merger will produce economies, because, among other reasons, the Department believes that equivalent economies can be normally achieved either through internal expansion or through a small firm acquisition or other acquisition not inconsistent with the standards herein.

19. *Mergers Creating Danger of Reciprocal Buying.*

(a) Since reciprocal buying (i.e., favoring one's customer when making purchases of a product which is sold by the customer) is an economically unjustified business practice which confers a competitive advantage on the favored firm unrelated to the merits of its product, the Department will ordinarily challenge any merger which creates a significant danger of reciprocal buying. Unless it clearly appears that some special market factor makes remote the possibility that reciprocal buying behavior will actually occur, the Department considers that a significant danger of reciprocal buying is present whenever approximately 15 percent or more of the total purchases in a market in which one of the merging firms ("the selling firm") sales are accounted for by firms which also make substantial sales in markets where the other merging firm ("the buying firm") is both a substantial buyer and a more substantial buyer than all or most of the competitors of the selling firm.

(b) The Department will also ordinarily challenge (i) any merger undertaken for the purpose of facilitating the creation of reciprocal buying arrangements, and (ii) any merger creating the possibility of any substantial reciprocal buying where one (or both) of the merging firms has within the recent past, or the merged firm has after consummation of the merger, actually engaged in reciprocal buying, or attempted directly or indirectly to induce firms with which it deals to engage in reciprocal buying, in the product markets in which the possibility of reciprocal buying has been created.

(c) Unless there are exceptional circumstances, the Department will not accept as a justification for a merger creating a significant danger of reciprocal buying the claim that the merger will produce economies, because, among other reasons, the Department believes that in general equivalent economies can be achieved by the firms involved through other mergers not inconsistent with the standards of this paragraph 19.

20. *Mergers Which Entrench Market Power and Other Conglomerate Mergers.* The Department will ordinarily investigate the possibility of anticompetitive consequences, and may in particular circumstances bring suit, where an acquisition of a leading firm in a relatively concentrated or rapidly concentrating market may serve to entrench or increase the market power of that firm or raise barriers to entry in that market. Examples of this type of merger include: (i) a merger which produces a very large disparity in absolute size between the merged firm and the largest remaining firms in the relevant markets, (ii) a merger of firms producing related products which may induce purchasers, concerned about the merged firm's possible use of leverage, to buy products of the merged firms rather than those of competitors, and (iii) a merger which may enhance the ability of the merged firm to increase product differentiation in the relevant markets.

Generally speaking, the conglomerate merger area involves novel problems that have not yet been subjected to as extensive or sustained analysis as those presented by horizontal and vertical mergers. It is for this reason that the Department's enforcement policy regarding the foregoing category of conglomerate mergers cannot be set forth with greater specificity. Moreover, the conglomerate merger field as a whole is one in which the Department considers it necessary, to a greater extent than with horizontal and vertical mergers, to carry on a continuous analysis and study of the ways in which mergers may have significant anticompetitive consequences in circumstances beyond those covered by these guidelines. For example, the Department has used Section 7 to prevent mergers which may diminish long-run possibilities of enhanced competition resulting from technological developments that may increase interproduct competition between industries whose products are presently relatively imperfect substitutes. Other areas where enforcement action will be deemed appropriate may also be identified on a case-by-case basis; and as the result of continuous analysis and study the Department may identify other categories of mergers that can be the subject of specific guidelines.

21. *Failing Company.* The standards set forth in paragraph 9 are normally applied by the Department in determining whether to challenge a conglomerate merger, except that in marginal cases involving the application of Paragraph 18 (a)(iii) and (iv) the Department may deem it inappropriate to sue under Section 7 even though the acquired firm is not "failing" in the strict sense.

Appendix B:
Report of the White House Task Force on Antitrust Policy

Summary

1. *We recommend specific legislation on the subject of oligopolies, or highly concentrated industries.*

The purpose of such legislation would be to give enforcement authorities and courts a clear mandate to use established techniques of divestiture to reduce concentration in industries where monopoly power is shared by a few very large firms. Up to now such measures have been employed only in the rare instances where the monopolistic structure of an industry takes the form of a single firm with an overwhelming share of the market. Specific legislation dealing with entrenched oligopolies would rectify the most important deficiency in the present antitrust laws.

Effective antitrust laws must bring about both competitive behavior and competitive industry structure. In the long run, competitive structure is the more important since it creates conditions conducive to competitive behavior. Competitive structure and behavior are both essential to the basic concern of the antitrust laws—preservation of the self-regulating mechanism of the market, free from the restraints of private monopoly power on the one hand and government intervention or regulation on the other. In one important respect, the antitrust laws recognize the necessity for competitive market structures; the 1950 amendment to Section 7 of the Clayton Act has effectively prevented many kinds of mergers which would bring about less competitive market structures. Our proposed remedy,

Note: Portions not pertinent to this study have been omitted.

Source: U.S. Congress, Senate, Committee on the Judiciary, Subcommittee on Antitrust and Monopoly, *Economic Concentration, Hearings before the Subcommittee on Antitrust and Monopoly*, 91st Cong., 2nd sess., 1970 (Washington: U.S. Government Printing Office, 1970), 5054–82.

which would deal with existing noncompetitive market structures, is a necessary complement to Section 7.

Highly concentrated industries represent a significant segment of the American economy. Industries in which four or fewer firms account for more than 70 percent of output produce nearly 10 percent of the total value of manufactured products; industries in which four or fewer firms account for more than 50 percent of output produce nearly 24 percent. An impressive body of economic opinion and analysis supports the judgment that this degree of concentration precludes effective market competition and interferes with the optimum use of economic resources. Past experience strongly suggests that, in the absence of direct action, concentration is not likely to decline significantly.

While new legal approaches might be developed to reduce concentration under existing law—a result which should be encouraged—the history of antitrust enforcement and judicial interpretation do not justify primary reliance on this possibility. For this reason, we recommend a specific legislative remedy directed to the reduction of concentration. Our proposed Concentrated Industries Act, which appears [later in] the Report, establishes criteria and procedures for the effective reduction of industrial concentration.

2. *We recommend additional legislation prohibiting mergers in which a very large firm acquires one of the leading firms in a concentrated industry.*

This legislation would supplement Section 7 of the Clayton Act, which prohibits mergers which may tend substantially to lessen competition. The primary impact of the new legislation would be on diversification or "conglomerate" mergers. Under Section 7 of the Clayton Act, such mergers may be prevented if adverse effects on competition can be anticipated. But the detection of such effects frequently depends on factual and theoretical judgments that are highly speculative. As a result, some mergers with potentially adverse effects on competition may escape attack and mergers which will not harm competition will be prohibited because the effects cannot readily be predicted. Because of the inherent limitations of the competitive standard of Section 7, the recently published Merger Guidelines do little to resolve these difficulties.

Our proposed legislation would prevent some possibly anticompetitive mergers which might have gone unchallenged because of the difficulty of applying Section 7 standards, and thus would act as an effective supplement to existing policy. In addition, the proposed legislation would have affirmative aspects in channelling merger activity into directions likely to increase competition. If large firms are prevented from acquiring leading firms in concentrated industries, they will seek other outlets for expansion which may be more likely to increase competition and decrease concentration. . . .

We therefore believe that restrictions on mergers should continue to be based on considerations related to competitive market structure. The policy we recommend would permit the continued growth of firms by diversification as well as by internal expansion but would, we believe, promote the development of more competitive market structures.

A draft of the Merger Act, implementing our recommendation, appears [later in] the Report. . . .

5. *We recommend that steps be taken to improve the quality and availability of economic and financial data relevant to the formulation of antitrust policy, the enforcement of the antitrust laws, and the operation of competitive markets.*

Specifically, we recommend formation of a standing committee of representatives of the Census Bureau and other Government agencies which gather or use economic information to consider (1) improving the gathering and presentation of economic information within the statutory limits on disclosure of information on individual firms; (2) new interpretations of existing law or, eventually, new legislation to minimize restrictions on disclosure of types of information which are not highly sensitive from the point of view of individual firms but are of great value in the formulation of policy and the application of law; and (3) machinery for developing information on the competitive structure of relevant economic markets, because such markets do not necessarily coincide with Census industry and product classifications. These recommendations could be implemented immediately, without new legislation or appropriations.

In addition, the role of financial information in the operation of competitive markets should be reflected in the formulation of financial reporting requirements by the Securities and Exchange Commission. These requirements are now imposed pursuant to the Securities Exchange Act of 1934, which is oriented to investor protection. We recommend that the Act be amended to recognize the role of financial information in the operation of a competitive economy, and to require that the SEC consult with antitrust enforcement agencies in formulating reporting requirements.

Pending adoption of this recommendation, the antitrust enforcement agencies should be requested to consider submitting recommendations to the SEC in connection with the current divisional reporting inquiry.

6. *We have a number of additional recommendations for further action or further study.*

These include advance notification of mergers and a reasonable statute of limitations on lawsuits attacking mergers; a limit on the duration of antitrust decrees; an examination of the effects of the income tax laws on merger activity and market concentration; a review of the extent to which competition may be substituted for regulation in the regulated industries; and the abolition of resale price maintenance.

I. Introduction

The antitrust laws reflect our Nation's strong commitment to economic freedom and the material benefits that flow from this freedom. The antitrust laws are based on the recognition that optimum use of economic resources and maximum choice and utility for consumers can best be obtained under competition. Moreover, they assume that the preservation of a large number and variety of decision-making units in the economy is important to ensure innovation, experimentation and continuous adaptation to new conditions. While consumer welfare is thus in the forefront of antitrust policy, important corollary values support the policy. Not only consumers, but those who control the factors of production—labor, capital and entrepreneurial ability—benefit when resources are permitted to move into the fields of greatest economic return; competition induces such movement and monopoly inhibits it. Antitrust policy also reflects a preference for private decision-making; a major value of competition is that it minimizes the necessity for direct Government intervention in the operation of business, whether by comprehensive regulation of the public utility type or by informal and sporadic interference such as price guidelines and other ad hoc measures.

The function of the antitrust laws in the pursuit of these goals is twofold: they are concerned both with preventing anticompetitive behavior and with preserving and promoting competitive market structures. Our Task Force has understood its assignment to be to examine the antitrust laws in broad perspective and consider ways in which they might be made more effective in this dual role.

In relation to the principal kinds of anticompetitive behavior, such as price-fixing, market division and other forms of collusive action among independent firms, we believe the present laws are generally adequate. Their effectiveness depends principally upon vigilance to provide sufficient enforcement resources and the vigorous use of enforcement power. . . .

Our consideration of the present state of the antitrust laws focuses to a considerable extent on problems of market structure. The principal laws presently concerned with competitive market structure are Section 7 of the Clayton Act, dealing with mergers, and Section 2 of the Sherman Act, which is addressed to cases of monopoly. We believe these laws can be made more effective by certain additional legislation on mergers and on oligopoly industries.

Market structure is an important concern of antitrust laws for two reasons. *First*, the more competitive a market structure (the larger the number of competitors and the smaller their market shares) the greater the difficulty of maintaining collusive behavior and the more easily such behavior can be detected. *Second*, in markets with a very few firms effects equivalent to those of collusion may occur even in the absence of collusion. In a market with numerous firms, each having a small share, no single firm by its action alone can exert a significant influence over price and thus output will be carried to the point where each seller's marginal cost equals the market price. This level of output is optimal from the point of view of the economy as a whole.

Under conditions of monopoly—with only a single seller in the market—the monopolist can increase his profits by restricting output and thus raising his price; accordingly, prices will tend to be above, and output correspondingly below, the optimum point. In an oligopoly market—one in which there is a smaller number of dominant sellers, each with a large market share—each must consider the effect of his output on the total market and the probable reactions of other sellers to his decisions; the results of their combined decisions may approximate the profit-maximizing decisions of a monopolist. Not only does the small number of sellers facilitate agreement, but agreement in the ordinary sense may be unnecessary. Thus, phrases such as "price leadership" or "administered pricing" often do no more than describe behavior which is the inevitable result of structure. Under such conditions, it does not suffice for antitrust law to attempt to reach anticompetitive behavior; it cannot order the several firms to ignore each other's existence. The alternatives, other than accepting the undesirable economic consequences, are either regulation of price (and other decisions) or improving the competitive structure of the market.

We believe that the goals of antitrust policy require a choice wherever possible in favor of attempting to perfect the self-regulating mechanism of the market before turning to public control. It is for this reason that we favor steps that will increase the effectiveness of the antitrust laws in promoting competitive market structure. Such steps are desirable, not only because the problem of concentrated industries is significant in economic terms, but because the existence of such concentration is a continuing (and perhaps increasing) temptation for political intervention. In a special sense, therefore, our recommendations have preventive as well as corrective purposes. . . .

II. Oligopoly, or Concentration in Particular Markets

The evils of monopoly are well known and the antitrust policy of the United States has sought from its beginning to provide safeguards against them. But those evils are not confined to situations conforming to the literal meaning of monopoly, i.e., an industry with but a single firm. In the years since the Sherman Act was adopted there has been growing recognition that monopoly is a matter of degree. A firm with less than 100 percent of the output of an industry may nevertheless have significant control over supply, and thus be in a position to impose on the economy the losses associated with monopoly: lower output, higher prices, artificial restraints on the movement of resources in the economy, and reduced pressure toward cost reduction and innovation. Likewise, a small number of firms dominating an industry may take a similar toll, either because the small number makes it easier to arrive at and police an agreement or because, without agreement, each will adopt patterns of behavior recognizing the common interest.

In general it may be said that the smaller the number of firms in an industry—at least where that number is very small or where a very small number is responsible for the overwhelming share of the industry's output—the greater the likelihood that the behavior of the industry will depart from the competitive norm.

These propositions have found general acceptance in economic literature in the past 25 or 30 years. They have also found recognition in the policy of the antitrust laws: a major aim of Section 7 of the Clayton Act, as amended in 1950 and as interpreted by judicial decisions and the new Merger Guidelines, is not merely to prevent monopolies but also to prevent all combinations of business firms that significantly increase market concentration or reduce the number of firms in an industry.

Interpretation of the Sherman Act itself, however, has lagged behind these developments. Early cases involving giant firms emphasized the purposes and methods by which a firm was created as the basis of illegality, and looked for evidence of predatory or abusive exercise of power rather than the power of a firm or group of firms to control prices and output. Decisions affecting market concentration were confined to instances, such as the old *Standard Oil* and *American Tobacco* cases, where a single firm commanding nearly the entire market had been assembled by mergers of many previous competitors. Even such major combinations as United States Steel Corporation, United Shoe Machinery Company, and the International Harvester Company escaped condemnation by the Supreme Court. An important advance was registered when Judge Learned Hand announced in the *ALCOA* case that a single firm, not resulting from merger, might be guilty of "monopolizing" merely by acquiring a sufficiently large market share and retaining its market share over a substantial period of time, if that market share was not the inevitable result of economic forces. That holding adopted and extended Judge Hand's early insight, in the *Corn Products* case of 1916, that "it is the mere possession of an economic power, acquired by some form of combination, and capable by its own variation in production, of changing and controlling price, that is illegal." The *United States Machinery* decision of 1953 applied and reinforced the new doctrine represented by the *ALCOA* case. In both of those cases, however, the monopoly section of the Sherman Act was invoked against a single firm with a predominant share of the market. While Judge Hand had intimated that a share as low as 65 percent might suffice, no subsequent case has tested that proposition or explored the limits of the *ALCOA* doctrine. Nor has any case yet provided a basis for treating as illegal the shared monopoly power of several firms that together possess a predominant share of the market, absent proof of conspiracy among them.

Thus a gap in the law remains. While Section 7 of the Clayton Act provides strong protection against the growth of new concentrations of market power in most instances, existing law is inadequate to cope with old ones.

This gap is of major significance. Highly concentrated industries account for a large share of manufacturing activity in the United States. . . .

If competitive pressures could be relied on to erode concentration in the reasonably foreseeable future, the direct reduction of concentration would be less urgent. But concentration does not appear to erode over time; rather, the evidence indicates that it is remarkably stable. In those industries with value of shipments greater than $100 million and four-firm concentration ratios by value of shipments greater than 65 percent in 1963, average concentration ratios were stable or declined the Clayton Act has generally been effective in forestalling increases in concentration through mergers and by other means, the antitrust laws and economic forces have not brought about significant erosion of existing concentration. The problem is not one which will disappear with time.

The adverse effects of persistent concentration on output and price find some confirmation in various studies that have been made of return on capital in major industries. These studies have found a close association between high levels of concentration and persistently high rates of return on capital, particularly in those industries in which the largest four firms account for more than 60 percent of sales. High profit rates in individual firms or even in particular industries are of course consistent with competition. They may reflect innovation, exceptional efficiency, or growth in demand outrunning the expansion of supply. Above-average profits in a particular industry signal the need and provide the incentive for additional resources and expanded output in the industry, which in due time should return profits to a normal level. It is the persistence of high profits over extended time periods and over whole industries rather than in individual firms that suggest artificial restraints on output and the absence of fully effective competition. The correlation of evidence of this kind with the existence of very high levels of concentration appears to be significant.

We recognize the need for further refinement of economic evidence of this type and for additional knowledge, theoretical and empirical, about the behavior of oligopolistic industries. It would be less than candid to pretend that economic science has provided a complete or wholly satisfactory basis for public policy in this field. But public policy must often be made on the basis of imperfect knowledge, and the failure to adopt remedial measures is in itself the acceptance of a policy. The judgment of most of the members of the Task Force is that enough is known about the probable consequences of high concentration to warrant affirmative government action in the extreme instances of concentration. Moreover, as we have noted, such action does not require acceptance of a new premise for public policy. A conviction that concentration is undesirable underlies the present stringent policy toward horizontal mergers. The same premise supports a policy of attempting, within conservative limits, to improve the competitive structure of industries in which concentration is already high and apparently entrenched.

Endorsement of such a policy implies a judgment that the potential gains from reducing market shares and increasing the number of competitors in an industry will not be offset by losses in efficiency. We think there is little basis for believing that significant efficiencies of production are dependent on generally maintaining existing high levels of concentration.

There is little evidence that economies of scale require firms the size of the dominant firms in most industries that are highly concentrated. Evidence to the contrary is the fact that in most such industries very much smaller firms have survived in competition with the larger firms. On the basis of studies covering a large number of industries Professor Stigler concluded that "In the manufacturing sector there are few industries in which the minimum efficient size of firm is as much as five percent of the industry's output and concentration must be explained on other grounds" (Stigler, *The Theory of Price*, 223, 3rd edition, 1966). Similarly, there is no evidence of any correlation between size or market concentration and research and development activities.

The success of very large firms may, of course, be explained on the basis of efficiencies other than economies of scale, such as superior management talent or other unique resources. To the extent that such efficiencies exist, however, they may ordinarily be transferred and thus would not necessarily be lost by reorganization of the industry into a larger number of smaller units. The same is true of advantages that inhere in legal monopolies, such as an accumulation of patents.

It must also be borne in mind that efficiencies belonging to or achieved by a firm with some degree of monopoly power may be reflected only in higher profits rather than lower prices. Reduction of concentration would increase the chance that such efficiencies would be passed on to consumers through competition; indeed, a net gain from the consumer standpoint might result even though some efficiencies were lost in the process of reducing concentration.

The statute we propose would, however, take account of possible adverse effects on efficiency resulting from divestiture by forbidding relief that a firm establishes would result in substantial loss of economies of scale. It would be expected that a court would consider, among other factors relevant on this issue, the minimum size that experience has indicated is necessary for survival in the industry.

For the foregoing reasons we conclude that remedies to reduce concentration should be made available as part of a comprehensive antitrust policy. To assist in translating that conclusion into workable legislation we have drafted in some detail a proposed statute embodying our views. That statute, entitled the Concentrated Industries Act, is attached to this report. While we believe, as hereafter noted, that some relief against concentration might be obtained through new interpretations of the Sherman Act, we also think that a statute such as the one we propose has several distinct advantages over reliance on existing law: (1) it would provide a clear determination of legislative policy and establish clear criteria for the application of that policy; (2) it would establish appropriate special procedures; (3) it would limit the policy to remedial ends.

The Act establishes clear criteria for its application. It applies only to those industries in which four or fewer firms have accounted for 70 percent or more of industry sales, and it provides for steps to reduce the market shares of firms with 15 percent market shares in such industries. The Act contains other provisions to limit its application to industries which are of importance in the economy as a whole and in which concentration has been high and stable over considerable periods of time. The criteria laid down in the Act are designed to minimize the likelihood that output levels over a short period of time will affect the applicability of the Act. Moreover, even if the Act does apply, there are no penalties but only prospective relief. Thus, the possibility is minimized that corporations will resort to output-restricting strategies in order to avoid application of the Act.

The Act also lays the basis for defining relevant markets in terms that are more closely related to economic penalties than are the definitions developed under existing antitrust laws. By and large, the Act limits the scope of industry to facts which are of relevance to its primary concern, the reduction of concentration, and which may be determined with reasonable precision. For these reasons, litigation under the Act should be relatively simple.

The Act establishes special procedures appropriate to the reduction of concentration. Under existing law, complex antitrust actions may be conducted by judges who have had little opportunity to become familiar with the kinds of questions involved, and who must rely on expert testimony offered by the parties. The Act would establish a special panel of district judges and circuit judges to conduct deconcentration proceedings. In addition, it would enable the court to draw on the specialized knowledge and experience of its own economic experts. This feature of the Act should be of importance in arriving at appropriate market definitions. In addition, court appointed experts would assist in evaluating the probable effect of proposed decrees.

Finally, the Act is limited to prospective relief designed to reduce concentration. Unlike existing law, it makes no provision for criminal penalties or for private actions seeking treble damages. The absence of these collateral effects makes the Act a more appropriate tool for reducing concentration.

Those who support the proposed Concentrated Industries Act believe, in varying degrees, that more can be done about concentration than has been done under existing law. We recommend that the Attorney General be encouraged to develop appropriate approaches under existing law and to bring carefully selected cases to test those theories.

Under existing law, three statutory provisions might be brought to bear. Section 2 of the Sherman Act prohibits monopolization or attempts to monopolize any part of interstate or foreign commerce. Section 1 of the Sherman Act prohibits any contract, combination, or conspiracy in restraint of interstate or foreign commerce. Section 7 of the Clayton Act prohibits acquisitions which may tend substantially to lessen competition. While existing precedents and the history of antitrust enforcement do not justify widespread use of these statutes against concentrated industries, we believe that appropriate precedents might be developed which would be useful in some cases.

Courts may be reluctant to expand the scope of these statutes, because their application would expose defendants to criminal penalties and treble damage liability. Moreover, existing law does not readily lend itself to the establishment of sufficiently clear and workable criteria. While expanded enforcement efforts might make some inroads in reducing concentration, they would not preclude the need for new legislation.

III. Conglomerates, or Large Diversified Firms

The initial mandate establishing the Task Force reflected concern with the current rate of merger activity, particularly diversification or "conglomerate" mergers. Current data confirm that the number and scale of mergers, and particularly of conglomerate mergers, have been accelerating rapidly and continue to accelerate. Individual firms have achieved spectacular growth in this way. There is no comparable trend toward reduction in corporate size through spinoffs of assets. The current rate and pattern of mergers is causing significant and apparently permanent changes in the structure of the economy, and the long-run impact of these changes cannot be readily foreseen.

A variety of legal and economic factors have contributed to the conglomerate merger movement. Relatively clear legal prohibitions on horizontal and vertical mergers, set forth in Section 7 of the Clayton Act and recently articulated in the Antitrust Division's Merger Guidelines, have channeled merger activity away from these more traditional forms while leaving conglomerate mergers relatively free from antitrust restraints. Although the Merger Guidelines identify some types of conglomerate mergers as likely candidates for antitrust attack and some conglomerate mergers have been successfully attacked on antitrust grounds, the antitrust laws leave relatively wide latitude for conglomerate mergers. This latitude reflects the fact that existing knowledge provides little basis for forecasting adverse effects on competition that support application of the merger prohibition of Section 7.

The economic forces encouraging conglomerate mergers are numerous and complex, and are not easy to identify in particular cases.

These appear to include desire of owners of smaller firms to convert their holdings into more readily marketable securities; the desire of management of large firms for growth for its own sake, apart from or in addition to growth in profits; the opportunity to bring more efficient management personnel or techniques to smaller or less successful firms; the possibility of reducing costs or increasing sales by meshing product lines or processes or methods of distribution; the desire to diversify business activities and reduce risks; the possibility of using one firm's cash flows or credit in another firm with limited access to capital; the tax advantages of direct reinvestment of earnings by corporations instead of distribution to stockholders for reinvestment through the general capital market; and the opportunity for speculative gains through mergers that immediately increase the per-share earnings of the surviving firm.

Whatever the causes, it is clear that many conglomerate mergers are not explainable in terms of obvious efficiencies in integrating the production or marketing facilities of the firms involved. The merger movement has contributed to and is furthered by a specialized "merger market" in business firms as such; merger candidates and independent experts actively seek out favorable opportunities to acquire or dispose of businesses through conglomerate mergers. The existence of such a market is not a sinister symptom; it merely emphasizes the volume and complexity of merger activity and its underlying causes. Indeed, an active merger market suggests a healthy fluidity in the movement of resources and management in the economy toward their more effective utilization. The existence of such a market may serve as a significant incentive for the establishment of smaller firms. It may partially overcome imperfections in the capital market which are not readily susceptible to other effective remedies. In many cases, merger activity may replace proxy fights as an effective means for changes in corporate control.

There are two types of possible antitrust objections to the current increase in merger activity: (1) mergers may have adverse effects on competitive structure and behavior in particular markets; (2) the volume and scope of merger activity may result in concentration of overall economic activity in a few large organizations and may substantially reduce the number of significant decision-making units within the economy.

As to the second point, the possibility that economic activity might become unduly concentrated in a few large firms would raise difficult and far-reaching questions of social policy. Fortunately, such a development is not now imminent. In spite of the high and increasing rate of merger activity, concentration of aggregate economic activity (which should not be confused with concentration in particular markets, referred to in part II of this Report) has changed only slowly over time. Preliminary FTC data allow that the share of total corporate manufacturing assets held by the 100 largest manufacturing firms has grown from 45.8 percent in 1957 to 47.7 percent in 1967; the share of the 200 largest has increased from 55.0 percent to 58.7 percent in the same period. Mergers have contributed somewhat to this trend; indeed, if no mergers had occurred, the shares of the largest firms would have declined somewhat during parts of the period. Nevertheless, it is clear that mergers are not solely responsible for the continued growth of the largest units in the economy, and have accounted for only a minor portion of such growth. Indeed, among the largest firms, the net effect of mergers has been to expand the size of smaller large firms relative to the top few. Further, the merger movement does not seem likely to cause the disappearance of smaller firms. The numbers of manufacturing firms with assets of $5 million to $10 million, $10 million to $25 million, and $25 million to $50 million have remained steady or increased somewhat during the period of greatest merger activity. Indeed, the numbers of nonmanufacturing firms have increased significantly.

In any event, the level of economy-wide concentration and numbers of firms that would be incompatible with the maintenance of a competitive market system is not known. Even very large firms may continue to grow as a result of desirable response to changing economic circumstances, and mergers—including conglomerate mergers—may result in important economic benefits. We are therefore not persuaded of the need to establish specific limits to the growth of large firms, either by merger or otherwise. Thus, we do not endorse the suggestion put forward at one time by Donald F. Turner, former Assistant Attorney General in charge of the Antitrust Division, that further expansion of larger firms by merger be prohibited.

Conglomerate mergers may affect competition in particular markets. Three possible types of anticompetitive effects of conglomerate mergers have been identified and are reflected in the new Merger Guidelines: (1) elimination of "potential competition" by a firm which, but for its acquisition of another firm, might have entered the latter firm's market in a way that would have increased competition in that market; (2) the creation of opportunities for "reciprocal dealing" relationships between the merged firm and other firms that may foreclose competitors of the conglomerate firm; and (3) the addition of large resources of a firm already dominant in a market, possibly insulating its position from erosion through competition.

The detection of these effects rests, in general, on factual and theoretical judgments that are more speculative than the findings usually relied upon in Section 7 cases; but to the extent that specific effects can be clearly identified in individual merger cases, present law and enforcement policies appear adequate. There are, however, two dangers in basing conglomerate merger policy entirely on the case-by-case substantiation of specific anticompetitive effects.

1. These or similar objections to conglomerate mergers may be pressed beyond the point where they are well founded, perhaps because of quite different objections, such as fear of the growth of individual large firms or of concentration of assets in very large firms, which are not explicitly recognized in the merger prohibition. The occurrence of these different objections may also lead to other distortions; for example, market definitions may be distorted to treat a conglomerate merger as horizontal and therefore subject to a more easily established prohibition. Such distortions would result in uncertainties in enforcement and unfairness to those affected.

2. Potentially anticompetitive mergers may be allowed to proceed because economic theory and analytical foresight are inadequate to predict anticompetitive effects in specific cases, even though there may be good reason for believing that some classes of mergers, considered in the aggregate, are harmful to competition.

Because of these difficulties, and because the incentives that have produced the current conglomerate merger movement can and should be directed to increase competition, we propose a statutory prohibition to supplement the merger prohibition of Section 7 of the Clayton Act. Such a prohibition should be clear and not rely on conjectural judgments of likely competitive effect in particular cases; it should prohibit or discourage mergers most likely to have anticompetitive consequences, and in doing so lessen reliance on extended and contrived interpretations of Section 7; and it should seek to direct the force of conglomerate merger activity into channels that will improve competitive structure to the maximum extent possible.

We propose that this be accomplished by forbidding mergers between very large firms and other firms that are already leading firms in concentrated markets significant in the national economy. A draft of a proposed statute outlining this recommendation, together with explanatory notes is attached to this report as Appendix B.

Such a rule satisfies our criteria for a supplementary prohibition. Unlike the Merger Guidelines applicable to conglomerate mergers, which rely on the difficult and conjectural questions referred to above, the proposed rule would provide clear criteria based solely on data as to market shares and sales or assets. It would apply to a large number of conglomerate mergers which might be attacked under existing law or under the law which might be developed in suits brought in accordance with the Guidelines. The existence of this simpler prohibition will lessen the pressure on enforcement agencies and courts to engage in the distorted extensions to which Section 7 lends itself. At the same time, the simpler prohibition will make enforcement simpler, and will prevent some mergers which would have gone unchallenged under Section 7 even though careful analysis or subsequent developments might have indicated a violation of Section 7.

In addition to these negative aspects of discouraging anticompetitive mergers, the proposed rule would have affirmative aspects in that it would channel merger activity into directions likely to improve competition. The proposed rule rests on the assumption that if large firms are prevented from acquiring leading firms in concentrated industries, they will seek other outlets for expansion. If the rule is adopted, a large firm wishing to expand into a particular concentrated industry may acquire a small firm with a view to enlarging the capacity and market share, or it may construct wholly new facilities in the industry. Either of these alternative courses of action is more likely to increase competition and to decrease concentration in a concentrated industry than if the large firm simply acquired a leading firm in the industry and settled for maintaining or modestly increasing the market shares of that firm.

As large firms become more diversified and more interested in further diversification, they become "potential entrants" into more and more industries. Although the probability that any one firm will enter is extremely small, the probability that a substantial number of diversified firms will enter a substantial number of concentrated industries is undoubtedly higher. The Guidelines and present enforcement based on the potential competition doctrine focus on the first probability alone, and must, therefore, be ineffectual or dependent on fictitious premises contrary to fact in many instances. If the potential competition doctrine under Section 7 is expanded to the extent indicated by the Guidelines and current enforcement policy, such firms may well be disqualified from expanding by merger into many markets, including some in which they might make contributions of general benefit to the economy. These contributions might take the form of new technology and competitive innovation, reduced costs, or simply the introduction of new and forceful competitive pressures. Our proposal focuses on the second probability, that a substantial number of large diversified firms will enter a substantial number of concentrated industries, and is intended to channel the potential competition of large firms along lines that are conducive to reducing levels of concentration in the American economy.

Thus, the rule has both negative and affirmative aspects that tend to strengthen competition. Members of the Task Force who support this proposal assess somewhat differently the relative values of the negative and affirmative effects of the rule, depending on their differing judgments about the likelihood that mere size and superior financial resources will confer unwarranted advantages on an acquired firm. They are agreed, however, as to the net beneficial effect of such a rule. Since the rule would leave even a very large firm free to enter a new market by acquiring a going concern in the new market, it would preserve wide opportunity for diversification and for exploitation of efficiencies that may be inherent in conglomerate mergers.

CONCENTRATED INDUSTRIES ACT

Section 1. Reduction of Industrial Concentration.

(a) It shall be the duty of the Attorney General and the Federal Trade Commission to investigate the structure of markets which appear to be oligopoly industries.

(b) When, as a result of such investigation, the Attorney General determines that a market appears to be an oligopoly industry and that effective relief is likely to be available under this Act, he shall institute a proceeding in equity for the reduction of concentration, to which all firms which appear to be oligopoly firms in such oligopoly industry shall be made parties.

(c) The court shall enter a judgment determining whether one or more markets are oligopoly industries and, if so, which of the parties are oligopoly firms in such oligopoly industries. Any party to the proceeding may appeal such judgment directly to the Supreme Court.

(d) In order to provide an opportunity for voluntary steps looking toward reduction of concentration, no affirmative relief shall be ordered against such oligopoly firms for a period of one year following entry or affirmance of such judgment.

(e) After such one-year period, further proceedings shall be conducted and a decree entered providing such further relief as may be appropriate, in light of steps taken or initiated during the one-year period, to achieve, within a reasonable period of time not in excess of four years, a reduction of concentration such that the market share of each oligopoly firm in such oligopoly industry does not exceed 12 percent. Such decree may include provisions requiring a party (i) to modify its contractual relationships and/or methods of distribution; (ii) to grant licenses (which may, in the discretion of the court, provide for payment of royalties) under and/or dispose of any patents, technical information, copyrights and/or trademarks; and (iii) to divest itself of assets, whether or not such assets are used in an oligopoly industry, including tangible assets, cash, stock or securities (including securities in existing firms or firms to be formed), accounts receivable and such other obligations as are appropriate for the conduct of business. The decree may also make such other provisions and require such other actions, not inconsistent with the purposes of this Act and the antitrust laws, as the court shall deem appropriate, including any provisions which would be appropriate in a decree pursuant to the antitrust laws. Such decree shall not require that a firm take any steps which such firm establishes would result in substantial loss of economies of scale.

(f)   Any decree entered pursuant to subsection (e) may be appealed directly to the Supreme Court.

(g)   Between four and five years after entry or affirmance of a decree pursuant to subsection (e) or a further decree pursuant to this subsection (g), proceedings shall be conducted to determine whether the decree has achieved the reduction of concentration referred to in subsection (e). If the court determines that it has not attained such end, it shall enter a further decree ordering additional steps to be taken. Such decree may be appealed directly to the Supreme Court.

(h)   Any decree entered pursuant to this Section 1 shall be subject to modification on the motion of any party acceding to the usual principles governing decrees in equity.

Section 2.   Regulated Industries.

(a)   No action may be brought pursuant to Section 1 of this Act with respect to any market which is subject to regulation under [specify federal regulatory statutes], unless, prior to the commencement of such action, a copy of the proposed complaint in such action shall have been furnished to the agency, commission, board or body vested with regulatory power pursuant to any of the Acts enumerated, and such agency, commission, board or body shall not have disapproved the commencement of such action within 90 days after receipt of such proposed complaint or shall have waived disapproval. No decree in any action pursuant to Section 1 of this Act may require divestiture of any assets used in any such regulated market, unless such agency, commission, board or body shall have been served with a copy of the proposed decree and shall not have objected thereto within 90 days after such service or shall have waived objection. No such disapproval or objection or the withholding or waiver thereof shall be considered to be either an adjudication or a rule-making proceeding for purposes of the Administrative Procedure Act or any Act of Congress establishing procedural requirements for determinations by any agency, commission, board or body.

(b)   No action may be brought pursuant to Section 1 of this Act with respect to a market (i) in which maximum prices or rates are subject to direct public utility regulation by any state, municipal, District of Columbia or territorial agency, commission, board or other body, and (ii) which consists of the furnishing of electricity, gas, water or telephone services, without the consent of each such agency, commission, board or body.

Section 3. Procedure.

(a) All proceedings under this Act shall be conducted by the Special Antitrust Court established pursuant to subsection (b) of this Section 3. Such proceedings shall be conducted in a judicial district or districts determined by the court or pursuant to rules established by the Court.

(b) The Chief Justice shall designate not more than ____ circuit judges and district judges to serve on the Special Antitrust Court for purposes of a specified proceeding or proceedings or for such period or periods of time as may be specified by the Chief Justice. The Chief Justice shall designate one such judge as Chief Judge of the Special Antitrust Court. Proceedings under this Act shall be conducted by panels consisting of one or more judges of the Special Antitrust Court designated by the Chief Judge of the Special Antitrust Court or by a judge or judges designated by the Chief Justice for the purpose. Such proceedings shall be conducted pursuant to the Federal Rules of Civil Procedure in effect at the time, subject to such additional rules (which may supersede or supplement the Federal Rules of Civil Procedure) as shall be adopted by the Special Antitrust Court for the purposes of proceedings under this Act.

(c) In any proceeding under this Act, the Special Antitrust Court may designate one or more economists or other persons to serve as expert witnesses to be called by the Court. Such witness or witnesses

    (i)   shall be furnished with all evidence introduced by any party;

    (ii)   may offer additional evidence subject to objection by any party;

    (iii) shall offer analyses of the issues, with particular reference to relevant markets;

    (iv) shall recommend appropriate provisions for decrees;

    (v)   shall be subject to cross-examination and rebuttal.

Section 4. Definitions as used in this Act.

(a) The term "oligopoly industry" shall mean a market in which

    (i)   any four or fewer firms had an aggregate market share of 70 percent or more during at least seven of the ten and four of the most recent five base years; and

    (ii) the average aggregate market share during the five most recent base years of the four firms with the largest average market shares during those base years amounted to at least 80 percent of the average aggregate market share of those same four firms during the five preceding base years, but shall not include any market in which the average aggregate sales of all firms during the five most recent base years declined by 20 percent or more from such average sales during the preceding five base years.

(b) The term "oligopoly firm" shall mean a firm engaged in commerce whose market share in an oligopoly industry during at least two of the three most recent base years exceeded 15 percent.

MERGER ACT

Section 1. Prohibited Acquisitions.

(a) No large firm shall directly or indirectly merge with, combine with, or acquire any equity security in any leading firm or directly or indirectly acquire all or substantially all the assets used by a leading firm in any market in which it is a leading firm.

(b) No leading firm shall directly or indirectly merge with, combine with, or acquire any equity security in any large firm or directly or indirectly acquire all the assets of a large firm or a part thereof sufficient to constitute a large firm.

(c) This section shall not apply to firms acquiring any equity security solely for investment and not using the same by voting or otherwise to bring about, or in attempting to bring about, control of firms in which any equity security is acquired. Nor shall anything contained in this section prevent firms from causing the formation of subsidiary firms for the actual carrying on of their immediate lawful business, or the natural and legitimate branches or extensions thereof, or from owning and holding all or a part of the stock of such subsidiary firms.

(d) If any acquisition is approved by any federal agency, commission, board or other body, such approval shall result in total or qualified exemption of such acquisition from this Act to the same extent such approval results in exemption from Section 7 of the Act entitled "An Act to supplement existing laws against unlawful restraints and monopolies, and for other purposes," approved October 15, 1914, as amended.

Section 2. Definitions as used in this Act.

(a) The term "large firm" shall mean a firm engaged in commerce which, giving effect to any acquisition or other transaction referred to in Section 1 of this Act and all acquisitions or other such transactions completed at or prior to the effective date of such acquisition or other transaction,

  (i)   had or would have had sales which exceeded $500 million during the most recent base year, or
  (ii) had or would have had assets which exceeded $250 million at the end of the most recent base year.

(b) The term "leading firm" shall mean a firm engaged in any market in which its market share was more than 10 percent during at least two base years, and in which the aggregate market share of any four or fewer firms during the same two base years was more than 50 percent, provided that the term "leading firm" shall not include a firm whose market share during the same two base years was not among the four largest in such market. . . .

ADDITIONAL LEGISLATION

1. *Amendment to Antitrust Civil Process Act to Require Premerger Notification.*
Section 3 of the Antitrust Civil Process Act is amended by adding thereto a new subsection (g) which shall read as follows:

(g) The Attorney General may by regulation require that any person or persons acquiring, or planning, proposing or agreeing to acquire, any other person or persons, or any person or persons being acquired by, or planning, proposing or agreeing to be acquired by, any other person or persons, and any officer, director or partner of any such person, file with the Attorney General, at such time or times, not earlier than 30 days prior to the effective date of an acquisition, as shall be specified in such regulation, such documentary material and other information as shall be specified in such regulation; *provided, however,* that such regulation shall not impose any requirement which, by reason of subsection (c) of this section 3, could not be contained in a civil investigative demand.

Comment: This provision authorizes the Attorney General to adopt regulations establishing advance reporting requirements for mergers, and imposing responsibility for compliance on specified officers of firms involved in such mergers.

Such reporting requirements will permit more efficient enforcement of the merger prohibitions in the antitrust laws and in merger legislation proposed in the Report. In many cases, particularly under legislation proposed in the Report, it should be possible to resolve merger actions before consummation of mergers, rather than unscrambling mergers after consummation. In order to prevent unduly burdensome requirements, the statute limits the timing of required reports to 30 days in advance of a merger, and it prevents the Attorney General from requiring any information privileged under the Antitrust Civil Process Act.

The regulations would probably not be as broad as the statute. For example, the formation of a subsidiary other than a joint venture would generally not be of antitrust significance. In addition, acquisitions involving a small acquiring or acquired firm should probably be excluded, as should most portfolio investments and some kinds of partial asset acquisitions. . . .

Phil C. Neal, Chairman   James W. McKie
William F. Baxter   Lee E. Preston
Robert H. Bork   James A. Rahl
Carl H. Fulda   George D. Reycraft
William K. Jones   Richard E. Sherwood
Dennis G. Lyons   S. Paul Posner, Staff Director
Paul W. MacAvoy

Appendix C:
Summary, Report of the Task Force on Productivity and Competition

We present here a summary of the recommendations of the Task Force on Productivity and Competition. These recommendations are elaborated and defended in the accompanying report.

1. We recommend that the President issue a general policy statement (a) establishing the Antitrust Division as the effective agent of the Administration in behalf of a policy of competition within the councils of the Administration and before the independent regulatory commissions; (b) urging those commissions to enlarge the role of competition in their industries; (c) marshaling public support for the policy of competition.

2. We urge the commission to permit free entry in the industries under regulation and to abandon minimum rate controls, whenever these steps are possible— and we think they usually are; and we urge the President, when occasion permits, to appoint at least one economist to membership in each of the major commissions, and institute effective procedures for the review of the performance of the commissions.

3. To enhance the effectiveness of the Antitrust Division, we urge the Attorney General and the Assistant Attorney General in Charge of Antitrust to insist that every antitrust suit make good economic sense, and to institute semi-public conferences to assist in the formulation and frequent reevaluation of enforcement guidelines.

4. We recommend that the Department of Justice establish close liaison with the Federal Trade Commission at the highest levels, with a view toward fostering

Source: U.S. Congress, Senate, Committee on the Judiciary, Subcommittee on Antitrust and Monopoly, *Economic Concentration, Hearings Before the Subcommittee on Antitrust and Monopoly*, 91st Cong., 2nd sess., 1970 (Washington: U.S. Government Printing Office, 1970), 5034–35.

a harmonious policy of business regulation.

5. We recommend that the Department bring a series of strategic cases against regional price-fixing conspiracies, which we believe to be numerous and economically important.

6. We cannot endorse, on the basis of present knowledge of the effects of oligopoly on competition, proposals whether by new legislation or new interpretations of existing law to deconcentrate highly concentrated industries by dissolving their leading firms. But we urge the Department to maintain unremitting scrutiny of highly oligopolistic industries and to proceed under section 1 of the Sherman Act—which in our judgment reaches all important forms of collusion—in instances where pricing is found after careful investigation to be substantially noncompetitive.

7. The Department of Justice Merger Guidelines are extraordinarily stringent, and in some respects indefensible. We suggest a number of revisions in the accompanying report.

8. We strongly recommend that the Department decline to undertake a program of action against conglomerate mergers and conglomerate enterprises, pending a conference to gather information and opinion on the economic effects of the conglomerate phenomenon. More broadly, we urge the Department to resist the natural temptation to utilize the antitrust laws to combat social problems not related to the competitive functioning of markets.

9. We recommend new legislation to increase the monetary penalties at present largely nominal, for price fixing.

10. We urge a new policy for antitrust decrees. . . . Save in exceptional circumstances, all decrees should contain a near termination date, ordinarily no more than 10 years from the date of entry. And the Department should undertake a review of existing decrees to determine which should be vacated as obsolete or inappropriate.

George J. Stigler, Chairman
Ward S. Bowman, Jr.
Ronald H. Coase
Roger S. Cramton
Kenneth W. Dam
Raymon H. Mulford
Richard A. Posner
Peter O. Steiner
Alexander L. Stott

Appendix D:
Directorships of Major U.S.
Corporations Tightly Interlocked

SENATE COMMITTEE ON GOVERNMENTAL AFFAIRS

For the first time in over a decade, a congressional committee has taken a comprehensive look at interlocking directorships among the nation's largest corporations. Initiated by Senator Lee Metcalf, Chairman of the Subcommittee on Reports, Accounting and Management, the study identifies 530 direct and 12,193 indirect interlocks among 130 of the nation's top industrial, financial, retailing, transportation, broadcasting, and utility companies. The companies in the study represented about 25 percent of the assets of all U.S. corporations.

A direct interlock occurs when two companies have a common director. An indirect interlock occurs when two companies each have a director on the board of a third company.

The study disclosed an extraordinary pattern of directorate concentration:

— 123 firms each connected on an average with half of the other major companies in the study.

— The 13 largest firms not only were linked together, but accounted for 240 direct and 5,547 indirect interlocks, reaching an average of more than 70 percent of the other 117 corporations. The 13 largest corporations ranked by assets were: AT&T, BankAmerica, Citicorp, Chase Manhattan, Prudential, Metropolitan, Exxon, Manufacturers Hanover, J. P. Morgan, General Motors, Mobil, Texaco, and Ford.

— The leading competitors in the fields of automotives, energy, telecommunications, and retailing met extensively on boards of America's largest financial institutions, corporate customers, and suppliers.

Source: Senate Committee on Governmental Affairs, press release, April 23, 1978.

—The largest commercial bankers clustered on major insurance company boards and insurance directors joined on the banking company boards.

—The nation's largest airlines and electric utilities were substantially interlocked with major lending institutions.

—The boards of four of the largest banking companies (Citicorp, Chase Manhattan, Manufacturers Hanover, and J. P. Morgan), two of the largest insurance companies (Prudential and Metropolitan), and three of the largest nonfinancial companies (AT&T, Exxon, and General Motors) looked like virtual summits for leaders in American business.

Notes

1. INTRODUCTION: A BRIEF HISTORY OF ANTITRUST POLICY TO 1950

1. General introductory information can be found in various business history texts. See for example, Alfred D. Chandler, Jr., *The Visible Hand: The Managerial Revolution in American Business* (Cambridge, MA: The Belknap Press, 1977), 315–20; Naomi R. Lamoreaux, *The Great Merger Movement in American Business, 1895–1904* (New York: Cambridge University Press, 1985), 1–8, 29–33, 87, 187–90; Martin J. Sklar, *The Corporate Reconstruction of American Capitalism, 1890–1916: The Market, the Law, and Politics* (New York: Cambridge University Press, 1988), 1–20; George David Smith, *From Monopoly to Competition: The Transformation of Alcoa, 1888–1986* (New York: Cambridge University Press, 1988), 45–60. For differing points of view among economists see William Lee Baldwin, *Antitrust and the Changing Corporation* (Durham, NC: Duke University Press, 1961).

2. *Wabash, St. Louis, and Pacific Railway v. Illinois*, 118 U.S. 557 (1886).

3. Kirk H. Porter and Donald Bruce Johnson, *National Party Platforms, 1840–1968*, 4th ed. (Urbana: University of Illinois Press, 1972), 78–80.

4. U.S. Congress, House, Antitrust Subcommittee of the Committee on the Judiciary, Staff Report, *The Antitrust Laws: A Basis for Economic Freedom* (Washington: U.S. Government Printing Office, 1965), 1–2.

5. For more detailed discussion of this First Great Merger Movement see Ralph L. Nelson, *Merger Movements in American Industry, 1895–1956* (Princeton, NJ: Princeton University Press, 1959); Lamoreaux. The reader will note that Nelson's narrative is primarily concerned with the first merger wave, with little information beyond 1920.

6. Chandler, 319–20, 331, 566.

7. *United States v. Jellico Mountain Coal and Coke Co., et al.*, 43 Fed 898 (1891); Hans B. Thorelli, *The Federal Antitrust Policy: Origination of an American Tradition* (Baltimore, MD: The Johns Hopkins University Press, 1955), 436–9.

8. Thorelli, 294–7. Depression information is available in most standard U.S. history texts. See, for example, William L. Barney, *The Passage of the Republic: An Interdisciplinary History of Nineteenth Century America* (Lexington, MA: D.C. Heath and Company, 1987),

399–401.

9.   *United States v. E.C. Knight Co., et al.*, 156 U.S.1 (1895); Thorelli, 445–8. Lamoreaux presents Charles W. McCurdy's explanation that the Supreme Court took the position that if manufacturing for interstate commerce was interstate commerce, the states would lose their power to regulate such corporations, since only the national government could regulate interstate commerce. Further, since the four acquired firms held Pennsylvania charters, and since the existence of monopoly had been acknowledged, the Fuller Court assumed that the state would proceed to invalidate their acquisition. Lamoreaux, 165–6.

10.   Federal Trade Commission, Staff Report, *Economic Report on Corporate Mergers* (Washington: U.S. Government Printing Office, 1969), 665. Because some mergers bring together only two companies, while others may involve the consolidations of several previously independent firms, the Federal Trade Commission has chosen to use *firms disappearing* as a more accurate indication of the significance of the merger movement. Lamoreaux, 1; Nelson, 103; Chandler, 334–6.

11.   *United States v. Trans-Missouri Freight Association et al.*, 166 U.S. 290 (1897). Thorelli, 452–7; Robert H. Bork, *The Antitrust Paradox: A Policy at War with Itself* (New York: Basic Books, 1978), 22–6.

12.   Thorelli, 457–8; Bork, 23–5. See Sklar, 127–48 for a more detailed discussion.

13.   *United States v. Joint Traffic Association*, 171 U.S. 505 (1898). Thorelli, 458–60; Bork, 23–4.

14.   *United States v. Addyston Pipe and Steel Co., et al.*, 85 Fed 271. Thorelli, 466–9; Bork, 26–30.

15.   *United States v. Addyston Pipe and Steel Co., et al.*, 175 U.S. 211. Thorelli, 469–70.

16.   Louis Galambos, *The Public Image of Big Business in America, 1880–1940* (Baltimore, MD: The Johns Hopkins University Press, 1975), 79–113; David Dale Martin, *Mergers and the Clayton Act* (Berkeley: University of California Press, 1959), 6–7.

17.   *United States v. Northern Securities Co., et al.*, 120 Fed 721. For background on the Northern Securities Company and Roosevelt's attitude, see Thorelli, 411–31, 470–1. Roosevelt's reputation as the "Trust Buster" derives from this case.

18.   *United States v. Northern Securities Co., et al.*, 193 U.S. 197 (1904). Thorelli, 471–5, 560–3.

19.   Jesse W. Markham, "Survey of the Evidence and Findings on Mergers," in *Business Concentration and Price Policy*, National Bureau of Economic Research (Princeton, NJ: Princeton University Press, 1955), 164–6; Chandler, 337–44; Lamoreaux, 141–2.

20.   In 1902, Ida M. Tarbell began her expose of the Standard Oil Company in a series of articles in *McClure's*. In that same year and magazine, Lincoln Steffens published "The Shame of the Cities," which unveiled corrupt alliances between business and several municipal governments. These were followed by attacks on the "Beef Trust" by Charles Edward Russell, and on Wall Street by Thomas W. Lawson, in *Everybody's Magazine* (1905 and 1906). Upton Sinclair's *The Jungle* (1906), revealing the horrible conditions in the meat-packing industry, became one of the best known books of the twentieth century. And David G. Phillips shocked an already startled nation by his series in *Cosmopolitan*, "The Treason of the Senate" (1906), in which he accused 75 of the 90 U.S. Senators of representing the trusts, not the people. These were a few of the more sensational revelations of the "muckrakers," those investigating journalists of the early Progressive period, whose writing heightened the fear of the "trusts" and whose agitation for reform pressured the politicians

and contributed in some degree to corrective legislation.

The Pure Food and Drug Act and the Meat Inspection Act are examples of this legislation. Discussion of the muckrakers and the Progressive Era legislation can be found in various general U.S. history or U.S. economic history texts. See, for example, Harold Underwood Faulkner, *American Economic History*, 8th ed. (New York: Harper and Brothers, 1960), 440–1. Various authors have noted that many business leaders sought federal regulation that would better structure their industry and, in some instances, force out their small competitors. See, for example, Gabriel Kolko, *The Triumph of Conservatism: A Reinterpretation of American History, 1900–1916* (Chicago: Quadrangle Books, 1963), 78; Lamoreaux, 159–62.

In 1906 the President asked Congress to pass legislation to regulate business engaged in interstate commerce, and in the following year the National Civic Federation called for the federal licensing or incorporation of firms in interstate commerce. The financial panic of 1907 further increased the public's fear of big business and business leaders' fear of instability in the economy. In his annual message to Congress in December 1907, Roosevelt asked for a federal incorporation law with a national commission to enforce it, and in 1908 the National Association of Manufacturers announced its support of such a law. Although Congress entertained a number of measures calling for federal incorporation, the Hepburn Bill of 1908 received most serious consideration. However, in its attempt to provide for all interests, especially those of labor, the bill was doomed to failure. Thus ended the first attempt to establish a national law for the chartering of corporations engaged in interstate commerce. Kolko, 133–8; Lamoreaux, 170–2; and Sklar, 228–84, provide information on the Hepburn Bill. The Panic of 1906–1907, coupled with various investigations and bills, contributed to the eventual establishment of the Federal Reserve System in 1913. Federal incorporation had been considered as early as 1899 by businessmen seeking nationwide uniformity, and as early as 1902 by President Theodore Roosevelt. Kolko, 63–4, 69; Sklar, 188–207.

21. *Standard Oil Company of New Jersey v. United States*, 221 U.S. 1 (1911); D. T. Armentano, *The Myths of Antitrust: Economic Theory and Legal Cases* (New Rochelle, NY: Arlington House, 1972), 63–85; Bork, 33–9; Kolko, 39–42; Lamoreaux, 173–6. From 1899 to 1911, Standard's refining percentage declined as over 100 competitors entered the market, including Pure, Texaco, Union, Sunoco, and Gulf.

22. Armentano, 95. Italics added.

23. *United States v. American Tobacco Company*, 221 U.S. 105 (1911). Armentano, 86–99; Bork, 33–41. Martin, 17, points out that in both cases the defendants were found to have violated the Sherman Act not because of a restraint of trade, but because of an *unreasonable* restraint of trade. Roosevelt had distinguished between "good" and "bad" trusts. See, for example, Kolko, 89, 129–30. Now it appeared that the courts would make that distinction according to the rule of reason.

24. Kolko, 175–8.

25. Faulkner, 443; Martin, 22–3, 29; Susan Wagner, *The Federal Trade Commission* (New York: Praeger Publishers, 1971), 14–5; Kolko, 260.

26. Kolko, 258–67; Bork, 47–8. See Martin, 20–56 for the legislative background of the Clayton Act.

27. Faulkner, 443–4, italics added. Big Business and bankers had opposed the inclusion of a prohibition on interlocks, although such a prohibition was supported by the National Chamber of Commerce. Kolko, 262–4. The extent of interlocks, especially between business and banks, and the revelation that the "Money Trust"—the large New York banking houses—

were the driving force behind many of the major mergers had been confirmed by the report of the Pujo Committee in 1913. The J. P. Morgan interests, for example, had organized U.S. Steel, General Electric, and American Radiator, and was one of seven groups that dominated railroads in the United States. The Morgan interests held 341 interlocking directorates at the time of the Pujo Committee. Faulkner, 447, 494. However, the prohibition against interlocks addresses direct competitors, thereby ignoring other possibilities, such as an executive of a manufacturing firm serving on the board of a bank, a railroad, and a raw materials supplier, all of which indirectly relate to the success of his corporation. The widespread existence of interlocking directorates continues to the present. (See Appendix D.)

28. Simon N. Whitney, *Antitrust Policies: American Experience in Twenty Industries,* Vol. 1 (New York: The Twentieth Century Fund, 1958), 15.

29. Bork, 48–9.

30. Kolko, 270–7; Wagner, 19–22; Arthur S. Link, *Woodrow Wilson and the Progressive Era, 1910–1917* (New York: Harper and Row, 1954), 74–6. Preparation for and the subsequent entry of the United States into World War I brought about a vast expansion of government involvement in almost every aspect of the economy. "Dollar-a-year" men presided over the War Industries Board and its various subordinate agencies, coordinating business efforts and coercing their fellow business leaders to cooperate. Antitrust was ignored.

31. J. Fred Weston, *The Role of Mergers in the Growth of Large Firms* (Berkeley: University of California Press, 1953), 39; Armentano, 103–6. The "Gary Dinners" were meetings of the top steel executives to maintain prices by gentlemen's agreement.

32. *United States v. United States Steel Corporation,* 251 U.S. 417 (1920).

33. William G. Shepherd, *Public Policies Toward Business,* 7th ed. (Homewood, IL: Richard D. Irwin, 1985), 189. The government would have to wait 25 years, until the *ALCOA* case in 1945, to overcome the concept of "good" and "bad" trusts.

34. Willard L. Thorp, "The Merger Movement," in *Monograph No. 27, The Structure of Industry,* Temporary National Economic Committee (Washington: U.S. Government Printing Office, 1941), 232–4; Willard L. Thorp, "The Changing Structure of Industry," in *Recent Economic Changes in the United States,* Report of the President's Conference on Unemployment, Vol. 1 (New York: McGraw Hill, 1929), 185–7. Although not a part of this study, the most awesome mergers during this period were those in the public utility industry. Over 3,700 firms disappeared during the years 1919 to 1927, with 1,029 disappearing in 1926 alone. Action to regulate this "power trust" began with the Public Utility Holding Company Act of 1935. Thorp, "Changing Structure," 187.

35. Information in the above four paragraphs from Faulkner, 611–14; Weston, 83; Samuel Richardson Reid, *Mergers, Managers, and the Economy* (New York: McGraw Hill, 1968), 57–8; Markham, 172–3; Willard L. Thorp, "The Persistence of the Merger Movement," *American Economic Review,* 21, No. 1, supplement (March 1931), 85–7; Carl Eis, *The 1919–1930 Merger Movement in American Industry* (Unpublished Ph.D. dissertation, University of Georgia, 1981), 78–89, 93. Merger for oligopoly is discussed in George Stigler, "Monopoly and Oligopoly by Merger," *American Economic Review Papers and Proceedings,* 40, No. 2 (May 1950), 31–2, in which Stigler states "the ghost of Senator Sherman is an ex officio member of the board of directors of every large company." Markham, 169–70, disagrees with Stigler, stating that "Merger for oligopoly presupposes an extremely high order of oligopolistic rationalization—a much higher order than events or logic can support." However, Eis, 86–134, strongly supports Stigler and refutes Markham.

Weston, 34–7, discusses oligopoly as a result of court dissolution or government investigative pressure, and oligopoly as a result of internal growth.

In addition to manufacturing and mining firms, the merger mania swept across the banking and public utility industries. Between 1921 and 1930, the number of banks in the United States declined from 30,812 to approximately 22,000. The Chase National Bank had become the largest bank in the entire world, while the National City Bank (now Citicorp) and the Bank of America had become financial giants. During those same years, over 4,300 public utility companies disappeared through merger. By the end of the decade, the twelve largest utility holding companies controlled approximately half of the power produced in the entire nation. The leading figure in this concentration of power was Charles Insull, who put together an electric power empire that affected 5,000 towns in 32 states. He built his empire by simply pyramiding holding company upon holding company so that a small amount of stock in one of the companies toward or at the top of the pyramid would control a large number of companies at a lower level. When his empire and others collapsed in 1932, thousands of investors lost millions of dollars. Thorp, "Changing Structure," 185–7; Faulkner, 610; Keith L. Bryant, Jr., and Henry C. Dethloff, *A History of American Business* (Englewood Cliffs, NJ: Prentice-Hall, 1983), 158.

36. *Federal Trade Commission v. Western Meat Company, Thatcher Manufacturing Company v. Federal Trade Commission, Swift & Company v. Federal Trade Commission*, 272 U.S. 554 (1926).

37. Ibid., 561, italics added; Thorp, "Persistence," 82; Martin, 105–12.

38. Morton Keller, "The Pluralist State: American Economic Regulation in Comparative Perspective, 1900–1930," in *Regulation in Perspective: Historical Essays*, edited by Thomas K. McCraw (Cambridge, MA: Harvard University Press, 1981), 76. After the three Section 7 decisions, the FTC, headed by the pro-business William E. Humphrey, with a Republican majority among the Commissioners, began to assist business through the sponsorship of trade-practice conferences. However, the FTC's investigation of public utilities, begun during this period, eventually led to the Public Utility Holding Company Act of 1935. For a brief review of the FTC under Humphrey, see Arthur M. Johnson, "The Federal Trade Commission: The Early Years, 1915–1935," in *Business and Government: Essays in 20th Century Cooperation and Confrontation*, edited by Joseph R. Frese and Jacob Judd (Tarrytown, NY: Sleepy Hollow Press, 1985), 168–81.

39. Information in the above four paragraphs is from Ellis Hawley, "Antitrust and the Association Movement, 1920–1940," in *National Competition Policy: Historians' Perspectives on Antitrust and Government-Business Relationships in the United States* (Washington: Federal Trade Commission, August 1981), 107–14; Thomas K. McCraw, ed., *Prophets of Regulation* (Cambridge, MA: The Belknap Press, 1984), 143–52; John D. Hicks, *Republican Ascendency, 1921–1933* (New York: Harper & Row, 1960), 65–7, 106–8; Eric F. Goldman, *Rendezvous with Destiny: A History of Modern American Reform* (New York: Vintage Books, pb, 1955), 237–9; George Soule, *Prosperity Decade: From War to Depression, 1917–1929* (New York: Rinehart and Company, 1947), 131–41; Johnson, 168–77. For detailed discussion of the associationist movement see Robert F. Himmelberg, *The Origins of the National Recovery Administration: Business, Government, and the Trade Association Issue, 1921–1933* (New York: Fordham University Press, 1976). It is interesting to note that during the 1920s Franklin D. Roosevelt had been instrumental in establishing a trade association—the American Construction Council—and served for seven years as its president. McCraw, 149.

40. Thorp, "Persistence," 83–4.

41. Ibid., 84–5; Keller, 76.

42. These figures confirm the relation between merger activity, prosperous times, and easy availability of funds, rather than the seemingly more logical belief that mergers would increase during periods of decreasing production and idle plant capacity. Thorp, "Prosperity," 85–7; Weston, 79–83.

43. Martin, 73–6, 126–7.

44. *International Shoe Company v. Federal Trade Commission*, 280 U.S. 291 (1930); Martin, 127–30.

45. *Arrow-Hart and Hegeman Electric Company v. Federal Trade Commission*, 291 U.S. 587 (1934); Martin, 118–21; Federal Trade Commission, *Report of the Federal Trade Commission on the Merger Movement: A Summary Report* (Washington: U.S. Government Printing Office, 1948), 4–5.

46. Martin, 148–9; FTC, *A Summary Report*, 5.

47. Ellis Hawley, *The New Deal and the Problem of Monopoly: A Study in Economic Ambivalence* (Princeton, NJ: Princeton University Press, 1966), 12–14. For a general treatment of the New Deal, see, for example, William E. Leuchtenburg, *Franklin D. Roosevelt and the New Deal* (New York: Harper & Row, 1963).

48. Hawley, *New Deal*, 84–5, 95–7, 293–301; Leuchtenburg, 67; Theodore Rosenof, "New Deal Pragmatism and Economic Systems: Concepts and Meanings," *The Historian*, 49, No. 3 (May 1987), 374–7.

49. Hawley, *New Deal*, 391–3, 411.

50. U.S. Temporary National Economic Committee, *Investigation of Concentration of Economic Power: Final Report and Recommendations of the Temporary National Economic Committee* (Washington: U.S. Government Printing Office, 1941), 11–20.

51. Ibid., 26, 35–40, 681–6. U.S. Temporary National Economic Committee, *Monograph No. 16: Antitrust In Action* (Washington: U.S. Government Printing Office. 1941) specifically addressed the need for increased funding of the Antitrust Agencies and the streamlining of antitrust procedures.

52. Hawley, *New Deal*, 420, 426–32.

53. Ibid., 440–3; Corwin D. Edwards, "Thurman Arnold and the Antitrust Laws," *Political Science Quarterly* 58 (September 1943): 343–55; U.S. Congress, Senate, Committee on the Judiciary, Subcommittee on Antitrust and Monopoly, *Economic Concentration, Hearings before the Subcommittee on Antitrust and Monopoly*, 91st Cong., 2nd sess., Part 8, 1970 (Washington: U.S. Government Printing Office, 1970), 4962. No mergers were challenged by the Justice Department in 1938, 1939, or 1943; one merger was challenged in 1940, two in 1941, and one in 1942. (No mergers were challenged by the FTC during these years.)

54. Richard Hofstadter, "What Happened to the Antitrust Movement?" in *The Business Establishment*, edited by Earl F. Cheit (New York: John Wiley and Sons, 1964), 147–8; Edwards, 339, 341, 353; Hawley, *New Deal*, 454.

55. J. Keith Butters, John Lintner, and William L. Cary, *Effects of Taxation: Corporate Mergers* (Cambridge, MA: Harvard University Press, 1951), 22–6, 249–54, 299. See also FTC, *A Summary Report*, 28, which indicates that 33 of the 200 largest corporations acquired more than five companies each, and 13 more than ten companies each.

56. U.S. Smaller War Plants Corporation, *Economic Concentration and World War II: Report of the Smaller War Plants Corporation* (Washington: U.S. Government Printing

Office, 1946), 62–3; FTC, *A Summary Report*, 59. The term *conglomerate* seems to have first appeared in U.S. Temporary National Economic Committee, *Monograph No. 27: The Structure of Industry* (Washington: U.S. Government Printing Office, 1941), 46.

57. Armentano, 107–22; George W. Stocking and Myron W. Watkins, *Monopoly and Free Enterprise* (New York: The Twentieth Century Fund, 1951), 288–93; Smith, 192–214; *United States v. Aluminum Company of America*, 148 F. 2d 416 (1945). This is the famous 90–64–30 response to what percentage of market control constitutes a monopoly. Judge Hand stated that 90 percent "is enough to constitute a monopoly; it is doubtful whether sixty or sixty-four per cent would be enough; and certainly thirty-three per cent is not." The Court did not order dissolution of the demonstrably efficient ALCOA but recommended that the government-owned aluminum plants constructed for the war effort be sold to competitors. They were later sold to the Reynolds and Kaiser Corporations.

58. *United States v. Columbia Steel Company*, 335 U.S. 495 (1948); Stocking and Watkins, 304–10.

59. FTC, *A Summary Report*, 1–8; Martin, 220–59; John C. Narver, *Conglomerate Mergers and Market Competition* (Berkeley: University of California Press, 1967), 33–55.

60. U.S. Congress, House, *The Antitrust Laws*, 6.

2. THE ISSUE: BUSINESS CONCENTRATION IN THE 1950s AND 1960s

1. The acquisition of large firms is important, not only because these firms own a substantial share of manufacturing assets, but because they usually hold the leading positions in their industries. A leading firm is one included among the top four, or sometimes eight, producers in one industry.

2. Federal Trade Commission, Staff Report, *Economic Report on Corporate Mergers* (Washington: U.S. Government Printing Office, 1969), 3, 42–5, 184–5. Although not a part of this study, there was also considerable merger activity during these years in retailing, transportation, and various service industries.

3. Samuel Richardson Reid, *Mergers, Managers, and the Economy* (New York: McGraw-Hill, 1968), 89, 102, 105; John F. Winslow, *Conglomerates Unlimited: The Failure of Regulation* (Bloomington: Indiana University Press, 1973), xvi–xix. Internal growth, with its increased capacity, new techniques, and new or improved products, bring social increases in terms of greater employment and even increased taxes. External expansion, though sometimes improving production through integration or other costs savings, does not generally increase capacity, may result in the elimination of some positions, and reduces the number of independent decision makers in the economy.

4. FTC, *Economic Report*, 41–2. The conglomerate firm will be discussed later in this chapter.

5. Ibid., 162–4, 169. Although there were about 175,000 additional manufacturing firms at this time, organized as partnerships or proprietorships, their combined assets as well as net profits totaled only about 1 percent of the whole. These concentration figures are actually understated since various joint ventures, nonconsolidated assets, and financial holdings are not included, and accounts receivable are not included.

6. Ibid., 45; Federal Trade Commission, *Statistical Report No. 4: Large Mergers in Manufacturing and Mining, 1948–1968* (Washington: Federal Trade Commission, April, 1969), 11.

7.   Willard F. Mueller, *The Celler-Kefauver Act: The First 27 Years* (Washington: U.S. Government Printing Office, 1979), 75–6. Federal Trade Commission, *Economic Report on Corporate Mergers*, 191–5. During this period, the 200 largest also acquired nonmanufacturing corporations whose combined assets totaled 41 percent of the assets of the manufacturing companies acquired.

8.   FTC, *Economic Report*, 54–6, 97–9, 237.

9.   Ibid., 205–8. Joint venture assets were not included in the above discussion of the concentration of assets.

10.   U.S. Cabinet Committee on Price Stability, *Study Paper Number 2: Industrial Structure and Competition Policy* (Washington: U.S. Government Printing Office, January 1969), 51–2; FTC, *Economic Report*, 194–201. See Appendix D for a 1978 Senate Committee press release pertaining to interlocking directorates.

11.   Cabinet Committee, 56–7.

12.   Ibid., 59, 98.

13.   Ibid., 58, 98.

14.   Ibid., 58–61.

15.   Mueller, 72–4.

16.   FTC, *Economic Report*, 214–8.

17.   Ibid., 220–4. Product class and major industry group are two categories in the Standard Industrial Classification (SIC) System. This system, developed and used by government and private industry, begins with a two-digit major industry group code and becomes progressively more narrow as more numbers are added. For example:

SIC Code	Designation	Name
20	Major Industry Group	Food and Kindred Products
201	Industry Group	Meat Products
2011	Industry	Meat Packing Plants
20111	Product Class	Fresh Beef

18.   Ibid., 238–41.

19.   Ibid., 477–81.

20.   Ibid., 482–4.

21.   Ibid., 475–7. This report mentions three acquired firms that had been the major employers in their area, but does not tell of the impact, positive or negative, resulting from the acquisition. Ibid., 494–7.

22.   Estes Kefauver, with the assistance of Irene Till, *In a Few Hands: Monopoly Power in America* (New York: Pantheon Books, 1965), 164–8.

23.   Ibid., 168–75. Many large corporations are sensitive to such criticisms about community involvement, and encourage their executives to participate in community activities.

24.   FTC, *Economic Report*, 473.

25.   U.S. Temporary National Economic Committee, *Monograph No. 27: The Structure of Industry* (Washington: U.S. Government Printing Office, 1941), 46; FTC, *Economic Report*, 59–60.

26.   Jesse W. Markham, *Conglomerate Enterprise and Public Policy* (Cambridge, MA: Harvard University Press, 1973), 8–11; U.S. Smaller War Plants Corporation, *Economic Concentration and World War II* (Washington: U.S. Government Printing Office, 1946), 62; FTC, *Report of the Federal Trade Commission on the Merger Movement: A Summary Report.* (Washington: U.S. Government Printing Office, 1948), 59; FTC, *Economic Report*

on Corporate Mergers, 60–2.

27. General Motors, for example, made automobiles, railroad locomotives, and airplane motors, but also made refrigerators and provided financial services. Chrysler also made air conditioners and outboard motors.

28. Winslow, xvi; Reid, 77, 95; Mueller, 91; Robert Sobel, *The Rise and Fall of the Conglomerate Kings* (New York: Stein and Day, 1984), 156.

29. Donald F. Turner, "Conglomerate Mergers and Section 7 of the Clayton Act," *Harvard Law Review* 98 (May 1965): 1394–5. Winslow, xx; Sobel, 157; and others have noted Turner's view. Alfonso Everett MacIntyre, "Conglomerate Mergers and Antitrust Law," Address before the Practicing Law Institute, New York, NY, December 2, 1966.

30. U.S. Congress, House of Representatives, *Investigation of Conglomerate Corporations, Hearings Before the Antitrust Subcommittee (Subcommittee No. 5) of the Committee on the Judiciary*, 91st Congress (Washington: U.S. Government Printing Office, 1970), 7; U.S. Congress, Senate, Committee on the Judiciary, Subcommittee on Antitrust and Monopoly, *Economic Concentration, Hearings Before the Subcommittee on Antitrust and Monopoly*, 91st Congress, 2nd sess, Part 8 (Washington: U.S. Government Printing Office, 1970), 5177.

31. The conglomerate corporation and its acts need not be, nor are they always, anticompetitive. Conglomerates may inject new competition into a market, thereby increasing efficiency and possibly reducing prices to consumers. However, by the late 1960s, even the word "conglomerate" usually generated ideas of greed or "badness," if not illegality.

32. Mueller, 100. For a broader discussion of reciprocity see, for example, Peter O. Steiner, *Mergers: Motives, Effects, Policies* (Ann Arbor: University of Michigan Press, 1975), 219–54.

33. FTC, *Economic Report*, 394–7.

34. *Federal Trade Commission v. Consolidated Foods Corporation*, 380 U.S. 594 (1965). This case will be discussed later in this study. Potential reciprocity was among the complaints in additional cases filed during these and subsequent years.

35. Although cross-subsidization is usually discussed in reference to a decrease in competition, it can also lead to an increase in competition, especially when barriers to entry are so high that only a conglomerate or otherwise powerful firm can enter into the specific product market.

36. *Federal Trade Commission v. Proctor & Gamble Co.*, 386 U.S. 568 (1967). This case will be discussed later in this study. The power of the parent firm to expend considerable sums on its newly acquired subsidiaries is frequently referred to as the "deep pocket" theory.

37. For a more detailed discussion see Steiner, 259–87; Mueller, 101–7; FTC, *Economic Report*, 458–71.

38. *United States v. El Paso Natural Gas Company*, 376 U.S. 651, 659 (1964). This case will be discussed later in this study.

39. *Federal Trade Commission v. Proctor & Gamble Co.*, 386 U.S. 568 (1967).

40. FTC, *Economic Report*, 256–64; For a more complete review see FTC, ibid., 500–43; Robert Sobel, 77–154.

41. Sobel accused Bluhdorn of showing "how to make millions of dollars by failing in attempted acquisitions." Ibid., 102.

42. Theodore Philip Kovaleff, *Business and Government During the Eisenhower Administration: A Study of the Antitrust Policy of the Antitrust Division of the Justice Department* (Athens, OH: Ohio University Press, 1980), 17.

43. U.S. Attorney General, *Report of the Attorney General's National Committee to Study the Antitrust Laws* (Washington: U.S. Government Printing Office, 1955), 116–25.

44. Ibid., 128, 346.

45. Kovaleff, 52–3.

46. Ibid., 71–2, 148; David Dale Martin, *Mergers and the Clayton Act* (Berkeley: University of California Press, 1959), 303–5. Premerger notification became law in 1976 with the passage of the Hart-Scott-Rodino Act.

47. Peter H. Schuck, *The Judiciary Committees: A Study of the House and Senate Judiciary Committees* (New York: Grossman Publishers, 1975), 62–6. The drug industry hearings, which resulted in the Kefauver-Harris Drug Industry Act of 1962, were primarily concerned with health and drug safety, not antitrust.

48. Ibid., 96. The subcommittee later was called the Antitrust Subcommittee. The four bills were concerned with an increase in fines, enabling the United States to recover damages for itself under the antitrust laws, finalizing the FTC's cease-and-desist orders, and giving automobile dealers more rights vis-à-vis the automobile manufacturers.

49. William Oscar Jenkins, Jr., *The Role of the Supreme Court in National Merger Policy: 1950–1973* (Unpublished Ph.D. dissertation, University of Wisconsin-Madison, 1975), 60–1; Schuck, 96–7.

50. *United States v. E.I. DuPont de Nemours & Company*, 351 U.S. 377 (1956); Kovaleff, 91–3; Jenkins, 58–61. The majority apparently became entangled in a theoretical discussion of cross-elasticity of demand rather than examining the actual demand for and use of the various products.

51. Since the Celler-Kefauver Act had not yet been passed, the reference is to the old Section 7. DuPont's purchase of the GM stock had been made 30 years prior to the filing of the case.

52. *United States v. E.I. DuPont de Nemours & Co., et al.*, 353 U.S. 586 (1957); Kovaleff, 94–9; Jenkins, 61–2; Martin, 276–80.

53. Kovaleff, 73–7; Martin, 296–300.

54. *United States v. Bethlehem Steel Corporation*, 168 F. Supp. 576 (1958); Mueller, 25–6; Kovaleff, 78–82. Since this case was not appealed to the Supreme Court, the antitrust agencies would have to wait until the 1960s for the first case under amended Section 7 to reach the highest court.

55. As the Eisenhower years drew to a close, 29 electrical equipment manufacturers, including General Electric, Westinghouse, and Allis-Chalmers, were successfully prosecuted for fixing prices of equipment such as transformers, generators, and switching devices. Almost $2 million in fines were imposed, seven executives were jailed, and others were given suspended sentences. Claims totaled over $400 million. Although this case drew considerable media attention, it is not included in this study because it pertained primarily to price fixing, not concentration. See, for example, Kovaleff, 119–34.

3. THE RESPONSE: THE EXECUTIVE

1. Federal Trade Commission, Staff Report, *Economic Report on Corporate Mergers* (Washington: U.S. Government Printing Office, 1969), 161–3; Jim Heath, *John F. Kennedy and the Business Community* (Chicago: University of Chicago Press, 1969), 10–11.

2. See Aggregate Concentration, Chapter 2, above, especially Figure 2.1.

3.   Kim McQuaid, *Big Business and Presidential Power: From FDR to Reagan* (New York: William Morrow, 1982), 30–2; Hobart Rowan, *The Free Enterprisers: Kennedy, Johnson and the Business Establishment* (New York: G. Putnam's Sons, 1964), 61–3. Although this study is primarily concerned with the manufacturing and mining industries, membership in the Business Advisory Council also included executives of firms in retailing, finance, transportation, and other areas.

4.   Hodges also requested the resignation of the BAC Chairman, Ralph Cordiner, Board Chairman of General Electric, because of the January 1961 price-fixing convictions of General Electric and some of its executives. Cordiner did resign and was replaced by Roger Blough, Chairman of U.S. Steel. McQuaid, 201–2; Heath, 17–8; Rowan, 63–4.

5.   McQuaid, 200–2; Heath, 17–8; Rowan, 61–9.

6.   McQuaid, 203–5; Heath, 18–9; Rowan, 61–77. Rowan credited Robert Kennedy for considerable influence in convincing the President to make an extensive effort to reassure the council members. Rowan, 71. Heath noted that corporate leaders, especially the steel executives, seeing Kennedy's reaction, may have decided that the President would condone the increase in prices which led to the "steel crisis" of 1962. Heath, 19.

7.   McQuaid, 215–8.

8.   Ibid., 223–36.

9.   Ibid., 242–55.

10.   Ibid., 254–5.

11.   Kirk H. Porter and Donald Bruce Johnson, *National Party Platforms, 1840–1968*, 4th ed. (Urbana: University of Illinois Press, 1972), 586–7, 609.

12.   Arthur M. Schlesinger, Jr., *A Thousand Days: John F. Kennedy in the White House* (Boston: Houghton Mifflin, 1965), 625; Bruce Miroff, *Pragmatic Illusions: The Presidential Power of John F. Kennedy* (New York: David McKay Co., 1976), 168; Heath, 49.

13.   Robert D. Cuff, "Antitrust Adjourned: Mobilization and the Rise of the National Security State," in *National Competition Policy: Historians' Perspectives on Antitrust and Government-Business Relationships in the United States* (Washington: Federal Trade Commission, August 1981), 226–9; Heath, 49.

14.   Richard Hofstadter, "What Happened to the Antitrust Movement?," in *The Business Establishment*, edited by Earl F. Cheit (New York: John Wiley & Sons, 1964), 131–3; U.S. President, *Public Papers of the Presidents of the United States* (Washington: U.S. Government Printing Office, 1962–1963), John F. Kennedy, 1962, 348.

15.   Ibid., 1961, 19–20, 86–7, 93, 182, 582; Paul Rand Dixon, Interview by John F. Stewart, August 7, 1968, John F. Kennedy Library Oral History Program, Boston, MA, 37–8.

16.   Letter, Representative Emanuel Celler to John F. Kennedy, April 28, 1961, White House Central Files, Box 13, BE 2–4, Monopoly and Antimonopoly: folder 1, John F. Kennedy Library, Boston, MA; Memorandum, Sam Hughes to Lee White, June 5, 1961, White House Central Files, Box 13, BE 2–4, Monopoly and Antimonopoly: folder 1, John F. Kennedy Library, Boston, MA.

17.   *Public Papers*, John F. Kennedy, 1962, 242. Premerger notification did not become law until the passage of the Hart-Scott-Rodino Act in 1976.

18.   Heath, 50–1; George Bookman, "Loevinger vs. Big Business," *Fortune*, January 1962, 93–114; Arthur M. Schlesinger, Jr., *Robert Kennedy and His Times* (New York: Ballantine Books, pb., 1968), 431–2.

19.   *Public Papers*, John F. Kennedy, 1961, 708, 774–5.

20. The "steel crisis" is adequately covered in Heath, 66–73; Miroff, 174–80; Dixon, Interview, 26–31; Luther H. Hodges, Interview by Dan B. Jacobs, March 21, 1964, John F. Kennedy Library, Oral History Program, Boston, MA., 56–60; Schlesinger, *A Thousand Days*, 634–40; and in contemporary newspapers and magazines.

21. The Research Institute of America on June 30, 1962, reported the results of a survey of 6,000 business executives. Fifty-two percent described the Kennedy Administration as strongly antibusiness, 36 percent as moderately antibusiness, and only 9 percent as neutral or probusiness. Schlesinger, *A Thousand Days*, 638.

22. In the wake of the steel episode, Congressman Celler proposed two bills amending Section 7 of the Clayton Act. His proposals will be presented in Chapter 4.

23. *Public Papers*, John F. Kennedy, 1962, 349–52.

24. Ibid., 470–75; Theodore Levitt, "The Johnson Treatment," *Harvard Business Review* 45 (Jan.-Feb. 1967): 121–4.

25. Lee Loevinger, Interview by Ronald J. Grele, May 13, 1966, John F. Kennedy Oral History Program, Boston, MA., 22–3; Emanuel Celler, Interview by Larry J. Hackman, April 11, 1972, Robert F. Kennedy Oral History Program, John F. Kennedy Library, Boston, MA., 4; Theodore Philip Kovaleff, *Business and Government During the Eisenhower Administration: A Study of the Antitrust Policy of the Antitrust Division of the Justice Department* (Athens, OH: Ohio University Press, 1980), 28, 147–8.

26. *Public Papers*, John F. Kennedy, 1961, 582; *Public Papers*, John F. Kennedy, 1962, 241; Heath, 54; Dixon, Interview, 38.

27. *Public Papers*, John F. Kennedy, 1962, 711.

28. Heath, 75; Miroff, 168, 174, 187–91, 197; Schlesinger, *Robert Kennedy*, 437; Rowan, 16–7.

29. Schlesinger, *Robert Kennedy*, 436; Rowan, 18.

30. Loevinger, Interview, 6; Victor S. Navasky, *Kennedy Justice* (New York: Atheneum, 1971), 167.

31. James E. Anderson and Jared E. Hazleton, *Managing Macroeconomic Policy: The Johnson Presidency* (Austin: University of Texas Press, 1986), 12, 227; Levitt, 114–28.

32. U.S. President, *Public Papers of the Presidents of the United States* (Washington: U.S. Government Printing Office, 1965), Lyndon B. Johnson, 1963–1964, 23–4.

33. Hugh Sidey, *A Very Personal Presidency: Lyndon Johnson in the White House* (New York: Atheneum, 1968), 93.

34. Dixon, Interview, 36.

35. Sidey, 93–4.

36. Dixon, Interview, 110–11; McQuaid, 236; Mark J. Green, Project Director and Editor, *The Closed Enterprise System: Ralph Nader's Study Group Report on Antitrust Enforcement* (New York: Grossman Publishers, 1970), 78–81. Again, in the 1964 Presidential election campaign, both parties had inserted antitrust planks in their platforms. It is interesting to note, however, that the Democrats had but one sentence promising vigorous enforcement of the antitrust laws. The Republicans, on the other hand, pledged constant opposition to monopoly, excessive concentration of power, and "improvement, and full enforcement, of the anti-trust statutes, coupled with long-overdue clarification of Federal policies and interpretations relating thereto." Both parties pledged assistance to small business. Porter and Johnson, 646–60, 684–5.

37. William H. Orrick, Jr., Interview by Larry J. Hackman, April 14, 1970, Robert F. Kennedy Oral History Program, John F. Kennedy Library, Boston, MA, 95.

38. David T. Bazelon, "Big Business and the Democrats," in *The Great Society Reader: The Failure of American Liberalism*, edited by Marvin E. Gettleman and David Mermelstein (New York: Random House, 1967), 142–50. Bazelon credits some movement of big business toward Johnson as the result of the Republican Party's nomination of Barry Goldwater for President.

39. Anderson and Hazelton, *Managing Macroeconomic Policy*, 31.

40. Schlesinger, *Robert Kennedy*, 431.

41. Loevinger, Interview, 4. Civil rights had not yet come to the forefront. Loevinger's use of the expression "secular religion" has been repeated in books and articles.

42. Heath, 50–1; Bookman, 93; Schlesinger, *Robert Kennedy*, 432.

43. Loevinger, Interview, 19–20; Schlesinger, *A Thousand Days*, 634–40; Schlesinger, *Robert Kennedy*, 433–8. The steel companies pleaded *nolo contendre* to the charges brought against them. Schlesinger, *Robert Kennedy*, 436.

44. Lee Loevinger, "Antitrust is Pro-Business," *Fortune*, August 1962, 96–7, 126.

45. Willard F. Mueller, *The Celler-Kefauver Act: The First 27 Years* (Washington: U.S. Government Printing Office, 1979), 131–3. On pages 125–83, Mueller gives a brief tabular summary of all mergers challenged by the Antitrust Division and FTC from February 1951 to December 1977. The Antitrust Division, because of its limited personnel resources, can only investigate a small fraction of the total number of mergers in a given period, and then challenge only a small percentage of that number. Therefore, only cases that may test a legal principle or establish a legal precedent and that the government has a reasonable chance of winning are chosen. It is estimated that less than 1 percent of all mergers are challenged. During the Kennedy-Johnson years, staff members within the Operations Office of the Antitrust Division each day compiled a list of proposed and completed mergers. Information on this list, taken from a variety of financial news sources, included the names of the companies involved, and relevant data pertaining to their size, products, and purpose of merger. Copies would then be sent to the various litigation sections (general, special, patent), where each merger would be assigned to a staff attorney for initial investigation and recommendation concerning possible department action. This attorney would investigate the degree of concentration and position of the firms within the industry, assemble additional pertinent information, and make a recommendation for challenge to the section chief, and if approved, to the operations chief. Additional steps, too detailed for the purpose of this study, would include seeking comments from other elements of the Antitrust Division (Economic Policy Office, Planning and Budget Office) and the Department of Justice (FBI assistance if required). If the investigation and recommendation for challenge survived these steps it would be referred to the Assistant Attorney General for Antitrust and the Deputy Attorney General, and finally to the Attorney General for approval. (The Assistant Attorney General for Antitrust can only recommend cases; the Attorney General must approve and file them.) At any point in this chain of command, a case could have been terminated for any reason. Thus, when a recommendation for challenge reaches the Attorney General, considerable data has been developed upon which to base a decision. William Oscar Jenkins, Jr., "The Role of the Supreme Court in National Merger Policy: 1950–1973 (Unpublished Ph.D. dissertation, University of Wisconsin-Madison, 1975), 24, 191–8; see also Suzanne Weaver, *Decision to Prosecute: Organization and Public Policy in the Antitrust Division* (Cambridge, MA: MIT Press, 1977).

46. Mueller, 131.

47. Ibid., 132; U.S. Department of Justice, *Annual Report of the Attorney General of*

the United States for the Fiscal Year Ended June 30, 1962 (Washington: U.S. Government Printing Office, 1962), 94–5; Robert M. Goolrick, *Public Policy Toward Corporate Growth* (Port Washington, NY: Kennikat Press, 1978), 37–8. In 1960, approximately 90 percent of Ling-Temco's sales and 75 percent of Chance Vought's sales had been to the U.S. government or to contractors to the U.S. government. Department of Justice, *Annual Report 1962*, 95.

48. Department of Justice, *Annual Report 1964*, 106; Mueller, 135; Peter O. Steiner, *Mergers: Motives, Effects, Policies* (Ann Arbor: University of Michigan Press, 1975), 156.

49. Mueller, 131–3; Department of Justice, *Annual Report 1961*, 109. Six of the 31 cases filed during Loevinger's tenure were against bank mergers, not included in this study.

50. Loevinger, Interview, 12. Price fixing had public attention when Loevinger came into office, due to the price-fixing scandal in the electrical equipment manufacturing industry (Chapter 2 above, note 55).

51. Department of Justice, *Annual Report 1962*, 98–9; Mueller, 23, 126. In 1963, Brown sold Kinney to F. W. Woolworth Co.

52. Lee Loevinger, "The Doctrine of Judicial Ratification," *Kentucky Law Journal* 51 (Spring 1963): 432–3; Schlesinger, *Robert Kennedy*, 432.

53. Loevinger, Interview, 6.

54. Robert F. Kennedy, "Introduction: The Antitrust Aims of the Justice Department," *New York Law Forum* 9 (March 1963): 3–4.

55. Schlesinger, *Robert Kennedy*, 432; Green, 74, 77–8; Jenkins, 186; Heath, 51.

56. Green, 78. Schlesinger, *Robert Kennedy*, 432; William H. Orrick, Jr., "Profile of an Antitrust Enforcement Program," Address Before the Antitrust Section of the New York State Bar Association, New York, NY, January 30, 1964, 2–3, 13; William H. Orrick, Jr., "Antitrust 1963," Address Before the Business Council, Hot Springs, VA, October 19, 1963, 11.

57. William H. Orrick, Jr., "The Clayton Act: Then and Now," Address Before the Antitrust Section of the American Bar Association, Washington, DC, April 17, 1964, 3, 6–7, 14.

58. Orrick, "Antitrust 1963," 5.

59. William H. Orrick, Jr., "The Impact of the Federal Antitrust Laws on Corporate Mergers," Address Before the Association for Corporate Growth, Inc., New York, NY, May 12, 1964, 4, 15.

60. William H. Orrick, Jr., "Antitrust and the Oil Industry: Recent Developments," Address Before the American Petroleum Institute, Bal Harbour, FL, June 10, 1964, 3.

61. Orrick, "Impact," 6; Orrick, "Antitrust and Oil," 9; William H. Orrick, Jr., "The Antitrust Division's Enforcement Program," Address Before the Antitrust Section of the New York State Bar Association, New York, NY, January 27, 1965, 8.

62. William H. Orrick, Jr., Testimony Before the Subcommittee on Antitrust and Monopoly, U.S. Senate, *Economic Concentration, Hearings*, April 21, 1965, 809–16.

63. Department of Justice, *Annual Report 1964*, 102–3; Mueller, 135. The government dropped the case in November 1966.

64. Department of Justice, *Annual Report 1964*, 100; Department of Justice, *Annual Report 1965*, 84; Mueller, 135–7.

65. Orrick, Interview, 95–104, 106, 111–2; Green, 79–80; Jenkins, 186; McQuaid, 236. As indicated above, following the assassination of President Kennedy, Robert Kennedy largely left the management of the Justice Department to his Deputy, Katzenbach, who succeeded to the position of Attorney General. To further understand the strained relation

between Orrick and Katzenbach, it must be noted that the Assistant Attorney General for Antitrust can only recommend cases; the Attorney General must sign and file them. As Orrick also points out, antitrust didn't have a "political constituency" at that time, as did civil rights and, later, the Vietnam War. In addition, the death of Senator Estes Kefauver, in 1963, removed one of the major champions of antitrust from the political scene.

66. Orrick, Interview, 110–12; Green, 42–4, 80–1. Mergers in the transportation industry are not included in this study.

67. Loevinger, Interview, 9–10, 16, 21; Orrick, Interview, 104–6; Nicholas deB. Katzenbach, Interview by Paige E. Mulhollan, Lyndon B. Johnson Oral History Collection, Lyndon B. Johnson Library, Austin, TX, 5.

68. Daily Report, Assistant Attorney General for Antitrust to the Attorney General, Papers of William H. Orrick, Jr., Box 5, folders: Daily Reports 8/63, 10/63, John F. Kennedy Library, Boston, MA.

69. White House Central Files, Papers of Lyndon Baines Johnson, President 1963–1969; Box 24, Judicial-Legal Matters, Gen JL2–11/23/65, Folder JL2–1 Antitrust Cases 11/22/63–7/29/65, Lyndon B. Johnson Library, Austin TX.

70. Letters from Senators Ribicoff and McClellan to the President, March 9, 1965, White House Central Files, Box 24, Judicial-Legal Matters, Gen JL2–11/23/65, Folder JL2–1 Antitrust cases 11/22/63–7/29/65, Lyndon B. Johnson Library, Austin, TX.

71. Green, 35–6, 41.

72. Turner had a reputation based upon his writings on antitrust. He and Carl Kayson had coauthored *Antitrust Policy: An Economic and Legal Analysis* (Cambridge, MA: Harvard University Press, 1959). Donald F. Turner, "Conglomerate Mergers and Section 7 of the Clayton Act," *Harvard Law Review* 98 (May 1965): 1313–95; Green, 82; Goolrick, 40.

73. Donald F. Turner, untitled, Address Before the Antitrust Section of the American Bar Association, Miami, FL, August 10, 1965, 2–5.

74. Jenkins, 188; Harold B. Meyers, "Professor Turner's Turn at Antitrust," *Fortune*, September 1965, 171.

75. Turner, "Conglomerate Mergers," 1394–5.

76. Turner, untitled address, August 10, 1965 (note 73 above), 8–9; Donald F. Turner, Testimony Before the Small Business Committee, U.S. Senate, April 6, 1967, 7. (Page number refers to copy of statement on file in the library of the Department of Justice, Washington, DC.)

77. Turner, Small Business Committee Testimony, 8–9. Like his predecessor, Turner advocated internal growth, viewing this as a source of increased efficiency, and the avenue by which many if not most firms have achieved economies of scale. Donald F. Turner, "The Role of Antitrust Among National Goals," Address Before the National Industrial Conference Board, New York, NY, March 3, 1966, 5; Donald F. Turner, "The Merits of Antimerger Policy," Address Before the Town Hall Forum, Los Angeles, CA, March 7, 1967, 13.

78. Green, 83–5; Jenkins, 187–8.

79. Richard Posner, "A Statistical Study of Antitrust Enforcement," *The Journal of Law and Economics* 13 (October 1970): 418–9.

80. Mueller, 139. In July 1974, the Supreme Court found that the acquisition of Tidewater by Phillips violated Section 7 and ordered divestiture. In August 1967, G&W accepted a consent judgment forcing the divestiture of the Desilu facilities.

81. Ibid., 141; Department of Justice, *Annual Report 1968*, 37.

82. Green, 90–1; Mueller, 134.

83. Donald F. Turner, "Advertising and Competition: Restatement and Amplification," Address Before the Annual Advertising Government Relations Conference, Washington, DC, February 8, 1967, 2–4, 7, 9, 12–3; Green, 93.

84. Letter, Representative Jerome R. Waldie to Nicholas Katzenbach, July 16, 1966, White House Central Files, Box 40, Papers of Ramsey Clark, folder Personal Papers of Ramsey Clark: Antitrust Division (1966–1967), Lyndon B. Johnson Library, Austin, TX; Green, 94.

85. Memo, Gardner Ackley to the President, June 29, 1967, White House Central Files, Box 4, GEN BE 2–1, folder BE 2–4 3/16/67–6/30/68, Lyndon B. Johnson Library, Austin, TX.

86. Goolrick, 43–5; Robert Sobel, *The Rise and Fall of the Conglomerate Kings* (New York: Stein and Day, 1984), 145–8.

87. Turner, untitled address, August 10, 1965 (note 73 above), 6–7.

88. Department of Justice, *Merger Guidelines*, May 30, 1968. For a discussion of the Merger Guidelines see Donald I. Baker, Chief Evaluation Section, Antitrust Division, Department of Justice, "The Department of Justice Merger Guidelines," Address Before the American Management Association, New York, NY, October 1, 1968.

89. Jenkins, 198–202; Goolrick, 46; Green, 86–7; Mueller, 91; Steiner, 156; John F. Winslow, *Conglomerates Unlimited: The Failure of Regulation* (Bloomington: Indiana University Press, 1973), xvi, 23, 30.

90. Edwin M. Zimmerman, "Views from the Antitrust Division," Address Before the Antitrust Section of the American Bar Association, Philadelphia, PA, August 7, 1968, 5, 8–9.

91. Edwin M. Zimmerman, "The Antitrust Laws in Your Future," Address Before the Association of the Bar of the City of New York, New York, NY, December 12, 1968, 4.

92. Zimmerman, "Views," 3, 10.

93. Mueller, 143.

94. Caspar Weinberger became Chairman on December 31, 1969. Dixon remained a Commissioner until September 24, 1974. Susan Wagner, *The Federal Trade Commission* (New York: Praeger Publishers, 1971), 25. Supposedly, the only favor Senator Kefauver asked of President Kennedy was the appointment of Dixon as FTC Chairman. Ibid., 223.

95. This dissension was noted in Edward F. Cox, Robert C. Fellmeth, and John E. Schulz, *"The Nader Report" on the Federal Trade Commission* (New York: Richard W. Baron, 1969), viii, and in an American Bar Association report prepared for President Nixon in 1969. Green, 322, 329–32; Wagner, 33, 222–4.

96. Jenkins, 210, 224; Green, 363–5; Harold B. Meyers, "The Root of the FTC's Confusion," *Fortune*, August 1963, 154; Robert Anthony Laudicina, "Judicial Influence and Group Behavior in National Merger Policy" (Unpublished Ph.D. dissertation, Columbia University, 1968), 56–7.

97. Wagner, 25; Green, 329, 342; Meyers, "The Root," 152–4.

98. Wagner, 33; Green, 328. Formal advisory opinions were initiated on June 1, 1962. This procedure binds the Commission to the opinion it has made regarding its view as to the legality or illegality of a proposed merger. Prior to this time, advisory opinions had been given by the staff but they were not binding on the Commission/Commissioners. Wagner, 53; Meyers, "The Root," 156; Mueller, 163–71.

99. Paul Rand Dixon, "Antitrust and Economic Freedom," Address Before the Rotary

Club, Houston, TX, September 17, 1964. Paul Rand Dixon, "Antitrust Compliance: The 'Will' to be Free," Address Before the Briefing Conference on Antitrust and Trade Regulation Law, Washington, DC, September 25, 1964. Paul Rand Dixon, "Conglomerate Merger Fever: The 1967 Virus," Address Before the Antitrust Section of the American Bar Association, Washington, DC, April 13, 1967. Paul Rand Dixon, Testimony Before Subcommittee #6 of the Select Committee on Small Business, U.S. House of Representatives, August 18, 1965; Dixon, Interview, 29.

100. Mueller, 164.

101. Ibid., 166.

102. Ibid., 169; FTC, *Annual Report 1968*, 22.

103. Mueller, 171.

104. Ibid., 164; Wagner, 123; Green, 364.

105. FTC, *Annual Report 1966*, 30; Mueller, 165.

106. Mueller, 57–8; Green, 348–9. Additional information regarding Folger may be found in Mueller, 58–61.

107. *Federal Trade Commission v. Proctor & Gamble Company*, 386 U.S. 568 (1967).

108. William G. Shepherd, *Public Policies Toward Business*, 7th ed. (Homewood, IL: Richard D. Irwin, 1985), 240; Green, 364–5; Mueller, 168.

109. Jenkins, 224; Shepherd, 239–40.

110. Dixon, Interview, 12, 41–3; Wagner, 212; Green, 351.

111. Samuel Richardson Reid, *The New Industrial Order* (New York: McGraw-Hill, 1976), 155; Wagner, 226. For some other examples of "political" pressure, see Green, 340–4.

112. Daily Report, Assistant Attorney General for Antitrust to the Attorney General, Papers of William H. Orrick, Jr., Box 5, folder: Daily Reports 6/63, Daily Report for June 12, 1963, John F. Kennedy Library, Boston, MA; Wagner, 227; Green, 369–70; Reid, 155. Reid indicates that Representative Gerald Ford was one of the influential Congressmen who opposed the study.

113. Dixon, Interview, 36.

114. Green, 170.

115. Ibid., 331, 351, 360.

116. Philip Elman, "Antitrust in an Expanding Economy," Address Before the Third Antitrust Conference of the National Industrial Conference Board, New York, NY, March 5, 1964, 7; Philip Elman, "Rulemaking Procedures in the Enforcement of the Merger Law," Address Before the Briefing Conference on Antitrust and Trade Regulation Law, Washington, DC, September 24, 1964, 10.

117. Mueller, 32, 158–9.

118. Ibid., 33–6.

119. Guidelines were also issued in the food distribution industry, January 3, 1967.

120. Mueller, 28–32; Green, 376–7.

121. FTC, *Annual Report 1968*, 36–8; Mueller, 50–3.

122. Memo, Ernest Goldstein to the President, October 6, 1967, White House Central Files, Box 362, EX FG 600/Task Force, folder FG 600 Task Force/Antitrust Policy, Lyndon B. Johnson Library, Austin, TX.

123. *Congressional Record*, November 16, 1967, copy, Office Files of James Gaither, Box 391, Lyndon B. Johnson Library, Austin, TX.

124. U.S. Cabinet Committee on Price Stability, *Study Paper Number 2: Industrial*

Structure and Competition Policy (Washington: U.S. Government Printing Office, January 1969), Foreword.

125. FTC, *Economic Report*, iv-v.

126. U.S. Congress, House of Representatives, Committee on the Judiciary, Antitrust Subcommittee, *Investigation of Conglomerate Corporations*, Staff Report, 92nd Cong., 1st sess., 1971 (Washington: U.S. Government Printing Office, 1971), 5, 429.

127. U.S. Cabinet Committee, *Study Paper Number 2*, 82–6.

128. U.S. President, *Economic Report of the President, January 1969* (Washington: U.S. Government Printing Office, 1969), 107–8.

129. U.S. Congress, Senate, Committee on the Judiciary, Subcommittee on Antitrust and Monopoly, *Economic Concentration, Hearings Before the Subcommittee on Antitrust and Monopoly*, 91st Cong., 2nd sess., 1970 (Washington: U.S. Government Printing Office, 1970), 5054–82. The report was not released to the public until May 21, 1969.

4. THE RESPONSE: THE CONGRESS

1.   Philip A. Hart, Box 577, Speeches, folder: Speeches Antitrust. Philip A. Hart Collection, Michigan Historical Collections, Bentley Historical Library, University of Michigan, Ann Arbor, MI. (Hereafter listed as Philip A. Hart Collection.)

2.   Thomas K. McCraw, ed., *Regulation in Perspective: Historical Essays* (Cambridge, MA: Harvard University Press, 1981), 17–22, 208. McCraw describes center firms as those that were technologically advanced in the sense that their production facilities were dominated by continuous process production. They were capital intensive and nearly all were vertically integrated. Thus they enjoyed some significant scale economy in production. Also, because of their enormous investment, they had a long-range perspective that involved five year plans, research and development, and complex managerial hierarchies (Standard Oil, American Tobacco, Carnegie Steel, International Harvester). Peripheral firms, on the other hand, were small, labor intensive, managerially thin, and bereft of economies of either scale or speed.

3.   See "Market Concentration," Chapter 2.

4.   See "The Conglomerate Movement," Chapter 2; Peter O. Steiner, *Mergers: Motives, Effects, Policies* (Ann Arbor: University of Michigan Press, 1975), 69–73.

5.   See "The Senate," this chapter, below.

6.   Morton Mintz and Jerry S. Cohen, *America, Inc.: Who Owns and Operates the United States* (New York: The Dial Press, 1971), 133.

7.   See Chapter 5, below.

8.   See Epilogue, below.

9.   Mintz and Cohen, 158, 207–8, 220; Mark J. Green, Project Director and Editor, *The Closed Enterprise System: Ralph Nader's Study Group Report on Antitrust Enforcement* (New York: Grossman Publishers, 1970), 19.

10.   Robert M. Goolrick, *Public Policy Toward Corporate Growth* (Port Washington, NY: Kennikat Press, 1978), ix-x. These comments are contained in the Foreword by Senator John V. Tunney, a member of the Senate Subcommittee on Antitrust and Monopoly during the Nixon years.

11.   Joseph Bruce Gorman, *Kefauver: A Political Biography* (New York: Oxford University Press, 1971), 300–1, 312.

12. Gorman, 299; Peter H. Schuck, *The Judiciary Committees: A Study of the House and Senate Judiciary Committees* (New York: Grossman Publishers, 1975), 64.

13. *Congressional Quarterly Almanac*, 84th Cong., 1st sess., 1955, Vol. 11 (Washington: Congressional Quarterly News Features, 1955), 546–54.

14. Gorman, 302–4, 311; Schuck, 64–5. The subcommittee also investigated concentration in sports, hearing aids, insurance, electrical equipment, and asphalt roofing.

15. Schuck, 64–5. The drug industry hearings, which resulted in the Kefauver-Harris Drug Industry Act of 1962, were primarily concerned with health and drug safety, not antitrust. Gorman, 309, points out that the hearings contributed to the establishment of consumer protection groups and the consumer legislation of later years.

16. Green, 56; Gorman, 302.

17. Schuck, 66–9; Green, 56.

18. Letter, Senator Philip A. Hart to Senator James O. Eastland, January 14, 1964, Box 443, Legislative Background Files, folder: Antitrust and Monopoly (Judiciary Subcommittee), Philip A. Hart Collection.

19. U. S. Congress, Senate, Committee on the Judiciary, Subcommittee on Antitrust and Monopoly, *Economic Concentration, Hearings before the Subcommittee on Antitrust and Monopoly*, 88th Cong., 2nd sess., 1964 (Washington: U.S. Government Printing Office, 1964), 1–2. The hearings would last until February 19, 1970, and fill over 5,000 printed pages.

20. Ibid., 499.

21. *Washington Post*, April 15, 1966, Box 495, Legislative Background Files, folder: Antitrust, Philip A. Hart Collection.

22. Mintz and Cohen, 133.

23. See "Toward the Legislative Process," Chapter 3.

24. *Sacramento Bee*, April 14, 1968. Box 495, Legislative Background Files, folder: Antitrust, Philip A. Hart Collection.

25. *New York Daily News Record*, October 2, 1968. Box 495, Legislative Background Files, folder: Antitrust, Philip A. Hart Collection.

26. Schuck, 91; Green, 61.

27. Philip A. Hart, Address Before the Law Forum, Duke University, Durham, NC, November 19, 1968, 21–2. Box 575, Speeches, folder: Hart speeches—1968 (3), Philip A. Hart collection.

28. Philip A. Hart, Address Before the National Council of Salesmens' Organizations, December 2, 1968, 11. Box 575, Speeches, folder: Hart Speeches—1968 (4), Philip A. Hart Collection.

29. See "The Justice Department" and "The Federal Trade Commission" in Chapter 3 above, and "Significant Antitrust Cases of the 1960s," Chapter 5 below.

30. Philip A. Hart, Address Before the National Council of Salesmens' Organizations, December 2, 1968, 11–13; and "Federal Incorporation," Address Before Professor Schulman's Law Class, Wayne State University, December 13, 1968, 1–12. Box 575, Speeches, folder: Hart Speeches—1968 (4), Philip A. Hart Collection.

31. Philip A. Hart, "Federal Incorporation," 10, 12.

32. Gabriel Kolko, *The Triumph of Conservatism: A Reinterpretation of American History, 1900–1916* (Chicago: Quadrangle Books, 1963), 63–4; Martin J. Sklar, *The Corporate Reconstruction of American Capitalism, 1890–1916: The Market, the Law, and Politics* (New York: Cambridge University Press, 1988), 188–207. Also see "The Period

Between: 1905–1918," Chapter 1, above.

33. Gorman, and Mintz and Cohen, indicate Hruska's support for business, while Schuck states that Hruska, while a Senator, received a salary as chairman of an insurance company, aided business clients of his former law firm, and paid approximately one-fifth the normal lease price for his Lincoln automobile. Mintz and Cohen also list numerous examples of Senators and Representatives who had received and given business favors. More pertinent to this study, however, is that during the Economic Concentration hearings of the Senate Subcommittee on Antitrust and Monopoly, Hruska denied that an increase in concentration existed. Using 1958 figures previously developed by the subcommittee, and acknowledging the existence of over 400 industry categories, he noted that market concentration had declined in some industries. Aggregate concentration, spurred by the conglomerate movement, and the concern of Senator Hart and others, Hruska dismissed as an issue of "bigness," *not properly the work of the subcommittee* (italics added). Further, he stated "bigness is not necessarily related to monopoly or even to concentration. . . . 6 of the 10 biggest companies in this country are oil companies, but the concentration ratio for the oil industry is not even particularly high" (Table 2.3). Thus, he concluded, the subcommittee would be "chasing wild geese." Gorman, 352; Mintz and Cohen, 208–31; Shuck, 69, 92; U.S. Congress, 2–6; Willard F. Mueller, *The Celler-Kefauver Act: The First 27 Years* (Washington: U.S. Government Printing Office, 1979), 72. See "The Legislative Branch: The Government-Business Environment," this chapter, above, for discussion of market and aggregate concentration.

34. One bill that did become law, the Bank Merger Act of 1966, did not broaden or strengthen antitrust coverage, but practically removed banks from antitrust prosecution. (Financial institutions are not included in this study.) However, some positive results were obtained from subcommittee hearings into the practices and high prices of funeral directors, price fixing among book wholesalers, and the worldwide prices of quinine (which led to action by the Common Market against the international quinine cartel). Schuck, 79–80, 86–8.

35. Schuck, 96–7. William Oscar Jenkins, Jr., "The Role of the Supreme Court in National Merger Policy: 1950–1973" (Unpublished Ph.D. dissertation, University of Wisconsin-Madison, 1975), 60.

36. See "The White House: The Government-Business Environment, the Kennedy Years," Chapter 3. Premerger notification did not become law until the passage of the Hart-Scott-Rodino Act in 1976.

37. Letter, Representative Emanuel Celler to Myer Feldman, April 17, 1962, White House Central Files, Box 469, Legislation, Business, Economics, folder: LE/BE 2–4, John F. Kennedy Library, Boston, MA. Although the letter indicated that the proposed bills were attached, no copies were attached or in the folder or box.

38. Schuck, 98. In a table on page 95, Schuck indicates only five days of hearings.

39. Ibid., 100; Green, 59.

40. Schuck, 97–102; Green, 36–7, 58–9.

41. See "Toward the Legislative Process," Chapter 3.

42. Mintz and Cohen, 154–5; Green, 19.

43. See "The Federal Trade Commission," Chapter 3.

44. U.S. Congress, House of Representatives, 5, 441–2.

45. Joseph S. Clark, *Congress: The Sapless Branch* (New York: Harper & Row, 1964), 22–3.

46. Ralph Nader and Mark J. Green, eds., *Corporate Power In America* (New York: Grossman Publishers, 1973), 32–3.

47. Edwin H. Sutherland, *White Collar Crime: The Uncut Version* (New Haven, CT: Yale University Press, 1983), 227–39. Sutherland had studied 70 large corporations. Forty-one had been convicted a total of 158 times. In addition, 822 adverse decisions of some type had been rendered against the 70. Mintz and Cohen, 255.

48. *Sacramento Bee*, April 14, 1968; Green, 56.

5. THE RESPONSE: THE SUPREME COURT

1. Further discussion regarding the Supreme Court as a policy maker may be found in Martin Shapiro, *Law and Politics in the Supreme Court* (New York: The Free Library Press of Glencoe, 1964), 253–63, 326–7; William Oscar Jenkins, Jr., "The Role of the Supreme Court in National Merger Policy: 1950–1973" (Unpublished Ph.D. dissertation, University of Wisconsin-Madison, 1975), 2–16.

2. It is estimated that less than 1 percent of all mergers are challenged by the Department of Justice or the Federal Trade Commission. Jenkins, 24.

3. *Brown Shoe Company v. United States*, 370 U.S. 294 (1962).

4. Ibid., 316–23.

5. Ibid., 300–4.

6. Ibid., 326–8, 336–9.

7. Ibid., 328, 334.

8. Ibid., 342–5.

9. Ibid., 346.

10. *United States v. Philadelphia National Bank, et al.*, 374 U.S. 321 (1963). An important issue in this case was the inclusion of banking under Section 7 and thus the decision that the Bank Merger Act of 1960 did not immunize banks from the federal antitrust laws. Ibid., 348–54. However, American bankers mounted a powerful lobbying effort to secure the enactment of the Bank Merger Act of 1966, which practically removed banks from antitrust prosecution. See Chapter 4, note 34, above. For a discussion of the efforts to secure the passage of this act, see, for example, Robert Anthony Laudicina, "Judicial Influence and Group Behavior in National Merger Policy" (Unpublished Ph.D. dissertation, Columbia University, 1968), 98–115.

11. *Philadelphia National Bank*, 331.

12. Ibid., 364.

13. *United States v. El Paso Natural Gas Company*, 376 U.S. 651 (1964).

14. Ibid., 652–7.

15. Ibid., 658.

16. Ibid., 659–61.

17. *United States v. Aluminum Company of America, et al.*, 377 U.S. 271 (1964).

18. Ibid., 273–7.

19. Ibid., 278–81.

20. *United States v. Penn-Olin Chemical Company, et al.*, 378 U.S. 158 (1964).

21. Justice Douglas, with Justice Black concurring, dissented, stating that a joint venture is an agreement among competitors to divide a market, and is therefore a per se violation of the Sherman Act. Thus, the case should have been immediately recognized as and disposed

of as a Sherman Act violation. Ibid., 177.

22. Ibid., 168–9.

23. Ibid., 167–77.

24. Final disposition of this case came on December 11, 1967. The District Court had previously ruled that the government had failed to prove that either parent would have entered the market in the absence of the joint venture. On appeal, the Supreme Court divided 4–4, thus affirming the lower Court's decision. *United States v. Penn-Olin Chemical Corp.*, 389 U.S. 308 (1967).

25. *United States v. Continental Can Company et al.*, 378 U.S. 441 (1964).

26. Ibid., 453.

27. Ibid., 457.

28. Ibid., 458.

29. Ibid., 465.

30. *Federal Trade Commission v. Consolidated Foods Corporation*, 380 U.S. 592 (1965).

31. Ibid., 593–4.

32. Ibid., 594, 599–601.

33. *United States v. Von's Grocery Company, et al.*, 384 U.S. 270 (1966), 272–7. Commenting on the *Von's Grocery* case, Turner stated that although the combined market share of the merged firms might be small, the merger moved the increasing trend toward concentration in food distribution one step further, and only a few more steps would be necessary to almost certainly weaken competition. "For if we wait out a growing trend to concentration until we find a merger about which we can honestly say, `*This* merger will probably substantially lessen competition,' we have already waited far too late." A series of mergers, uncontested on the basis that no one of them is likely to cause harm, would materially alter the structure of that market and frustrate the purpose of the antitrust laws. Donald F. Turner, "The Merits of Antimerger Policy," Address Before the Town Hall Forum, Los Angeles, CA, March 7, 1967, 11–12.

34. *Federal Trade Commission v. Proctor & Gamble Company*, 386 U.S. 568 (1967), 570–3.

35. Ibid., 574–9.

36. In addition to the cases discussed above, there were three bank merger cases, plus *United States v. Pabst Brewing Corporation*, 384 U.S. 546 (1966); *Federal Trade Commission v. Dean Foods*, 384 U.S. 597 (1966); *Cascade Natural Gas v. El Paso Natural Gas*, 386 U.S. 129 (1967); and *United States v. Baltimore and Ohio Railway*, 386 U.S. 372 (1967). This record of government victories would continue until 1974. Jenkins, 4.

37. Laudicina, 79. See note 21 above regarding Justices Douglas' and Black's dissent in *Penn-Olin*.

6. CONCLUSIONS

1. Quoted in William H. Orrick, Jr., Untitled Address Before the Conference on the Government's Role in Consumer Protection, University of Toledo, Toledo, OH, April 24, 1964, 13. Public Speeches of Assistant Attorneys General, Antitrust Division, Department of Justice, Washington, DC.

7. EPILOGUE

1.   See "Toward the Legislative Process," Chapter 3, and Appendix B.
2.   U.S. Congress, Senate, Committee on the Judiciary, Subcommittee on Antitrust and Monopoly, *Economic Concentration, Hearings Before the Subcommittee on Antitrust and Monopoly*, 91st Cong., 2nd sess., 1970 (Washington: U.S. Government Printing Office, 1970), 5034–52.
3.   Robert M. Goolrick, *Public Policy Toward Corporate Growth* (Port Washington, NY: Kennicat Press, 1978), 57–9.
4.   John F. Winslow, *Conglomerates Unlimited: The Failure of Regulation* (Bloomington: Indiana University Press, 1973), 18. U.S. Congress, House of Representatives, Committee on the Judiciary, Antitrust Subcommittee, *Investigations of Conglomerate Corporations*, Staff Report, 92nd Cong., 1st sess., 1971 (Washington: U.S. Government Printing Office, 1971), 7.
5.   Willard F. Mueller, *The Celler-Kefauver Act: The First 27 Years* (Washington: U.S. Government Printing Office, 1979), 144–5. No other merger cases significant to this study were contested in 1969 by the Antitrust Division, and none were contested by the Federal Trade Commission.
6.   Winslow, 23.
7.   U.S. Congress, House, *Investigations*, 428.
8.   Mueller, 144; Robert Sobel, *The Rise and Fall of the Conglomerate Kings* (New York: Stein and Day, 1984), 177–81.
9.   Mueller, 144–5; Sobel, 184–7; Goolrick, 7–9. McLaren had tired of the political intrigue, and had sought and received an appointment as a District Judge in late 1971. Peter O. Steiner, *Mergers: Motives, Effects, Policies* (Ann Arbor: University of Michigan Press, 1975), 163.

Glossary

ADMINISTERED PRICE. Prices agreed upon by the dominant firms in an industry rather than having been arrived at by the free market forces of demand and supply.

ANTITRUST. Government opposition to business firms, or combinations thereof, that are engaging in activities that may reduce competition. Such activities may be mergers, price fixing, patent abuses, production quotas, etc. (Although the "trust" form of business operation became obsolete by the late 1890s, the term *antitrust* has remained to the present.)

ANTITRUST ENFORCEMENT AGENCIES. In the United States, the two antitrust agencies of the federal government are the Antitrust Division of the Department of Justice and the Federal Trade Commission (FTC).

BARRIER TO ENTRY. Any obstacle that may prevent or make it very difficult for a potential producer to enter an industry. Control over natural resources, excessive start-up costs, size of plant required for cost-effective operation, and market power of leading firms are examples of entry barriers.

CIVIL INVESTIGATIVE DEMAND. An Antitrust Division request for information, enforced by a court order.

COLLUSION. The act of firms cooperating to establish the price and/or production level for a particular product or service.

CONCENTRATION. Economic strength acquired legally and/or illegally, which gives a firm or firms great power in their industry and in the economy. Political power usually accompanies such economic strength.

Aggregate Concentration. The total assets held by the 200 largest corporations in the United States. (The FTC uses the number 200 for its various statistical purposes.)

Market Concentration/Concentration Ratio. The share of total industry output produced by the four leading firms in a given industry.

CONSENT DECREE/ORDER. An agreement negotiated between the government's attorneys and those of the defendant. The agreement specifies certain actions or procedures to which the firm must agree. In return, the government agrees to terminate litigation. The agreement must be approved by the Court. When negotiated by the Department of Justice, the agreement is referred to as a consent decree; when negotiated by the FTC, the agreement is called a consent order.

CROSS-SUBSIDIZATION. The use of profits obtained in one product, industry, or geographic location, to offset losses incurred in another. It is a type of price discrimination and/or predatory pricing.

DEEP POCKETS. Phrase used to describe the concept that a large firm has an advantage over smaller ones because it has greater financial resources. Such large firms are able to temporarily subsidize losses in one product or market, or selectively reduce prices or increase advertising, which smaller competitors may not be able to do. The phrase is also used to describe the capability of a parent firm to spend considerable sums on behalf of a newly acquired subsidiary.

DIVESTITURE. Separation of a part of an organization from the rest of the organization in order to create or increase competition. The separation usually is the result of a court order. The separated part or unit may be sold to another firm or may be established as a new enterprise.

EXTERNAL GROWTH/EXPANSION. Growth or expansion of an organization by the acquisition of other producers. Though sometimes improving productive efficiency and output, external growth does not of itself increase total capacity or employment, and may result in the elimination of some positions and a reduction in competition.

FORBEARANCE. Refraining from active competition. Companies touching in many markets recognize that aggressive competition in one area can precipitate retaliation in another area.

HOLDING COMPANY. An organization established to control other corporations by owning all or a portion of their stock.

INTERLOCKING DIRECTORATES. This occurs when Boards of Directors are "interlocked" through the representation of directors or executives of one corporation on the board of another corporation. Although such interlocking among competitors is forbidden by the Clayton Act, combinations of bankers, lawyers, suppliers, etc. sitting on boards of supposed competitors has not been declared illegal by Congress.

INTERNAL GROWTH. Growth or expansion of an organization accomplished by the introduction of new products and/or techniques, or expanded capacity, which may result in increased employment and market competition.

JOINT VENTURE. A relationship or new organization formed by two or more companies in order to pursue some mutually advantageous business purpose. By strengthening already existing relations or establishing new ones, joint ventures contain the potential for reducing both actual and potential competition. Business partners in one market might be less inclined to compete aggressively in other markets.

LEADING FIRM. One included among the four largest sellers in an industry.

MERGER. A bringing together of formerly independent firms. Because a merger may join two or more companies, the FTC uses the concept of firms "disappearing as a result of merger" for its statistical analyses.

Horizontal Merger. Unites former competitors in the same line of business, e.g., the merger of two formerly independent food processors.

Vertical Merger. Unites suppliers and users at different stages in the production process. For example, a food processor may merge backward into the acquisition of farms that grow the food, or merge forward into the acquisition of retail outlets that sell the food to the final consumer.

Conglomerate. Generally refers to the merger of firms with non-related end products, e.g., the food processor diversifying into clothing and auto parts manufacturing. The conglomerate corporation and its acts need not be, nor are they always, anticompetitive. The conglomerate may inject new competition into a market, thereby increasing efficiency and possibly reducing prices to consumers. However, by the late 1960s, even the word "conglomerate" usually generated ideas of greed or "badness," if not illegality.

MONOPOLY. One firm controlling an entire industry or geographical market. (Illegal, except where permitted by government, e.g., public transportation.)

OLIGOPOLY. A condition in which a relatively small number of firms control the market. Dominant form (in terms of assets and profits) of business in the United States today. Automobiles, steel, petroleum, chemicals, electronics, etc.

POTENTIAL COMPETITION/POTENTIAL ENTRANT. Theory that states that organizations with the resources to enter an industry or market exert pressures that maintain competition among the existing producers. Merger with a potential competitor would not only end the threat of entry, but could result in a single organization capable of increasing market share at the expense of the other competitors.

PREDATORY PRICING. The practice of deliberately charging a price below cost in order to force a competitor out of business, or to discourage new entrants into the industry or geographic area.

PRICE DISCRIMINATION. The practice of charging different prices to different buyers for the same product or service. There are no differences in quality or production costs to account for the difference in price.

RECIPROCITY. A condition that exists when one firm purchases goods or services from another firm that is an actual or potential customer for the former's products.

STANDARD INDUSTRIAL CLASSIFICATION (SIC) SYSTEM. This system, developed and used by government and private industry, begins with a two-digit major industry group code and becomes progressively more narrow as more numbers are added. For example:

SIC Code	Designation	Name
20	Major Industry Group	Food and Kindred Products
201	Industry Group	Meat Products
2011	Industry	Meat Packing Plants
20111	Product Class	Fresh Beef

TOE-HOLD MERGER. This condition occurs when a potential entrant into an industry or market, not wishing to internally develop the production capability, acquires one of the smaller competitors in that industry or market. If the acquiring firm has sufficient resources (deep pocket theory), it can exert considerable competitive pressure on the existing producers.

TRUST. A legal entity in which firms gave their voting stock to a central board of trustees. The board members were thereby authorized to vote the stock as they wished, while the dividends continued to be paid to the shareholders, who had exchanged their stock for trust certificates. The trustees used the power vested in them to coordinate production, distribution, and prices, thus establishing a monopoly over the products made. Such arrangements were declared illegal by the Sherman Act of 1890.

Selected Bibliography

PRIMARY SOURCES

Manuscript sources

John F. Kennedy Library
    White House Central Files
    Personal Papers:
        Walter Heller (Chairman, Council of Economic Advisors)
        Robert F. Kennedy: The Attorney General's Papers
        Theodore Sorensen (Special Counsel and Speechwriter)
    White House Staff Files:
        Myer Feldman (Deputy Special Counsel to the President)
    Oral History Interviews:
        Emanuel Celler (U.S. Representative, D–NY)
        Paul Rand Dixon (Chairman, Federal Trade Commission, 1961–1969)
        Luther H. Hodges (Secretary of Commerce)
        Lee Loevinger (Assistant Attorney General, Antitrust Division, 1961–1963)
        William Orrick (Assistant Attorney General, Antitrust Division, 1963–1965)
Lyndon B. Johnson Library
    White House Central Files
    Personal Papers:
        Ramsey Clark (Attorney General, 1966–1969)
    White House Aides Files:
        James Gaither (White House Assistant)
        Harry McPherson (Special Counsel to the President)
        Task Force on Antitrust Policy
    Administrative History:
        Department of Justice, Antitrust Division (1963–1968)
        Federal Trade Commission, Division of Mergers (1963–1968)

Oral History Interviews:
  Nicholas Katzenbach (Attorney General, 1964–1966)
Department of Justice
  Public Speeches of Assistant Attorneys General, Antitrust Division
Federal Trade Commission
  Public Speeches of Federal Trade Commissioners

U.S. Government Documents

Cuff, Robert D. "Antitrust Adjourned: Mobilization and the Rise of the National Security State." In *National Competition Policy: Historians' Perspectives on Antitrust and Government-Business Relationships in the United States*. Washington: Federal Trade Commission, August, 1981.

Federal Trade Commission. *Annual Report of the Federal Trade Commission for the Fiscal Year Ended June 30, 1961–1969*. Washington: U.S. Government Printing Office, 1961–1969.

_____. *Report of the Federal Trade Commission on the Merger Movement: A Summary Report*. Washington: U.S. Government Printing Office, 1948.

_____. Staff Report. *Economic Report on Corporate Mergers*. Washington: U.S. Government Printing Office, 1969.

_____. *Statistical Report No. 4: Large Mergers in Manufacturing and Mining, 1948–1968*. Washington: Federal Trade Commission, April, 1969.

Hawley, Ellis. "Antitrust and the Association Movement, 1920–1940." In *National Competition Policy: Historians' Perspectives on Antitrust and Government-Business Relationships in the United States*. Washington: Federal Trade Commission, August, 1981.

Mueller, Willard F. *The Celler-Kefauver Act: The First 27 Years*. Washington: U.S. Government Printing Office, 1979.

Thorp, Willard. "The Merger Movement." In *Monograph No. 27: The Structure of Industry*. Temporary National Economic Committee. Washington: U.S. Government Printing Office, 1941.

U.S. Attorney General. *Report of the Attorney General's National Committee to Study the Antitrust Laws*. Washington: U.S. Government Printing Office, 1955.

U.S. Cabinet Committee on Price Stability. *Study Paper Number 2: Industrial Structure and Competition Policy*. Washington: U.S. Government Printing Office, January 1969.

U.S. Congress. House of Representatives. Committee on the Judiciary. Antitrust Subcommittee, Subcommittee No. 5. *Investigation of Conglomerate Corporations*. Hearings Before the Antitrust Subcommittee. 92nd Cong., 1st sess., 1971. Washington: U.S. Government Printing Office, 1971.

_____. Senate. Committee on the Judiciary. Subcommittee on Antitrust and Monopoly. *Economic Concentration. Hearings Before the Subcommittee on Antitrust and Monopoly*. 88th Cong., 2nd sess., 1964—91st Cong., 2nd sess., 1970. Washington: U.S. Government Printing Office, 1964–1970.

U.S. Department of Justice. *Annual Report of the Attorney General of the United States for the Fiscal Year Ended June 30, 1961–1969*. Washington: U.S. Government Printing Office, 1961–1969.

U.S. President. *Economic Report of the President, January 1969.* Washington: U.S. Government Printing Office, 1969.

_____. *Public Papers of the Presidents of the United States.* Washington: U.S. Government Printing Office, 1962–1963. John F. Kennedy, 1961–1962.

_____. *Public Papers of the Presidents of the United States.* Washington: U.S. Government Printing Office, 1965. Lyndon B. Johnson, 1963–1964.

U.S. Smaller War Plants Corporation. *Economic Concentration and World War II: Report of the Smaller War Plants Corporation.* Washington: U.S. Government Printing Office, 1946.

U.S. Temporary National Economic Committee. *Investigation of Concentration of Economic Power: Final Report and Recommendation of the Temporary National Economic Committee.* Washington: U.S. Government Printing Office, 1941.

_____. *Monograph No. 16: Antitrust in Action.* Washington: U.S. Government Printing Office, 1941.

_____. *Monograph No. 27: The Structure of Industry.* Washington: U.S. Government Printing Office, 1941.

SECONDARY SOURCES

Books and Book Chapters

Alexander, Charles C. *Holding the Line: The Eisenhower Era, 1952–1961.* Bloomington: Indiana University Press, 1975.

Anderson, James E., and Jared E. Hazleton. *Managing Macroeconomic Policy: The Johnson Presidency.* Austin: University of Texas Press, 1986.

Armentano, D. T. *The Myths of Antitrust: Economic Theory and Legal Cases.* New Rochelle, NY: Arlington House, 1972.

Baldwin, William Lee. *Antitrust and the Changing Corporation.* Durham, NC: Duke University Press, 1961.

Barney, William L. *The Passage of the Republic: An Interdisciplinary History of Nineteenth Century America.* Lexington, MA: D. C. Heath, 1987.

Bazelon, David T. "Big Business and the Democrats." In *The Great Society Reader: The Failure of American Liberalism,* edited by Marvin E. Gettleman and David Mermelstein. New York: Random House, 1967.

Benston, George J. *Conglomerate Mergers: Causes, Consequences and Remedies.* Washington: American Enterprise Institute for Public Policy Research, 1980.

Bork, Robert H. *The Antitrust Paradox: A Policy at War with Itself.* New York: Basic Books, 1978.

Brozen, Yale. *Concentration, Mergers, and Public Policy.* New York: Macmillan, 1982.

Bryant, Keith L., Jr., and Henry C. Dethloff. *A History of American Business.* Englewood Cliffs, NJ: Prentice-Hall, 1983.

Butters, J. Keith, John Lintner, and William L. Cary. *Effects of Taxation: Corporate Mergers.* Cambridge, MA: Harvard University Press, 1951.

Canterbery, E. Ray. *Economics on a New Frontier.* Belmont, CA: Wadsworth Publishing Co., 1968.

Chandler, Alfred D., Jr. *The Visible Hand: The Managerial Revolution in American Business.* Cambridge, MA: The Belknap Press, 1977.

Clark, Joseph S. *Congress: The Sapless Branch.* New York, Harper & Row, 1964.

Congressional Quarterly Almanac, 84th Cong., 1st sess., 1955, Vol. 11. Washington: Congressional Quarterly News Features, 1955.

Cox, Edward F., Robert C. Fellmeth, and John E. Schulz. *"The Nader Report" on the Federal Trade Commission.* New York: Richard W. Baron, 1969.

Faulkner, Harold Underwood. *American Economic History.* 8th ed. New York: Harper and Brothers, 1960.

Fusilier, H. Lee, and Jerome C. Darnell. *Competition and Public Policy: Cases in Antitrust.* Englewood Cliffs, NJ: Prentice-Hall, 1971.

Galambos, Louis. *The Public Image of Big Business in America, 1880–1940.* Baltimore, MD: The Johns Hopkins University Press, 1975.

Galbraith, John Kenneth. *The New Industrial State.* Boston: Houghton Mifflin, 1967.

Goldman, Eric F. *Rendezvous with Destiny: A History of Modern American Reform.* New York: Vintage Books, 1955.

Goolrick, Robert M. *Public Policy Toward Corporate Growth.* Port Washington, NY: Kennikat Press, 1978.

Gorman, Joseph Bruce. *Kefauver: A Political Biography.* New York: Oxford University Press, 1971.

Green, Mark J., Project Director and Editor. *The Closed Enterprise System: Ralph Nader's Study Group Report on Antitrust Enforcement.* New York: Grossman Publishers, 1970.

Harris, Richard. *The Real Voice.* New York: Macmillan, 1964.

Harris, Seymour. *The Economics of the Kennedy Years and a Look Ahead.* New York: Harper & Row, 1964.

Hawley, Ellis. *The New Deal and the Problem of Monopoly: A Study in Economic Ambivalence.* Princeton, NJ: Princeton University Press, 1966.

Heath, Jim. *John F. Kennedy and the Business Community.* Chicago: University of Chicago Press, 1969.

Hicks, John D. *Republican Ascendancy, 1921–1933.* New York: Harper & Row, 1960.

Himmelberg, Robert F. *The Origins of the National Recovery Administration: Business, Government, and the Trade Association Issue, 1921–1933.* New York: Fordham University Press, 1976.

Hofstadter, Richard. *The Age of Reform: From Bryan to FDR.* New York: Vintage Books, 1955.

————. "What Happened to the Antitrust Movement?" In *The Business Establishment*, edited by Earl F. Cheit, New York: John Wiley & Sons, 1964.

Johnson, Arthur M. "The Federal Trade Commission: The Early Years, 1915–1935." In *Business and Government: Essays in 20th Century Cooperation and Confrontation*, edited by Joseph R. Frese and Jacob Judd. Tarrytown, NY: Sleepy Hollow Press, 1985.

Katzman, Robert A. *Regulatory Bureaucracy: The Federal Trade Commission and Antitrust Policy.* Cambridge, MA: The MIT Press, 1980.

Kaysen, Carl and Donald F. Turner. *Antitrust Policy: An Economic and Legal Analysis.* Cambridge, MA: Harvard University Press, 1959.

Kefauver, Estes, with the assistance of Irene Till. *In A Few Hands: Monopoly Power in America.* New York: Pantheon Books, 1965.

Keller, Morton. "The Pluralist State: American Economic Regulations in Comparative Perspective, 1900–1930." In *Regulation in Perspective: Historical Essays*, edited by

Thomas K. McCraw. Cambridge, MA: Harvard University Press, 1981.

Kolko, Gabriel. *The Triumph of Conservatism: A Reinterpretation of American History, 1900–1916.* Chicago: Quadrangle Books, 1963, pb. 1967.

Kovaleff, Theodore Philip. *Business and Government During the Eisenhower Administration: A Study of the Antitrust Policy of the Antitrust Division of the Justice Department.* Athens, OH: Ohio University Press, 1980.

Lamoreaux, Naomi R. *The Great Merger Movement in American Business, 1895–1904.* New York: Cambridge University Press, 1985.

Leuchtenburg, William E. *Franklin D. Roosevelt and the New Deal.* New York: Harper & Row, 1963.

Link, Arthur S. *Woodrow Wilson and the Progressive Era, 1910–1917.* New York: Harper & Row, 1954.

Low, Richard E., ed. *The Economics of Antitrust: Competition and Monopoly.* Englewood Cliffs, NJ: Prentice-Hall, 1968.

Markham, Jesse W. *Conglomerate Enterprise and Public Policy.* Cambridge, MA: Harvard University Press, 1973.

———. "Survey of the Evidence and Findings on Mergers." In *Business Concentration and Price Policy*, National Bureau of Economic Research. Princeton, NJ: Princeton University Press, 1955.

Martin, David Dale. *Mergers and the Clayton Act.* Berkeley: University of California Press, 1959.

Matusow, Allen J. *The Unraveling of America: A History of Liberalism in the 1960s.* New York: Harper & Row, 1984.

McCraw, Thomas K., ed. *Prophets of Regulation.* Cambridge, MA: The Belknap Press, 1984.

———. *Regulation in Perspective: Historical Essays.* Cambridge, MA: Harvard University Press, 1981.

McQuaid, Kim. *Big Business and Presidential Power: From FDR to Reagan.* New York: William Morrow, 1982.

Meier, Kenneth J. *Regulation: Politics, Bureaucracy, and Economics.* New York: St. Martin's Press, 1985.

Mintz, Morton, and Jerry S. Cohen. *America, Inc.: Who Owns and Operates the United States.* New York: The Dial Press, 1971.

Miroff, Bruce. *Pragmatic Illusions: The Presidential Power of John F. Kennedy.* New York: David McKay Co., 1976.

Nader, Ralph, and Mark J. Green, eds. *Corporate Power in America.* New York: Grossman Publishers, 1973.

Nader, Ralph, Mark J. Green, and Joel Seligman. *Taming the Giant Corporation.* New York: W. W. Norton & Co., 1976.

Narver, John C. *Conglomerate Mergers and Market Competition.* Berkeley: University of California Press, 1967.

Navasky, Victor S. *Kennedy Justice.* New York: Atheneum, 1971.

Nelson, Ralph L. *Merger Movements in American Industry, 1895–1956.* Princeton, NJ: Princeton University Press, 1959.

Pearson, Drew, and Jack Anderson. *The Case Against Congress: A Compelling Indictment of Corruption on Capitol Hill.* New York: Simon and Shuster, 1968.

Porter, Kirk H., and Donald Bruce Johnson. *National Party Platforms, 1840–1968.* 4th ed. Urbana: University of Illinois Press, 1972.

Reid, Samuel Richardson. *Mergers, Managers, and the Economy*. New York: McGraw-Hill, 1968.

————. *The New Industrial Order*. New York: McGraw-Hill, 1976.

Rowan, Hobart. *The Free Enterprisers: Kennedy, Johnson and the Business Establishment*. New York: G. Putnam's Sons, 1964.

Schlesinger, Arthur M., Jr. *Robert Kennedy and His Times*. New York: Ballantine Books, pb., 1968.

————. *A Thousand Days: John F. Kennedy in the White House*. Boston: Houghton Mifflin, 1965.

Schuck, Peter H. *The Judiciary Committees: A Study of the House and Senate Judiciary Committees*. New York: Grossman Publishers, 1975.

Schwartz, Bernard. *Super Chief: Earl Warren and His Supreme Court—A Judicial Biography*. New York: New York University Press, 1983.

Shepherd, William G. *Public Policies Toward Business*. 7th ed. Homewood, IL: Richard D. Irwin, 1985.

Shapiro, Martin. *Law and Politics in the Supreme Court*. New York: The Free Press of Glencoe, 1964.

Sidey, Hugh. *A Very Personal Presidency: Lyndon Johnson in the White House*. New York: Atheneum, 1968.

Sklar, Martin J. *The Corporate Reconstruction of American Capitalism, 1890–1916: The Market, the Law, and Politics*. New York: Cambridge University Press, 1988.

Smith, George David. *From Monopoly to Competition: The Transformation of Alcoa, 1888–1986*. New York: Cambridge University Press, 1988.

Sobel, Robert. *The Rise and Fall of the Conglomerate Kings*. New York: Stein and Day, 1984.

Soule, George. *Prosperity Decade: From War to Depression, 1917–1929*. New York: Rinehart and Company, 1947.

Steiner, Peter O. *Mergers: Motives, Effects, Policies*. Ann Arbor: University of Michigan Press, 1975.

Stelzer, Irwin M. *Selected Antitrust Cases: Landmark Decisions*. 4th ed. Homewood, IL: Richard D. Irwin, Inc., 1972.

Stocking, George W., and Myron W. Watkins. *Monopoly and Free Enterprise*. New York: The Twentieth Century Fund, 1951.

Sutherland, Edwin H. *White Collar Crime: The Uncut Version*. New Haven, CT: Yale University Press, 1983.

Thorelli, Hans B. *The Federal Antitrust Policy: Organization of an American Tradition*. Baltimore, MD: The Johns Hopkins University Press, 1955.

Thorp, Willard L. "The Changing Structure of Industry." In *Recent Economic Changes in the United States*, Report of the President's Conference on Unemployment. Vol. 1. New York: McGraw-Hill, 1929.

Van Cise, Jerrold G. *The Federal Antitrust Laws*. 3rd ed. Washington: American Enterprise Institute for Public Policy Research, 1975.

Vatter, Harold G. *The U.S. Economy in World War II*. New York: Columbia University Press, 1985.

Wagner, Susan. *The Federal Trade Commission*. New York: Praeger Publishers, 1971.

Weaver, Suzanne. *Decision to Prosecute: Organization and Public Policy in the Antitrust Division*. Cambridge, MA: MIT Press, 1977.

Weston, J. Fred. *The Role of Mergers in the Growth of Large Firms*. Berkeley: University of California Press, 1953.

Whitney, Simon N. *Antitrust Policies: American Experience in Twenty Industries*. New York: The Twentieth Century Fund, 1958.

Winslow, John F. *Conglomerates Unlimited: The Failure of Regulation*. Bloomington: Indiana University Press, 1973.

Articles

Bookman, George. "Loevinger vs. Big Business." *Fortune*, January, 1962, 93–114.

Bork, Robert, and Ward S. Bowman, Jr. "The Crisis in Antitrust." *Fortune*, December 1963, 138–201.

Chandler, Alfred D., Jr. "The Structure of American Industry in the Twentieth Century: A Historical Overview." *Business History Review* 43 (Autumn 1969): 255–98.

Didrichsen, Jon. "The Development of Diversified and Conglomerate Firms in the United States, 1920–1970." *Business History Review* 46 (Summer 1972): 202–19.

Edwards, Corwin D. "Thurman Arnold and the Antitrust Laws." *Political Science Quarterly* 58 (September 1943): 338–55.

Elman, Philip. "The Need for Certainty and Predictability in the Application of the Merger Law." *New York University Law Review* 40 (October 1965): 613–22.

Kennedy, Robert F. "Introduction: The Antitrust Aims of the Justice Department." *New York Law Forum* 9 (March 1963): 1–4.

Levitt, Theodore. "The Johnson Treatment." *Harvard Business Review* 45 (Jan.–Feb. 1967): 114–28.

Loevinger, Lee. "Antitrust in 1961 and 1962." *Antitrust Bulletin* 8 (May–June 1963): 349–79.

_____. "Antitrust is Pro-Business." *Fortune*, August 1962, 96–126.

_____. "The Doctrine of Judicial Ratification." *Kentucky Law Journal* 51 (Spring 1963): 422–33.

Marcus, Sumner. "New Weapons Against Business." *Harvard Business Review* 43 (Jan.–Feb. 1965): 100–8.

Markham, Jesse. "Antitrust Trends and New Constraints." *Harvard Business Review* 41 (May–June 1963): 84–92.

Merkel, Edward W. "The Other Anti of Antitrust." *Harvard Business Review* 46 (March–April 1968): 53–60.

Meyers, Harold B. "LBJ's Romance with Business." *Fortune*, September 1964, 131–33.

_____. "Professor Turner's Turn at Antitrust." *Fortune*, September 1965, 168–90.

_____. "The Root of the FTC's Confusion." *Fortune*, August 1963, 114–58.

Posner, Richard. "A Statistical Study of Antitrust Enforcement." *The Journal of Law and Economics* 13 (October 1970): 365–419.

Rosenof, Theodore. "New Deal Pragmatism and Economic Systems: Concepts and Meanings." *The Historian* 49, No. 3 (May 1987): 368–82.

Stern, Lewis W. "Mergers Under Scrutiny." *Harvard Business Review* 47 (July–Aug. 1969): 18–36.

Stigler, George. "Monopoly and Oligopoly by Merger." *American Economic Review* 40, No. 2 (May 1950): 23–34.

Thorp, Willard L. "The Persistence of the Merger Movement." *American Economic Review* 21, No. 1, supplement (March 1931): 77–89.
Turner, Donald. "Conglomerate Mergers and Section 7 of the Clayton Act." *Harvard Law Review* 98 (May 1965): 1313–95.

Dissertations

Didrichsen, Jon Christian. "Business-Government Interaction in the Evolution of Antitrust Policy Toward Diversification." Unpublished D.B.A. dissertation, Harvard University, 1974.
Eis, Carl. "The 1919–1930 Merger Movement in American Industry." Unpublished Ph.D. dissertation, City University of New York, 1968.
Goldberg, Lawrence. "The Effect of Conglomerate Mergers on Competition." Unpublished Ph.D. dissertation, University of Chicago, 1972.
Goodman, Jon P. "An Exploratory Investigation of Some Effects of Mergers on Selected Organizations." Unpublished Ph.D. dissertation, University of Georgia, 1981.
Jenkins, William Oscar, Jr. "The Role of the Supreme Court in National Merger Policy: 1950–1973." Unpublished Ph.D. dissertation, University of Wisconsin—Madison, 1975.
Laudicina, Robert Anthony. "Judicial Influence and Group Behavior in National Merger Policy." Unpublished Ph.D. dissertation, Columbia University, 1968.
Looney, Robert E. "Antitrust Mergers: An Economic Analysis of Some Recent Court Decisions." Unpublished Ph.D. dissertation, University of California at Davis, 1969.

Case Index

Subject Index

About the Author

JAMES R. WILLIAMSON is a retired U.S. Army officer and retired Professor of History and Business, Gwynedd-Mercy College. Presently, he is Adjunct Professor of History and Political Science at the University of Scranton and Adjunct Professor of History and Business at Wilkes University. He coauthored *Zebulon Butler: Hero of the Revolutionary Frontier* (Greenwood Press, 1995).